A COMMENTARY ON

THE BOOK OF THE REVELATION

A COMMENTARY ON

THE BOOK OF THE REVELATION

BASED ON A STUDY OF TWENTY-THREE PSYCHIC DISCOURSES OF EDGAR CAYCE

A.R.E. Press • Virginia Beach • Virginia

11th Printing, May 1995

Printed in the U.S.A.

A.R.E. Press
Sixty-Eighth & Atlantic Avenue
P.O. Box 656
Virginia Beach, VA 23451-0656

ISBN 0-87604-003-2

Cover design by Richard M. Boyle

Preface

This volume of The Revelation study has been rearranged, as to format, but contains the same material as previous publications. The changes are as follows:

1. The "direct references" to passages of The Revelation given by Edgar Cayce have been placed on pages opposite the appropriate verses.

2. For convenience of study, this volume is in three sections; viz.:

A—Edgar Cayce readings on The Revelation.

B—The Book of the Revelation with appropriate readings extracts.

C—The Book of the Revelation with a New York group's symbology and interpretation.

3. A glossary by Esther Wynne has been added at the end of the volume.

EDGAR CAYCE FOUNDATION
Virginia Beach, Virginia

This collection comprises twenty-three psychic readings given by Edgar Cayce on the subjects of The Revelation and the Endocrine Glands.

The following case numbers are included:

281-16
281-28
281-29
281-30
281-31
281-32
281-33
281-34
281-36
281-37
281-38
281-46
281-47
281-48
281-49
281-51
281-52
281-53
281-54
281-55
281-57
281-58
281-63

The Book of

THE REVELATION

WITH THE EDGAR CAYCE READINGS

281-16

This psychic reading given by Edgar Cayce at the Edmonds' home, 611 Pennsylvania Ave., Norfolk, Va., this 13th day of March, 1933, in accordance with request made by Norfolk Study Group #1, for their opening meeting at which approximately fifty people were present—9:00 to 9:50 P.M., Eastern Standard Time.

Mrs. C: You will give at this time an interpretation of the Book of Revelation as recorded in the King James version of the Bible, explaining the general plan and theme, the significance of the Book, and give such explanations of the symbols used as will make this book of personal value to those present seeking to awaken and develop the inner life. You will then answer the questions which will be asked regarding various parts of this Book.

Mr. C: Yes, we have the text written in the Revelation, as recorded in the King James version of same.

In making this worthwhile in the experience of individuals who are seeking for the light, for the revelation that may be theirs as promised in the promises of same, it would be well that there be considered first the conditions which surrounded the writer, the apostle, the beloved, the last of those chosen; writing to a persecuted people, many despairing, many fallen away, yet, many seeking to hold to that which had been delivered to them through the efforts and activities of those upon whom the spirit had fallen by the very indwelling and the manifestations that had become the common knowledge of all.

Remember, then, that Peter—chosen as the rock, chosen to open the doors of that known today as the church—had said to this companion, "I will endeavor to keep thee in remembrance; even after my demise I will return to you."

The beloved, then, was banished to the isle, and was in meditation, in prayer, in communion with those saints who were in that position to see, to comprehend the greater needs of those that would carry on.

And, as given in the beginning, "I was in the Spirit on the Lord's day, and beheld, and heard, and saw, and was told to *write.*"

Why, then, ye ask now, was this written (this vision) in such a manner that is hard to be interpreted, save in the experience of every soul who seeks to know, to walk in, a closer communion with Him?

For the visions, the experiences, the names, the churches, the places, the dragons, the cities, all are but emblems of those forces that may war within the individual in its journey through the material, or from the entering into the material manifestation to the entering into the glory, or the awakening in the spirit, in the inter-between, in the borderland, in the shadow.

Hence we find, as the churches are named, they are as the forces that are known as the senses, that must be spiritualized by the will of the individual made one in the very activities in a material world.

And the elders and the Lamb are the emblems, are the shadows of those acceptances or rejections that are made in the experiences of the individual.

As we find, in the various manners and forms that are presented as the vision or visions proceed, every force that is manifest is of one source; but the soul, the will of the individual, either makes such into a coordinating or cooperating influence in bringing about more and more manifestations in the material world of those experiences that are seen from the spiritual conditions, or the opposite.

Why, then, is it presented, ye ask, in the form of symbols? Why is there used those varied activities? These are for those that were, or will be, or may become, through the seeking, those initiated into an understanding of the glories that may be theirs if they will but put into work, into activity, that they know in the present.

In seeking, then, do individuals find from the beginning that there is presented, in every line, in every form, that good and bad (as termed) that arises from their activity, in what they do about that knowledge they have respecting the law, the love, the mercy, the understanding of the wherefore of the Lamb's advent into the world that they, through His ensample set, may present themselves before that throne even as He, becoming—as given—heirs, joint heirs with Him, as the sons of God, to that *everlasting* glory that may be had in Him.

Then, seek to know to what self is lacking, even as given in the first four chapters (as divided in the present).

What is lacking in self? Are ye cold? Are ye hot? Have ye been negligent of the knowledge that is thine? Are ye stiff-necked? Are ye adulterous in thought, in act, in the very glories that are thine?

Then, again—may ye not have had through the varied experiences those presentations before the throne, even as the elders twenty and four that are represented by the figures within thine own head, that which is shown in the physical forces of self? Has it not been given to thee, or has not the message come as the rider of the pale, the black, the white, or the red horses that are the figures of the messages that have come to thee in thine varied experiences? Or, art thou among the figures represented in the Babylon, or in the rivers of blood, or in the trees of life?

These we see, then, represent *self;* self's body-physical, self's body-mental, self's body-spiritual; with the attributes of the body-physical, attributes of the body-mental, attributes of the body-spiritual, and they are *one* in thee—even as the Father, the Son and the Holy Spirit is one in Him.

Then, dost thou seek to enter into the glories of the Father? Whosoever will may come, may take of the water of life freely—even as flows from the throne of the Lamb. For, the very leaves of the trees are for the healing of the nations, and—if ye will accept—the blood cleanses from all unrighteousness. How? From what? Saves self from what? To what are ye called? To know that only from the falling away of self may ye be saved. Unto the glorifying of self in Him may ye be saved.

Then, whosoever will, come!

Ready for questions.

Q-1. Please interpret the fall of Babylon as referred to in the 14th, 17th, and 18th chapters of Revelation.

A-1. Babylon represented the individual; those periods through which every soul passes in its delving into the varied mysteries that are the experiences of the carnal-mental, the spiritual-mental forces of the body; and, as viewed from that presented, may come to the knowledge only through the *cleansing* that is shown must come to those that would be saved from the destructions that are given there.

Q-2. What did the angel mean when he said: "I will tell thee the mystery of the woman, and of the beast that carrieth her"?

A-2. That which is understood by those that follow in the way of the Lamb, that come to know how man separates himself through the desires to become as the procreator in the beasts; which made the necessity of the shedding of blood for redemption, for it brought sin *in* the shedding—and only through same may there be the fulfilling; and, as given, the heavens and the earth may pass, but His law, His love, His mercy, His grace, endureth for those who *will* seek to know His will.

Q-3. Where are the dead until Christ comes? Do they go direct to Him when they die?

A-3. As visioned by the beloved, there are those of the saints making intercession always before the throne for those that are passing in and out of the inter-between; even as He, the Christ, is ever in the consciousness of those that are redeemed in Him.

The passing in, the passing out, is as but the summer, the fall, the spring; the birth into the interim, the birth into the material.

Q-4. In what form does the anti-Christ come, spoken of in Revelation?

A-4. In the spirit of that opposed to the spirit of truth. The fruits of the spirit of the Christ are love, joy, obedience, long-suffering, brotherly love, kindness. Against such there is no law. The spirit of hate, the anti-Christ, is contention, strife, fault-finding, lovers of self, lovers of praise. Those are the anti-Christ, and take possession of groups, masses, and show themselves even in the lives of men.

Q-5. Will we be punished by fire and brimstone?

A-5. That as builded by self; as those emblematical influences are shown through the experiences of the beloved in that builded, that created. For, each soul is a portion of creation—and builds that in a portion of its experience that it, through its physical-mental or spiritual-mental, has builded for itself. And each entity's heaven or hell must, through *some* experience, be that which it has builded for itself.

Is thy hell one that is filled with fire or brimstone? But know, each and every soul is tried so as by fire; purified, purged; for He, though He were the Son, learned obedience through the things which He suffered. Ye also are known even as ye do, and have done.

Q-6. Is this the period of the great tribulation spoken of in Revelation, or just the beginning, and if so just how can we help ourselves and others to walk more closely with God?

A-6. The great tribulation and periods of tribulation, as given, are the experiences of every soul, every entity. They arise from influences created by man through activity in the sphere of any sojourn. Man may become, with the people of the universe, ruler of any of the various spheres through which the soul passes in its experiences. Hence, as the cycles pass, as the cycles are passing, when there *is* come a time, a period of readjusting in the spheres (as well as in the little earth, the little soul)—seek, then, as known, to present self spotless before that throne; even as *all* are commanded to be circumspect, in thought, in act, to that which is held by self as that necessary for the closer walk with Him. In that manner only may each atom (as man is an atom, or corpuscle, in the body of the Father) become a helpmeet with Him in bringing that to pass that all may be one with Him.

Q-7. What is meant by the four beasts?

A-7. As given, the four destructive influences that make the greater desire for the carnal forces, that rise as the beasts within self to destroy. Even as man, in his desire to make for companionship, brought those elements within self's own experience. These must be met. Even as the dragon represents the one that separated self so far as to fight with, to destroy with, those that would make of themselves a kingdom of their own.

Q-8. What is meant by "a new heaven and a new earth"?

A-8. Former things have passed away, when there is beheld within self that the whole will of the Creator, the Father, the place of abode, the forces within and without, make for the *new* heaven, the *new* earth.

We are through.

281-28

This psychic reading given by Edgar Cayce at his home on Arctic Crescent, Virginia Beach, Va., this 26th day of October, 1936, in accordance with request by those present—11:55 A.M. to 12:25 P.M. Present: Edgar Cayce; Gertrude Cayce, Conductor; Gladys Davis, Steno.; Helen Ellington, Esther Wynne, Hannah Miller, Frances Y. Morrow, Edith & Florence Edmonds, Elizabeth Perry, Sallie Jones, Margaret Wilkins, Ruth LeNoir, Myrtle Demaio, and Hugh Lynn Cayce.

Mrs. C: You will have before you the Glad Helpers, members of which are present here. First you will give affirmations to be sent those on the prayer list; next you will consider the study which has been made by this group for several weeks on the Book of Revelation in attempting to follow the suggestions given through this channel that the references in this book should be applied to experiences in the physical, mental and spiritual bodies of individuals. [See 2501-6.] You will answer the questions which will be presented on Revelation.

Mr. C: Yes, we have the group as gathered here, as a group, as individuals; their work with others, which—first—we would commend. For there has been, is being and may be accomplished, a great deal of hope, of cheer, in the lives and in the experiences of individuals.

And in this manner may this group find within themselves that peace, that harmony, that is the promise from Him who hath given, "That as ye ask, as ye seek in my name, that may the Father do, that I may be glorified through you in the material world."

Be then faithful to that thou hast purposed in thy heart. For many there be who are weak, discouraged, troubled, that ye may aid. And as ye do it unto the least of thy brethren ye do it unto thy Maker. For as He hath given, "Ye that minister to the sick, to the disconsolate, to those in prison, to those in turmoils and strife, minister unto me."

The affirmations in the present are these:

OUR FATHER, OUR GOD, HEAR THE PRAYER OF THY SERVANTS; THAT WE MAY KNOW, THAT WE MAY UNDERSTAND, THAT WE MAY BE WHAT THOU WOULD HAVE US BE.

Again: FATHER OF MERCY, OF LOVE, OF PATIENCE, HEAR THY HUMBLE SERVANT. THOU KNOWEST THE NEEDS OF MY BODY, MY MIND, MY HEART. SUPPLY FROM THE BOUNTY. FOR WE ASK IN THE CHRIST-NAME.

Again: FATHER, GOD, IN HUMBLENESS OF HEART I SEEK. I PRAY THY MERCY, THY LOVE AT THIS PERIOD: NOT ONLY FOR MYSELF BUT ALL THAT SEEK TO KNOW THY WAYS.

Again: FATHER OF MERCY, OF GRACE, LET THY PROTECTION BE WITH ALL THOSE THAT SEEK, IN THE NAME OF THE CHRIST.

Again: FATHER, WHO ART IN HEAVEN, BLESSED BE THY NAME! MAY THY LOVE, THY GRACE, THY MERCY, FILL MY LIFE AND MAKE IT THAT THOU, O GOD, WOULD HAVE IT BE!

Again: FATHER OF LOVE, OF GRACE AND MERCY, KEEP MY FEET LEST THEY FALTER IN THY WAYS. KEEP MY MIND AND MY BODY THAT THEY GO NOT IN THE WAY OF DOUBT OR DESPAIR.

Again: FATHER, GOD, IN THY SON THOU HAST PROMISED THAT WHAT WE ASK WE MAY RECEIVE. MAKE MY BODY, MY MIND, OF SUCH AN ATTITUDE AND

ACTIVITY AS TO BE WORTHY OF THOSE PROMISES!

Again: FATHER, WHO AM IN HEAVEN, BE THOU NEAR TO THOSE THAT FALTER, TO THOSE THAT ARE AFRAID. STRENGTHEN THOU THROUGH THY LOVE MY PURPOSES, THAT I MAY BE A LIGHT, A HELP, A STRENGTH TO MANY.

Again: FATHER, MERCY! MERCY UPON THOSE THAT ARE WAYWARD, THAT IN THEIR NOT UNDERSTANDING FALTER. BE PATIENT, BE KIND WITH ALL!

In considering then the studies that have been made with this group, in the understanding of the Revelation as given by the beloved of Him: These as we find have been well, and as you each become conscious in your own experience of the movement *of* the influences *through* the body upon the various stages of awareness, there comes a determination, a desire, a longing for the greater light. To him, to her that is faithful, there shall be given a *crown* of light. And His Name shall be above every name: For ye that have seen the light know in whom thou hast believed, and know that in thine own body, thine own mind, there is set the temple of the living God, and that it may function in thy dealings with thy fellow man in such measures that ye become as rivers of light, as fountains of knowledge, as mountains of strengths, as the pastures for the hungry, as the rest for the weary, as the strength for the weak. Keep the faith. Ready for questions.

Q-1. Are we using the correct methods of breathing and intonation in our group meditations?

A-1. As has been given in Meditation, to some, *this* then is the correct manner; As has been given so oft of old, purge ye your bodies, washing them with water, putting away those things of the mind and of the body; for tomorrow the Lord would speak with thee.

Hence in this group make thy mind, thy body, as a fit subject for a visit of thy Lord, thy God. Then as ye seek *ye know*, as He hath given, that the wedding feast is prepared and thou hast bid the guests, and that ye have come with the garments of the feast with thy Lord, thy Master, thy King, thy Savior.

For lowly as He was in His earthly ministry, He honored all such that gathered for the commemoration of a union of body, a union of mind, a union of strength for their worship, their sacrifice, their meeting with their God.

So do ye in thy meditation. For thy prayer is as a supplication or a plea to thy superior; yet thy meditation is that thou art meeting on *common* ground!

Then prepare thyself!

In breathing, take into the right nostril, STRENGTH! Exhale through thy mouth. Intake in thy left nostril, exhaling through the right; opening the centers of thy body—if it is first prepared to thine *own* understanding, thine *own* concept of what *ye* would have if ye would have a visitor, if ye would have a companion, if ye would have thy bridegroom!

Then, as ye begin with the incantation of the Ar-ar-r-r-r—the e-e-e, the o-o-o, the m-m-m, *raise* these in thyself; and ye become close in the presence of thy Maker—as is *shown* in thyself! They that do such for selfish motives do so to their own undoing. Thus has it oft been said, the fear of the Lord is the beginning of wisdom.

Wisdom, then, is fear to misapply knowledge in thy dealings with thyself, thy fellow man.

For as ye are honest, as ye are patient, as ye are sincere with thyself in meeting with thy God, thy Savior, thy Christ, in thy meditation, ye will be in thy dealings with thy fellow man.

We are through for the present.

281-29—10/28/36, 3:40 to 4:15 P.M. Continuing:

Yes, we have the Glad Helpers Group, as a group, as individuals; and the study that has been made by same on Revelation. In adding to *some* of those things as have been applied, let each consider how and why that such application would be made by the Beloved in a message of the nature and character. First, the body of the Christ represented to the world a channel, a door, a mediation to the Father. Hence this then may become as the study of self in its relationship to the material world, the mental world, the spiritual world. And this is the manner that has been presented as the way through which each individual would make application of same, of the life of the Christ in his or her own experience.

Q-1. Are we correct in interpreting the seven churches as symbols of seven spiritual centers in the physical body?

A-1. Correct.

Q-2. Do we have these correctly placed? As each is called, comment on each in relation to an individual's development and experiences in connection with these centers. Gonads—Ephesus; Lyden—Smyrna; Solar Plexus—Pergamos; Thymus—Thyatira; Thyroid—Sardis; Pineal—Philadelphia; Pituitary—Laodicea.

A-2. Rather than the commenting, it is well that these are correctly placed, but each individual's *experience* in the application of that gained by each in his or her experience will be different. To give an interpretation that the opening or activity through a certain center raises or means or applies this or that, then would become rote. But know the way, then each may apply same as his or her environment, ability, experience, gives the opportunity. For know, in all and through all, the activity of self is only as a channel—and God giveth the understanding, the increase, to such; and in the manner as is best fitted for the individual. It is not then as a formula, that there are to be certain activities and certain results. These are true in the sense that they each represent or present the opportunity for the opening to the understanding of the individual, but the application is as to the individual. For, as has been given, man is free-willed. And only when this is entirely given, and actively given, to the will of the Father may it be even as the life of the Christ.

Q-3. Which is the highest gland in the body—the pineal or the pituitary?

A-3. The pituitary!

Q-4. Are we correct in interpreting the twenty-four elders as the twenty-four cranial nerves of the head especially related to the five senses?

A-4. Correct.

Q-5. Is the frequent reference to the throne indicating the head in which are found the higher gland centers?

A-5. Correct.

Q-6. Are we correct in interpreting the four beasts as the four fundamental physical natures (desires) of man which must be overcome? Give us more light on each of these.

A-6. Correct. In all of these, let this be understood: These are symbolized; they are as in these representing the elemental forces—as the body is of the earth, is of the elements. For as has so oft been given, and as may be found in man, every element or every influence that is outside of man is found in the *living* man—not a dead one but a *living* man! For the *living* force is that *of* which all that is *was* brought into being. Hence all the influences, all the forces, all the activities are in that. And in man, man's experience, there never has been, never will be found in material activity an instrument, an action, that is not shown as a replica or expression or manifestation of that in a living man; whether it be in this, that or the other of the forces of nature, of activity. For when such is active, unless found in man—or an answer to something within, it would not be cognizable by man.

Q-7. Do we have these four beasts placed correctly in relation to the centers in the body and the ancient elementals? Air—Eagle—Thymus?

A-7. These are *relatively*, yes. Relatively correct.

Q-8. Fire—Lion—Solar Plexus?

A-8. Correct.

Q-9. Water—Man—Lyden?

A-9. Yes.

Q-10. Earth—Calf—Gonads?

A-10. Yes.

Q-11. Is the book with the seven seals the human body with the seven spiritual centers?

A-11. This is correct.

Q-12. Do we have the opening of the seals correctly placed in our chart? As each is called, give advice that will help us in properly opening these centers.

A-12. [Interrupting] First, let's give as this: Do not attempt to open any of the centers of the book until self has been tried in the balance of self's own conscious relationship to the Creative Forces and not found wanting by the spiritual answer in self to that rather as is seen in the manner in which the book itself becomes as that in the whole body which may be assimilated by the body, when taken properly. In these then there has been set as ye have in thine outline. These are well. *Do not* misuse them!

Q-13. Gonads—White Horse?

A-13. Yes.

Q-14. Lyden—Black Horse?

A-14. Yes.

Q-15. Solar Plexus—Red Horse?

A-15. Yes.

Q-16. Thymus—Pale Horse?

A-16. Yes. For a reference to these, let each in your study of these, as in relation to the centers themselves, consider the effect of the color itself upon thine own body as ye attempt to apply same by either concentration, dedication or meditating upon these. For as has been given, color is but vibration. Vibration is movement. Movement is activity of a positive and negative force. Is the activity of self as in relationship to these then positive? Proceed.

Q-17. Thyroid—Souls slain for Word of God?

A-17. Correct.

Q-18. What color here?

A-18. Gray.

Q-19. Pineal—Upheavals?

A-19. Correct, but this would have to be *relatively* so. For these are at those periods when, in the colors that these arise to—which are of the purple, they become rather such that there *must* be the *disseminating* or the giving away of the egoism of self. Consider as an example in thy study of same, the servant Moses. For these become as may be found even for and from that record as ye have, the stumbling block at Meribah.

Q-20. Pituitary—Silence?

A-20. Silence, golden; the forces upon which the greater expression has been set of all the influences of might and power as may be seen in man's experience—*Silence* if ye would hear the Voice of thy Maker!

Q-21. Do the planets as placed in our chart have proper relation and significance? Pituitary—Jupiter; Pineal—Mercury; Thyroid—Uranus; Thymus—Venus; Solar Plexus—Mars; Lyden—Neptune; Gonads—Saturn?

A-21. These are very well done. These vary, to be sure, according to the variation of an *experience*. For these are the variable forces in the very nature of man himself, for he partakes of all and from all the influences and forces. For remember as has been given, it is not that the planets rule the man; rather has man, as man of God, ruled the planets! For he's a portion of same.

Then, these are as we have given; only relative. Relatively, these are correct. At times these are represented by others. It is here the application of these influences in the experience of the individual rather than there being set, as it were, a blanket to cover each and every individual.

Q-22. Does the outline of the Lord's Prayer as placed on our chart have any bearing on the opening of the centers?

A-22. Here is indicated the manner in which it was given as to the purpose for which it was given; not as an *only* way but as a way that would answer for those that sought to be—as others—seekers for a way, *an* understanding, to the relationships to the Creative Forces. It bears in relationships to this, then, the proper place.

Q-23. Pituitary—Heaven?

A-23. Correct. In all of its activities these open, for the upward lift of the thoughts of man as in relationships to that which becomes—how has it been given?—"He is alpha, omega, the beginning and the end." Hence as we find in its relationships to man, it becomes then the beginnings, the endings, of all things.

Q-24. Pineal—Name?

A-24. Relatively, yes.

Q-25. Thyroid—Will?

A-25. Correct.

Q-26. Thymus—Evil?

A-26. Correct.

Q-27. Solar Plexus—Debts?

A-27. Yes.

Q-28. Lyden—Temptation?

A-28. Correct

Q-29. Gonads—Bread?

A-29. Right,

Q-30. How should the Lord's Prayer be used in this connection?

A-30. As in feeling, as it were, the flow of the meanings of each portion of same throughout the body-physical. For as there is the response to the mental representations of all of these in the *mental* body, it may build into the physical body in the manner as He, thy Lord, thy Brother, so well expressed in, "I have bread ye know not of."

Q-31. What is meant by the seven lamps of fire burning before the throne, described as the seven spirits of God—Ch. 4:5?

A-31. Those influences or forces which in their activity in the natures of man are without, that stand ever before the throne of grace—or God, to become the messengers, the aiders, the destructions of hindrances; as the ways between man's approach to—as was represented in the ways of dividing man's knowledge of or between—good and evil. Hence they work ever as those influences or forces that stand between, as it were; being the helpful influences that become as the powers of activity in the very nature or force of man.

Q-32. What is meant by the angels at the four corners of the earth as given in Ch. 7?

A-32. These are only as from the body-forces ever. There are those four influences or forces in the natures of man from his source; as in environment, heredity as of the earth and as of the mental and spiritual. These are as the four corners that become represented here as the very natures or forces to which all approaches to all these influences are made in the very nature of man.

Q-33. Are we correct in interpreting the 144,000 who were sealed as being spiritualized cellular structure of the twelve major divisions of the body?

A-33. Correct. And this is as of a man, and the name of same.

Q-34. Are the zodiacal divisions of the body proper and do they have any relation to this?

A-34. Only relatively. For this is as we have given again and again in reference to same; for as they have been set as the zodiacal signs, correct. As they have moved in their orb or their sphere about the earth, these have just recently passed and have become—as has been indicated—a very different nature to them.

Q-35. Is the multitude before the throne as described in Ch. 7 the rest of the cellular structure in process of spiritualization?

A-35. This is correct.

Q-36. Are we correct in interpreting the sounding of the seven angels as the experience during physical purification?

A-36. Correct.

We are through for the present.

281-30

This psychic reading was given by Edgar Cayce at his home on Arctic Crescent, Va. Beach, Va., this 17th day of Feb., 1937, requested by the Glad Helpers of the Ass'n for Research and Enlightenment, Inc. 3:15 to 3:50 P.M. Present: Edgar Cayce; Gertrude Cayce, Conductor; Gladys Davis, Steno; Florence and Edith Edmonds, Esther Wynne, Hannah Miller, Helen Ellington, Hugh Lynn Cayce, Noah Miller, Margaret Wilkins, Ruth Denny, and Virginia Twiford.

Mrs. C: You will have before you the Glad Helpers of the Ass'n for Research and Enlightenment, Inc., members of which are present here; and their study of the Book of Revelation together with the information given them through this channel on Oct. 26, 1936 and Oct. 28, 1936, in connection with this study. You will answer the questions regarding this study which will be asked.

Mr. C: Yes, we have the work of the Glad Helpers, together with their study of Revelation, and the information which has been given respecting same. In the beginning again we would give this, that it may be clarified in the minds of those who seek to have the interpretation of *the* Revelation in their own experience:

Know first that the knowledge of God is a growing thing, for ye grow in grace, in knowledge, in understanding *as* ye apply that ye KNOW. But remember, as has been given by Him, to know to do good and do it not is sin.

In the interpretation then of the Revelation as given by John in Patmos: This was John's revelation of *his* experience, and interpreted in the individual by the application of the body of self as a pattern with the attributes physically, mentally, spiritually, in their respective spheres for thine *own* revelation.

For this to be practical, to be applicable in the experience of each soul, it must be an individual experience; and the varied experiences or activities of an entity in its relationship to the study of self are planned, builded, workable in the pattern as John has given in the Revelation.

Each attribute of the body, whether organ or functioning or the expression of same, becomes then in the experience of each soul as a seeker first. Seek and ye shall find, knock and it shall be opened unto you!

Then in thy study, for those who would become Glad Helpers, in the physical, in the moral, in the mental, in the spiritual life of each soul: Condemn no one. Love all. Do good. And ye may experience it all.

Ready for questions.

Q-1. Please discuss more fully the relation of colors to the seven major glandular centers. Do the colors vary for each center with different individuals, or may definite colors be associated with each center?

A-1. Both. For to each—remember, to study each of these in the light not only of what has just been given but that as is a practical experience in the material world—as is known, vibration is the essence or the basis of color. As color and vibration then become to the consciousness along the various centers in an individual's experience in meditation made aware, they come to mean definite experiences. Just as anger is red, or as something depressing is blue; yet in their shades, their tones, their activities, to each they begin with the use of same in the experience to mean those various stages. For instance, while red is anger, rosy to most souls means delight and joy—yet to others, as they are formed in their transmission from center to center, come to mean or to express what *manner* of joy; whether that as would arise from a material, a mental or a spiritual experience. Just as may be seen in the common interpretation of white, but with all manner of rays from same begins or comes to mean that above the aura of all in its vibration from the body and from the activity of the mental experience when the various centers are vibrating to color.

Q-2. If so, give color for: (1) Gonads (2) Lyden (3) Solar Plexus (4) Thymus (5) Thyroid (6) Pineal (7) Pituitary.

A-2. These come from the leaden, going on through to the highest—to that as is the halo. To each they become the various forces as active throughout, and will go in the regular order of the prism.

Q-3. What is the significance of the color of the four horses associated with four lower centers; pale horse for Thymus; red for Solar Plexus; black for Lyden; white for Gonads?

A-3. That comes as has just been given as the illustration of same from the *emotions* or physical forces that ride forth to their expression in the higher forces of the activity.

Q-4. *Please explain what was meant in reading of Oct. 28 [281-29], regarding the "relative" connection of Name in the Lord's Prayer with the Pineal gland.*

A-4. This might occupy a whole period of several hours, if the full conclusion were to be given; but each must reach this. There is a Name to each soul. For He hath called His own by *name!* What name? All the names that may have been as a material experience through an earthly sojourn, or all the names that may have been through the experience of an entity in that environ or those relative associations of Venus, Mars, Jupiter, Uranus, Saturn, Sun, Moon, or what! Or a Name that is above *every* name!

Then as has been indicated this becomes relative, as is signified in the indication as given to the number, which is of John's own. But as has been given, every influence—you see—is *relative!* Hence the name is relative to that which is accomplished by the soul in its sojourn throughout its whole experience; whether in those environs about this individual sphere or another—this individual sphere meaning thine own sun, thine own planets with all of their attributes (does an earth mind comprehend such?) and it carried through with what is its *relative* force to that which has been or is the activity of the entity-soul (not a body now at all!) toward Constructive Force or God, or God's infinitive force to that integral activity of the soul in its sojourn. Hence it becomes *relative.* And for the finite mind to say Jane, John, Joe, James or Jude would mean only as the *vibrations* of those bring the *relative* force or influence to which, through which an entity's sojourns have brought the concrete experience in any one given or definite period of activity!

Was one named John by chance? Was one named Joe or Llewellyn by chance? No; they are relative! While it may be truly in the material plane relative because you have a rich aunt by that name, or relative because an uncle might be named that—but these carry then the vibrations of same; and in the end the name is the sum total of what the soul-entity in all of its vibratory forces has borne toward the Creative Force itself.

Hence each soul has a definite influence upon the experiences through which it may be passing. This ye have illustrated in thine own secret organizations, in thy papal activities in the religious associations, and in each vibration. For when ye have set a vibration by the activity of thy *soul's* force, ye are then either in parallel, in direct accord, or in opposition to constructive force—whatever may be the position or activity of the soul in infinity. For ye *are* gods! But you are becoming devils or real gods!

Q-5. What was meant in the reading of Oct. 28 [281-29], in connection with 144,000 who were sealed as being spiritualized cellular structure of the twelve major divisions of the body, when the reading gave, "Correct. And this is as of a man, and the name of same." Please explain.

A-5. Just as has been illustrated or given, as to the relative force of the vibratory forces of the individual; which is shown in an individual soul or entity by its name and its activity in all the influences or environs through which it passes in that which is a shadow in man (active, living) to those influences that are relative to the infinitive position of a soul's activity in a universe.

Q-6. In connection with the symbols of Revelation, what are the twelve major divisions of the body?

A-6. Those that are of the general construction and those that are of the keeping alive physical, and those that are in keeping with the influences to the mental, to the material, to the spiritual; and the illustrations are shown in the bodily forces that are opened for those activities in a material plane.

Q-7. What is meant by the symbol of the angel with the golden censer and incense described in Rev. 8:3-5?

A-7. As the influence is visualized in the experience of each soul by the name as implied in "angel," or the good that goes out from the individual soul in its relationships to the influences or forces about same, so is it called or given as the angel with the censer of the activities that emanate from each individual. And as has been given in other illustrations, that ye ARE—that of good—rises ever as an incense, sweet before the throne of mercy. Or to take the back track, as it were, and take the angel with the censer, with the incense that is before the image of a soul seeking to become one with the Creative Forces or God—that which has been kind, gentle, patient, merciful, long-suffering in self's experience during a day, rises before the throne of the mercy seat within self to that of an incense of satisfaction. Why? Hate, unkindness, harshness, all such become as base in thine own experience, and as usual one condemns self by saying, "Why can't I do this or that?" And, "What is the use?" Well—and the censer is broken!

Q-8. Do the seven angels described in Rev. 8-9 represent spiritual forces governing the various dimensional planes through which souls pass between incarnations on the earth? Please explain.

A-8. This is a very good interpretation. Yes. While this explanation becomes a portion of another group's study and activity in the lesson just being approached on *happiness*, it may be best explained in this; as to how this must indeed be interpreted in the experience of each soul, whether considered in a material plane in which there is found the real essence of happiness or that in the interim when ye are looked over, or when the promises become more and more as has been interpreted from that given by others—to be absent from the body-physical is to be present in the grace and glory and presence of divinity; or to be those influences that make for an activity in an influence without self.

Now ye are studying yourself! Do not confuse the interpretation with that outside of thyself, but happiness is love of something outside of self! It may never be obtained, may never be known by loving only things within self or self's own domain!

Then the expression that has been given by an entity in a sojourn in the earth becomes as a portion of that activity as has been given, "He hath given His angels charge concerning thee, lest at any time ye dash thy foot against a stone."

Hence we find that in the expression then of those interims where there are the guiding influences of that we have loved, we have love—for this becomes then very definite.

If ye have loved self-glory, if ye have loved the honor of the people more than those thoughts of the mental and spiritual and moral welfare, what manner of angels will direct thee between thy interims?

Think on the study then of self, in thy body—but let it all become as has been *so oft* given:

Study to show thyself approved unto God, the God in self, the God in thine own consciousness—that is creative in its essence; rightly divining and dividing the words of truth and light; keeping self unspotted from the world. And ye become lights to those that sit in darkness, to those that wander.

Though ye may be reviled, revile not again. Though ye may be spoken of harshly, smile—SMILE! For it is upon the river of life that smiles are made. Not grins! No Cheshire cat activities bring other than those that are of the earth, of such natures that create in the minds and the experiences those things that become repulsive. But the smile of understanding cheers on the hearts of those who are discouraged, who are disheartened. It costs so little! It does thee so much good, and lifts the burdens of so many!

We are through for the present.

281-31

This psychic reading given by Edgar Cayce at his home on Arctic Crescent, Virginia Beach, Va., this 12th day of March, 1937, in accordance with request made by the Glad Helpers of the Ass'n for Research and Enlightenment, Inc., 3:35 to 4:00 P.M. Present: Edgar Cayce; Gertrude Cayce, Conductor; Gladys Davis, Steno; Florence and Edith Edmonds, Hannah Miller, Frances Y. Morrow, Helen Ellington, and Hugh Lynn Cayce.

Mrs. C: You will have before you the Glad Helpers of the Ass'n for Research & Enlightenment, Inc., members of which are present here; and their study of the Book of Revelation together with the information already given them through this channel in connection with this study. You will continue answering the questions which have been prepared.

Mr. C: Yes, we have the Glad Helpers Group, and their study of Revelation; and the information that has been given here respecting same.

Ready for questions.

Q-1. Please interpret the 2nd Chapter, 17th verse of Revelation. "To him that overcometh will I give to eat of the hidden manna, and will give him a white stone, and in the stone a new name written, which no man knoweth saving he that receiveth it."

A-1. In giving the interpretation of this particular portion of the Revelation, it must all be kept in mind that, as has been indicated, while many of the references—or all—refer to the physical body as the pattern, there is that as may be said to be the literal and the spiritual and the metaphysical interpretation of almost all portions of the Scripture, and especially of the Revelation as given by John.

Yet all of these to be true, to be practical, to be applicable in the experiences of individuals, must coordinate; or be as one, even as the Father, the Son and the Holy Spirit.

In the interpretation of the Name, then: Each entity, each soul, is known— in all the experiences through its activities—as a name to designate it from another. It is not only then a material convenience, but it implies—as has been given, unless it is for material gain—a definite period in the evolution of the experience of the entity in the material plane.

Then as each entity under a given name makes its correlating of that it does about the Creative Forces in its experience, it is coming under those influences that are being fed by the manna—which is a representation of the universality as well as the stability of purposes in the Creative Forces as manifested to a group or a nation of peoples.

So it becomes that as the Master gave, "Ye shall not live by bread alone but by every word that proceedeth from the mouth of the Father."

That indeed is the holy manna which each entity, each soul in each experience must make a part of its mental and spiritual self. Thus it becomes as is indicated, in that the name—as in each experience—bears a relative relationship to the development of the individual entity in each experience.

Then in the end, or in those periods as indicated, it is when each entity, each soul has so manifested, so acted in its relationships as to become then as the new name; white, clear, known only to him that hath overcome. Overcome what? The world, even as He.

For what meaneth a name? John, Jane, Peter, Andrew, Bartholomew, Thaddeus, Rhoda, Hannah? All of these have not only the attunement of a vibration but of color, harmony; and all those relative relationships as one to another.

Then as has been asked, and has been indicated in another portion of Revelation, all those that bear the mark, those that have the name, those that have the stone—these are representatives then of the same experience in the various phases of an individual experience for its activity.

Then the interpretation is that they *have* overcome, they *have* the new name, they *have* the manna, they *have* the understanding, they *have* their relationships as secure in the blood of the Lamb!

Q-2. Continuing with the references to the seven angels described in Rev. 8:9, are we correct in interpreting the sounding of these seven angels as the influence of spiritual development in these other planes becoming through the vibrating centers of the physical body during the process of purification?

A-2. Correct. But these are not always interpreted in individual experiences as the true sound, true tone.

Now, this is not to confuse but rather to clarify for those who are studying these, in the relationships to what takes place as the various centers in the body are opened, that are represented by the Spirit's activative forces upon same; that these may be the more perfectly understood:

Just as the individual who has by practical application gained the correct pitch, correct tone in a musical composition. This may be as a soul-expression or a mechanical expression; and only when it is in the true accord, as from the soul, is it perfectly understood. See?

Q-3. Do the seven angels govern in order the major glandular centers of the physical body?

A-3. In their order, as they have been set.

Q-4. Please explain the meaning of some of the symbols in the sounding of the seven angels: (1) Hail and fire, blood and one-third of earth burned. What is the earth in this connection?

A-4. As has been intimated or given in the first interpretations of what the elements represent, that are apparent or a portion of the First Cause; as the Earth, Air, Water and the like. These are then as has just been given, ever to represent or be symbolical of the same influences or forces throughout; else we may become confused as to their place. Earth—that as we represent as being in a state of transition, or as earthy. Not necessarily lowly or unduly a condition that would belie development. But as Fire is purifying, as Hail is the crystallization of the water, the Air and the temperaments, so all of these then represent those as figuratives of that as may be purified by the fires of Nature; as may be represented by the earth when they are met and conquered and used for the development—as in the Hail and the like becoming purifying in their natures for the crystallization and the oneness of the individual's purposes and desires.

For to go back just a bit, that we may ever keep what is the purpose of the Revelation: Was it for the purpose of confusing, of being mysterious? (This has been gone over before, to be sure.) Rather was it not to present it that each entity, each soul, might find within itself that which answers to that within, that makes the real answer to that as was before stated, "My Spirit beareth witness with thy spirit"? And until the answer is in accord, in attune, is there the consciousness of the prompting of the ability in a manifested material world to make same practical?

Then as the progress is made, as the understanding comes more and more, *never, NEVER* does it make the manifested individual entity other than the more humble, the more meek, the more long-suffering, the more patient. Of this ye may be sure.

Then in all of the experiences of the opening of the centers as are represented, and those vibrations that find expression in the various temperaments of individual souls, these come not as justifications in *self* but justification in the Lamb of God!

Q-5. (2) Mountain of fire in sea, sea becomes blood.

A-5. Again as the body elements that become conflicting one with another, which shows the overcoming within the individual activities of the influences that are constantly warring within.

How has it been said? "O today there is life and death, good and evil— Choose thou." This may be said to be symbolical then of these conflicting forces within the influences that are ever present, or as given by another, "The Spirit is willing, the flesh is weak." These are symbolical then, one interpreting the other.

Q-6. (3) Great star falls from heaven. What are the one-third part of the rivers and fountains that it falls upon?

A-6. The star signifies simply the coming of the influence from without to the influences from within, as is signified by "His Star have we seen." Then this becomes that as falls upon the third, or that is a third portion of the bodily activities—and as interpreted in the experience of the individual, ye have made so many steps as it were along the way.

Q-7. One-third part of sun smitten and one-third of stars.

A-7. These are symbolical and represent in the experience of the individual that of life and heat, beauty and that as given in another portion, "The stars declare the glory of God, the firmament showeth His handiwork." These then represent in the experiences the vibrations of the emotions that are being aroused, as has just been given. Again less and less then is it of self, and more and more unto the glory of the Father.

Q-8. Star from heaven, Key to bottomless pit. What are the locusts as described in this sounding? King Apollyon in this connection?

A-8. As has been given as to how each of these vibratory forces arises from the lower portion, or as has been put in another setting—that which represents in the bodily forces the most uncomely, or that from the depths of the bottomless pit, or from out the presence of God, again has the spirit of man arisen to the glory of the star as in the Son (not sun, but Son), to those glories that become as the natures of the bodily forces, and every influence as comes through the earthly natures becomes lost in that beauty in the Son.

Q-9. Voice from four horns before the throne.

A-9. As indicated by the horns of the altar, as indicated by the four forces in nature, as indicated by the four influences in the experiences of the individual soul which cry then in the voice raised as a sweet incense, or as the essence of the purifying that has come to the individual entity or soul to arise before the Throne of Him who is Lord of Lords and King of Kings, for His love as given, as shown in that as accomplished in the raising of self in the Christ, the Son, in Jesus.

We are through for the present.

281-32

This psychic reading given by Edgar Cayce at his home on Arctic Crescent, Virginia Beach, Va., this 24th day of March, 1937, in accordance with request made by the Glad Helpers of the Ass'n for Research & Enlightenment, Inc., 3:00 to 3:25 P.M. Present: Edgar Cayce; Gertrude Cayce, Conductor; Gladys Davis, Steno; Helen Ellington, Florence and Edith Edmonds, Hannah Miller, Esther Wynne, and Hugh Lynn Cayce.

Mrs. C: You will have before you the Glad Helpers, members of which are present here, who come seeking at this time further light and understanding on the Book of Revelation. You will continue to answer the questions which will be presented on this study.

Mr. C: Yes, we have the group, the Glad Helpers, and their study and their seeking in the study and understanding of Revelations; together with that which has been given respecting this. Ready for questions.

Q-1. What is meant by the four angels bound in the river Euphrates in connection with the sounding of the sixth angel? [Gen. 2:14; Rev. 9:14, 16:12]

A-1. As has been given, each reference in the Revelation is to some portion of the body as in its relative position to the emotions physical, mental, material; and their activities through portions of the system, as places that represent conditions in some phase of manifestation or development of the entity. Or the whole (to be put in another way and manner) is an experience of man as known to those who were being spoken to by the writer.

Then we find, as in the beginning, the Euphrates—or *the good river* [Frat], or *the river* of the fiat [covenant Gen. 15:18]—is being represented as being sounded now for the beginnings of the changes which have been effected by the activities of those who have preceded, who have acted upon the various influences or forces by the opening of centers and the emotions and the understandings and the conditions of the individual entity.

Hence it represents now, as it were, to the individual—that ye now begin again to make practical or applicable, mentally, spiritually, materially, with that which has been thus far attained.

Q-2. What are the four angels that are bound in the river Euphrates?

A-2. As has been indicated, the four influences that are as the Air, the Earth, the Fire, the Water; being influences now that are—as understood by the entity, the soul, the individual—as a portion of itself again.

Q-3. What is meant by the symbol of the Euphrates in relation to the body, if it may be connected?

A-3. As has just been given, it represents that as a boundary of its beginnings, or a beginning, or an end, from the material standpoint.

Q-4. What is meant by the symbols of the horsemen who were to kill one-third part of men, in connection with the sounding of the sixth angel?

A-4. That as a place, as a condition, an experience through which the influences are acted upon by the emotions in which the changes are wrought by the application of those very forces or conditions that have been spoken of in the experience of the individual, see?

Or, as put by another, "When I was a child I did as a child, when I was a man I did as a man," the same as in the beginning and the same as in the activities, or the same as in the relationships to all of these then as has been given heretofore—they must be as one, they must be compatible, they must be coordinant, they must be in the relative relationships one to another. These then become as destroying influences within the individual, a third portion of that which has been set as such a necessary force for a material body. How hath it been given throughout? The Father, the Son, the Holy Spirit—which is the third. They are all one, and yet a third. The same as the death of those influences or forces or activities within the emotional, the physical, the material forces. All of these then are as representatives of these, or the activities from the fourfold elements that are activative in the experience of each entity, each soul.

Q-5. Do we interpret correctly the angel described in Rev. 10, with the little book, as a guardian of the book of knowledge?

A-5. This is a very good interpretation; or we come to that point in the experience of each soul—know ye have passed through the experiences of attaining to the understanding of thine emotions, the understanding of the needs of thy physical body, the understanding of thy relationships to the spiritual forces; and know ye come to that which is to be—what will ye do with that knowledge?

It might be set or interpreted as the guardian force, for as is understood by each and every one that have studied in these influences or forces, all force, all power, all knowledge (constructive) is from a one source—is it not?

Then the guardian force is that ability to use or abuse that which has been combined in the book; or the book may be the *body,* see, as an illustration of that, as a parallel of that. Know ye have gained these, know ye are to use these in thine own experience.

Q-6. Is the little book described in Rev. 10—Power of Creative Thought?

A-6. As has just been given, it may be that of the whole influence or that of the body itself, or—yes—that of creative thought itself; for these are one.

Q-7. What is the significance of John eating it up and of the verse, "Thou must prophesy again before many peoples, and nations, and tongues, and kings"?

A-7. As illustrated in that as indicated, and as from the use of same. Know ye have it—what will ye do with it? It becomes part and parcel, by the eating up. It is very beautiful to look upon, very beautiful to be desired; but in the application of same at times very bitter.

As is seen in the very manner in which—How did the Son in the earth become as an intermediator between sinful man and an All-Wise, All-Merciful God? By going through or experiencing, or in giving to, through the very sufferings in the body, the right, the purpose, the aim to be in that position!

Now, man having attained same by this study must prophesy—apply—prophesy *is* apply—before many in many experiences, in many ways, in many environs, in many lands. All of these are a part and parcel of same. How did He put it as He gave, "I will bring to your remembrance *all* things, from the foundations of the world."

Then as it has been experienced by those who have taken hold of, who have combined the book (that is the book of Life), into the experience, it becomes within its body then a part and parcel of—and is to be expended in its relationships to the environs in that of prophecy, yes; in experiences before kings, yes; yea as beggars; yea as rulers; yea as those in authority; yea as those authoritative over.

Think of how this is shown in the life of the Master Himself; He that made man, yet under the authority and the will of man by the mere giving of self in the experience of passing through same. Not that these were needed other than that it might be fulfilled, what? Prophecy, as had been given in man's search for God.

Then as this has been found, as is illustrated here by John, in the taking of the book and in becoming these, each then must pass in its experience through the same sources.

Q-8. What is meant by the symbol of the "reed like unto a rod" with which John was told to measure the temple? Rev. 11. Please explain.

A-8. How again has it been given by Him? "With what measure ye mete it shall be measured to thee again." Know that he had acceded to the point wherein he is to set the metes and bounds (John as an individual). Ye, your own souls as individuals, who will you put in your heaven? Ye of a denomination, ye of a certain creed, ye of a certain measurement, with what measure ye mete it is measured to thee again.

This then is an illustration that to each there is given, what? All power to set that as the metes and bounds of what heaven in itself shall be to those who would gather these, or those, or the self. What would be heaven to a soul that built it for its individual self? Heaven, yes—but alone!

Those that will measure then, those that will set metes and bounds—how has it been given oft? When ye name a name, or when ye give metes and bounds, ye forget that God's force, God's power is *Infinite!* and this is beyond the comprehension of the finite mind. Yet as is illustrated here to John, as is illustrated to thee, thou art given—with the understanding—as to what the metes and bounds shall be. As to the numbers as seen, as understood, these become as parts of its *own* understanding.

Q-9. Is the temple here the physical body?

A-9. Rather the *mental* in which is the pattern as of the tabernacle; or the holy mount—or that as set by a *unified* service of the body-mind, the body-physical, the body-spiritual; that vehicle that is without nails (as was the tabernacle as a pattern), not bound together, yet a covering, a place, an understanding for a *unified* activity with Creative Forces, or the power of God. The veil without, the holy within, and the holy of holies—knowing that there must be the cleansing, there must be the purifying, there must be the consecration. All of these are as patterns, they are as conditions, they are as experiences for each and every soul.

Q-10. Is the court referred to the body apart from the spiritual centers?

A-10. As indicated, rather is it as the environ without—the body-physical and mental within for its sacrificial forces, and then to the spiritual force within as to the holy of holies.

Q-11. Are the Gentiles here those not seeking spiritual development?

A-11. Rather do the Gentiles here refer to that without the court. Not necessarily not seeking, but—remember the measuring rod He hath set. These do not change because if thou art worthy, Christ-like in the material, ye are Christ-like in the broader sense in the mental—and how much greater in the spiritual! The same as in those who are very devout without—as a Catholic, as a Protestant—as of such and such creed or faith; how much smaller have they grown within!

We are through for the present.

281-33

This psychic reading given by Edgar Cayce at his home on Arctic Crescent, Virginia Beach, Va., this 31st day of March, 1937, in accordance with request made by the Glad Helpers of the Ass'n for Research & Enlightenment, Inc., 3:00 to 3:30 P.M. Present: Edgar Cayce; Gertrude Cayce, Conductor; Gladys Davis, Steno; Florence and Edith Edmonds, Esther Wynne, Hannah Miller, Margaret Wilkins, and Hugh Lynn Cayce.

Mrs. C: You will have before you the Glad Helpers, members of which are present here, and their study of the Book of Revelation. You will continue to answer the questions which have been prepared.

Mr. C: Yes, we have the Glad Helpers, as a group, as individuals; and their study of Revelation, with that which has been given as respecting same.

In considering the study, the seeking of the Group as here, and that as has been given: The Book thus far, as has been given, is the study of the body, the mind, the soul; the physical body, its attributes; the mental body, its associations and attributes; the soul body and its attributes.

Now we have reached the point as implied by the book as eaten, the rod as given to John; that these understandings are now to be, and are, applied in the experience of the individual *entity*—in its relationships to its fellow man.

Hence we see in the symbolized form that as now gives place to the references as to the influences from without, that have had, do have, their influences upon these activative forces in the human experience—or the individual experience in this material life.

Now: In the study of the rest or the last half of the Revelation, we find this is referring to the application, the effect, the influence—and, as in the end, "Whosoever will may come, drink of the water of life and be whole in Him."

Ready for questions.

Q-1. What is meant by the two witnesses mentioned in Rev. 11:3? Are they the mental and emotional bodies of the soul of man?

A-1. As has been made reference, now—the Book of Life has been eaten. It is in the mouth, sweet; in the belly (or the body), bitter.

This may be the interpretation then: the mental or the subconscious; but rather is it the *conscious PHYSICAL* lives, or the attributes and the consciousness in the *experience* of the soul in the attributes of a physical consciousness!

Do not confuse self; and many of you are wondering just what it is. Then, as has been so oft given, all of this was recognized by John. Hence all of this is given in form, ritual, the emblems, what we may term numerology, astrology, and all the forms of the ancient wisdoms; yet it is represented by the activities of same upon a physical being.

As has so oft been given, an individual experience in the earth plane is motivated by that which arises from its sojourns in the influences of the consciousnesses outside of the physical being—or as ye would say astrologically the sojourn in the environ of Venus, Jupiter, Mars, Neptune, Saturn, Uranus, Sun, Moon, and the constellations and those effects upon same—emotionally from the *innate* forces; *and* by the *emotional* effect from sojourns in the earth. Both of these are witnesses.

As the Book of Life then is opened, there is seen the effect of that which now has been attained by the opening of the system, the body, the mind; all of those effects that have been created by the ability of the entity to, in the physical being, attune self to the consciousness of being at-one with the Divine within.

Now we see those in the material world using these influences for self-exaltation, self-indulgence, self-glorification; and yet we see those using same for the glory, the understanding, the knowledge, the wisdom of the Father.

These then are the witnesses. The innate and the emotional; or the spiritual-mental, the physical-mental; the subconscious, the superconscious.

Q-2. Explain the symbol of the death of the two witnesses.

A-2. As is the symbol of—Does the individual, unless—Let's illustrate by what has been given: The Master gave, "Before the world was, I AM! Now if ye abide in me and I in the Father, then I will bring to thy remembrance ALL *THINGS*—from the foundations of the world!"

Yet these are as dead, or the only consciousness that arises from same is that which is fanned into life or activity by the application of the laws concerning same. Hence they are as dead, yet become alive again by remembrance, by the application of thought. In what? The light of that which has been attained by the entity or soul that has applied the former lessons in its experience.

Q-3. What is meant by the "great city which is called Sodom and Egypt, where also our Lord was crucified"?

A-3. As has been so often given, all places—as Egypt or Sodom or the Crucifixion, or the Lord—are conditions, circumstances, experiences, as well as individual places. Then in the minds of those who would attempt or that would seek knowledge, they represent their own experiences. Thus these to the people represent—Egypt, the release from bondage; Gomorrah, as a reckoning with sin—as the Lord was crucified there. As has been given, there has never been an experience when His Christ-mass, His death, His birth, wasn't an experience of the age, the people. Though it may go under many names, as an individual may be under many names, in many environs, there is one—ONE—that ever comes as is shown in that later given as to those who have the name in the hand, in the head or in the forehead and the like; that is, what is the intent and purpose. Just as the Savior of the world, as Lord, as Christ—what do these as names indicate? That which is as a help in a time of trouble alone? or that to glory in, in thy joy, thy gladness, thy happiness? How many, O how many have there been that have laughed with God, that have wept with Jesus, that have gloried with the Christ! or rather has it been, "My happiness and my joy is of myself"?

No condemnation; but rather is there the pattern pointed to as was set by Him. He was *all* things to *all* men; rejoiced with those that did rejoice; He wept with those that wept. He was glad, He was happy, He was sorry, He kept the faith.

Q-4. What is signified by the revival of these witnesses?

A-4. How hath He given? "If ye meditate on these things, I will bring to thy remembrance all things." The reviving, the renewing, by the abilities of the soul to take hold upon the witnesses of the life itself! And what is life? God!

Q-5. What is meant by the sounding of the seventh angel? How should time be interpreted as given?

A-5. Remember, as has been given to him that was given a measure, as a mete, as a rod to measure heaven—as to how large his heaven would be. All right! Then we have as to how much time—What is time? Is it a record merely of the events of self or of the glory of God? What is the extent of the glory of thy heaven or of thy God? This is as a reckoning. Yet as is shown by the indication of so many days, so many weeks, it is the *inclination* of the individual mind in materiality to set (as was said of John) metes and bounds; and we judge from—How many days or years have ye set? Nineteen thirty-seven [1937] is what? And thy Lord has been continuous! yet ye say only 1937!

Q-6. In Rev. 12 we find the symbols of the Woman, Dragon and Child. Do these represent the part played by souls in the creation and fall of man? Please explain the reference of these symbols.

A-6. Rather is the reference given to show to the individual entity that from which or through which soul in the earth has passed in its creation, its activity in the earthly sojourn, see?

For as we go on or interpret further we find: The war was in heaven, see? The woman—or the mother—earth; the source from which all materiality is to become a conscious thing—and these are brought forth.

Now, as is given, ye have reached to that understanding of thy perfection with God; how in materiality ye may attune the attributes of self.

Now from what have ye risen? These are emblems, significant of that as given as the name of Satan, the Devil, the Dragon or the like, through which man's rebellious forces arise, even though he has attained to the Book even itself in his body! And these are the experiences then to be met.

Q-7. What is meant here by the war in heaven between Michael and the Devil?

A-7. As has just been given, as is understood by those here, there is first—as is the spiritual concept—the spiritual rebellion, before it takes mental or physical form. This warring is illustrated there by the war between the Lord of the Way and the Lord of Darkness—or the Lord of Rebellion.

Q-8. What is meant by the symbols of the wings of eagle given to the woman for escape and "the time and times and half a time"?

A-8. This is as the entrance into or the flight from materiality into those influences through which the body may rest within itself; as physical, or the mental flight, or that to the astral forces as about its various changes. It is figurative of the transitions from the various spheres of mental experience; by mind, the spiritual influences as arise—and are as the use of same. Remember, all of these should be then in accord with that ye have attained to, that the Book of Life is given thee. What is the Book of Life?

The record of God, of thee, thy soul within and the knowledge of same.

We are through for the present.

281-34

This psychic reading given by Edgar Cayce at his home on Arctic Crescent, Virginia Beach, Va., this 21st day of April, 1937, in accordance with request made by the Glad Helpers of the Ass'n for Research & Enlightenment, Inc., 3:00 to 3:30 P.M. Present: Edgar Cayce; Gertrude Cayce, Conductor; Gladys Davis, Steno; Florence & Edith Edmonds, Helen Ellington, Esther Wynne, Margaret Wilkins, Hannah Miller, Ruth Denney, and Hugh Lynn Cayce.

Mrs. C: You will have before you the Glad Helpers, members of which are present here, and their work in studying the Book of Revelation. You will continue to answer the questions which have been prepared on this Book.

Mr. C: Yes, we have the group as gathered here and the work of the Glad Helpers with their study of the Revelation; and that which has been given.

In continuing the interpretations of the symbols, and the experiences of John as written to those in the various churches in Revelation; these portions—or the last half of same, as has been indicated—are the application of what is gained by the analyzing of self and the emotions and the effects of activities through the physical being—as is applied by and to the individuals in the application of the truths gained in their material, their mental, their spiritual relations.

Ready for questions.

Q-1. What is meant by the symbol of the child in Rev. 12?

A-1. That which is the outgrowth of the application of the Word, or the Book, upon self. For as the child it is born of application of the elements in the body (physical, mental and spiritual) of the individual.

Q-2. Explain the flood as caused by the serpent to destroy the woman and the help given by the earth. Rev. 12:15-16.

A-2. The flood is the emotions upon the influences of the body in all of its relationships to the activities in its relationships to others; and destroys the baser forces—aided by the application in the earth; which represents the elements of material manifestations in the experiences of the individual.

For, how hath He given? The children of earth are wiser in their generation than the children of light, or from the very growth of what is the experience of the individual in the earth in its seeking for light. Or as He gave in the parable, for impunity's sake or for custom's sake, or for the help that the influence may bring, He will arise and give.

So in the experience of the individual, know that there constantly arises within the sojourn in the life or in an experience in the earth the flood of emotions that make for doubt, fears, tribulation, disturbances, anxieties. For the very same of that as becometh then impunity, the earth aids in the quieting of the influence as is illustrated here.

Q-3. Please explain the symbol of the beast like a leopard with seven heads and ten horns. Rev. 13.

A-3. As has been described in the Revelation as to how the influences of the knowledge as gained arise through the various forces and centers of the body. Now we find them visualized by John the revelator as representing the beast, or by the beast that makes for the fears as given in the minds of many by the representing of same in the forms as given, working as it were upon those very forces that have been aroused by the application in the seeking for the understanding of the book, or of the body, or of the relationship of the individual to the relationships borne by the individual. For it is all as individual, yet is applicable to every force or influence that is in the earth in an individual experience.

Q-4. Explain what is meant by those whose names are not written in the Book of Life.

A-4. Those not written are those who have climbed up some other way, or have only for impunity's sake or only for the momentary conscience's sake, as from the influence about them, acknowledged the Way. For as we see later more definitely given, whosoever *will* may take of the water of life.

But as has been given, there are those who from the first—as he that is last to be bound—had the import to do evil. Then those who have followed closely after the flesh, or the indulgences of the emotions of the body alone, without the considerations of others, without other than self's own interest—as is shown by the beast that is loosened—these are they whose names are not written, and these are they who are easily led about by every wind that bloweth, unstable as it were in those as represented in a portion or one of the churches; not hot, not cold, but allowing today, tomorrow, the circumstance of the moment to sway—without purpose, without direction, without the Name. For there is only given under heaven that Name whereby men may be saved, by their belief, their faith, their trust, their works in Him. Hence those who do them not, those who are seen about the individuals striving, are not to be by the individual lamented so much as that the individual loses his own way, but rather knowing that God, the merciful Father, the loving Father of the Christ, in His own time, His own way, will bring those necessary influences.

Be YE then, as is given, in the same association by the promptings of that ye have gained. Having tasted of the tree of life, the knowledge of God, make thyself and thy calling and thy election SURE in that ye faint not when ye see these troubles, these disturbances that are only of the earth-earthy, that only are the emotions of the desires of self's own show coming to pass in thine experience.

Q-5. Explain the symbol of the second beast with two horns, having the power to perform miracles. Rev. 13.

A-5. As has been given by Him, the power as attained by the study that has been shown in the first portions is to be applied, or may be applied unworthily—as is shown by the beast with two ways, two horns. Then here, how hath it been given? One Lord, one faith, one God, one baptism, one way! Yet in the experiences as ye watch about you there are constantly shown the influences by the very forces of the beast with the double-mindedness, as showing wonders in the earth yet they must come even as He hath given, "Though ye may have done this or that, though ye may have healed the sick, though ye may have cast out demons in my name, I know ye not; for ye have followed rather as the beast of self-aggrandizement, self-indulgence, self-glorification," even as the beast shown here.

Q-6. Do these two beasts as described in Rev. 13 have relation to the subconscious and conscious minds of man?

A-6. They work in and through these influences, to be sure; the subconscious forces that become as a portion, and the consciousness that works through the elements—for self or for God. They work *through* these but not as directing, as being the beast.

Q-7. What is meant by the mark of the beast in the right hand, or forehead?

A-7. These are as signs or symbols of this or that grouping, or of the organizations that become as a part of the vows or obligations to those who have joined in with the work of the beast.

Hence the warning that if these come to mean more in the experience they stand as that which condemns, rather than that which is the helpful experience.

For having the mark of the beast and the mark of the Lamb becomes the difference between the consciousness of the indwelling presence of the Christ and the hoped for yet not seen or known.

Q-8. What is meant by the number of the beast is the number of a man, 666?

A-8. Just as has been given, that when it is taken on as being the exercise of the man without reference to or realizing the influence which has brought same—though it may be in an organization, in a group, in any influence that becomes the work of man's hands—then it is the number of a man and is numbered as may be the days of man, but lacks that consciousness of God and God alone directing.

For as in each organized work or each association, or each group—it should never be as is said as of any man, but how hath He given? God that worketh in and through Him. Thus is the mark of the beast effaced from the workings of the hand or the activities of the head, and it becomes not as the name or the number of a man but the trust alone in God.

Q-9. Explain "Here is wisdom" mentioned in this connection.

A-9. That as ye have gained by the analysis or the study of the activity and influence of the spirit of truth throughout the whole members of thy body, physical, mental and spiritual, and have come to the knowledge of that which has first been given, that there is only *one* God, *one* Christ, one faith, one baptism; or as Christ hath given—this is the whole law; to love the Lord thy God with all thy mind, thy body, thy soul; thy neighbor as thyself. This is the whole law. This is wisdom. This is knowledge. Knowing that those things which have been put on through the activities of the elements within thine own forces of thy body and mind are but as the stepping-stones to the knowledge that no man, no number, no force, is above that knowledge that God is in and through ALL—and in Him ye live and move and have thy being. When this is fully comprehended, fully understood, ye have the working knowledge of God in the earth.

We are through for the present.

281-36

This psychic reading given by Edgar Cayce at his home on Arctic Crescent, Virginia Beach, Va., this 28th day of July, 1937, in accordance with request made by those present—12:05 to 12:25 P.M. Present: Edgar Cayce; Gertrude Cayce, Conductor; Gladys Davis, Steno; Edith and Florence Edmonds, Ruth LeNoir, Esther Wynne, Helen Ellington, Myrtle Demaio, Edna B. Harrell, and Hugh Lynn Cayce.

Mrs. C: You will have before you the Glad Helpers, members of which are present here, and their work in studying the Book of Revelation. You will continue to answer the questions prepared on this Book.

Mr. C: Yes, we have the group as gathered here, as a group and as individuals, with the information that has been given the group respecting the Revelation—and its application in the experience of the individual.

In continuing, as has been given, the portions now begin with that assurance to the individual having put on the whole armor, with the full understanding of what is meant by the various activities that are given as emblematical experiences in the affairs and conditions of the earth, of which each material entity then is a part.

These assurances become rather as the great help in those periods of temptation or trial.

Ready for questions.

Q-1. In Rev. 14 do the harpers as mentioned symbolize the souls or spiritual beings that took part in the early attempts to stop the fall of man, but who have not entered the earth plane?

A-1. These have entered the earth plane but were those that in the beginning were as the sons of God *in* the earth plane; and hence are referred to as the *first* of those redeemed.

Q-2. What is the meaning of the new song of the harpers?

A-2. The new experience that comes to each soul. Let's keep it individual, see? The new experience that comes to each soul, as to the assurance of that help when necessary of the saints of the Father.

Q-3. Please explain the symbols of the angels mentioned in Rev. 14. What is meant by the symbols of the sickles and reaping?

A-3. That those individuals who have and are a part of the active force in a material world are to work, to give forth, to give out of their strength, their selves in active service and not as those that would rest (from the material angle); but as the reapers, as the harvesters—which to the individual mind means labors for a definite purpose and service.

Q-4. What is meant by "Blessed are the dead which are in the Lord from henceforth, yea, saith the spirit, that they may rest from their labors, and their words do follow them." Rev. 14:13.

A-4. As referred to or given, the changes that have come and the assurance that has come to each individual who has recognized that the Lamb (or the Christ), or the activities of Jesus becoming the Christ are the assurance of the activity of the Christ in the passage from the material plane to the celestial. For as He preached to those bound even in the shadows of death, loosened that which made it possible for them to become again conscious of the opportunities for reconstructing of themselves in the experiences through which error had come, so blessed then are they who die in the Lord—for the body alone is bound.

Q-5. What is meant by the angels with the seven last plagues, in Rev. 15?

A-5. These are the activities that come to those who have begun and have found and have known the experiences of the activities and influences as indicated, and even have put on and become a part of—or are still in the active forces in the materiality—these see the pouring out of that which is the meeting of self in individuals yet in the earth, see? that is, the angels are the figures of that influence as of the wrath; that is, then the law, see? and this becomes necessary for the fulfilling of that "He hath not willed that any soul shall perish but hath with every ill provided a means, a way." Hence the pouring out, the meeting—and the great work or service that those may render who have named the Name, those who have known the song, those that are one with Him.

Q-6. Is the temple or tabernacle of testimony, Rev. 15:5, referring to Akashic Records?

A-6. That as you may term the Akashic Record, or the Book of Life, or the Book of Revelation; that is, of the individual, see?

Q-7. What is meant by the temple filled with smoke, Rev. 15:8? Is the temple the body and are these final steps in the process of spiritualization of the body?

A-7. These are the final steps in the abilities of the individuals for their effective service, or filled with the smoke as the glory of the Father, see? This is the temple of the body, and—as such—where the Lord hath promised to meet those that are faithful and true.

Q-8. What is meant by the angels with the seven vials, Rev. 16?

A-8. This again is that fulfilling of the law. This is as the carrying forth in the earth of those influences that bring the wrath in the active forces, in the experience of the individuals.

Q-9. What is the symbol of the first vial and the pouring of it?

A-9. These all are as the same, though are represented as the effective activity upon the various conditions that have become a part of the errors in those that have the mark of the beast.

Q-10. In Rev. 17 does the woman here symbolize the cause of the fall of spiritual man? Please explain with reference to Creation.

A-10. It represents rather that which made for the projecting of man into matter through the associations that brought carnal relationships in those very activities. Not as a spiritual but as a material giving or bringing spiritual activity in the desire of the individual or soul.

Q-11. Do the seven heads and mountains have any reference to the spiritual centers of the body, Rev. 17:9?

A-11. These have reference to the spiritual centers, as has been indicated; and indicate and show in the latter portion of same as to how these have become purified in the redeeming forces of the Lamb.

Q-12. Does Babylon symbolize self?

A-12. Babylon symbolizes self.

Q-13. Does Rev. 18 give some idea in symbols of the effect of the fall of self—selfishness?

A-13. It does.

Q-14. Does the marriage of the Lamb symbolize the complete spiritualization of the body? Please explain.

A-14. As there has been given through the whole portion of Revelation; first how the symbols of the activity of the body mentally, spiritually, physically, are affected by influences in the earth—and as to how now the body has been raised to the realizations of the associations with spirit and matter through mind, the builder, and comes now to that as represented by the Lamb—or the mind, spiritual—that has now so raised the body as to become as a new being; or as was given by Him—the body is the church, the Christ Consciousness is that activity which motivates same within the individual.

We are through for the present.

281-37

This psychic reading given by Edgar Cayce at his home on Arctic Crescent, Virginia Beach, Va., this 8th day of September, 1937, in accordance with request made by those present—3:30 to 4:00 P.M. Present: Edgar Cayce; Gertrude Cayce, Conductor; Gladys Davis, Steno; Florence and Edith Edmonds, Hannah Miller, Esther Wynne, Frances Y. Morrow, Ruth LeNoir, Helen Ellington, Margaret Wilkins, Sallie Jones, Ruth Denney, and Hugh Lynn Cayce.

Mrs. C: You will have before you the Glad Helpers, members of which are present here, and their work in studying the Book of Revelation. You will continue to answer the questions they have prepared on the last few chapters.

Mr. C: Yes, we have the group as gathered here; as a group, as individuals, and their work on the study of Revelation.

In continuing with that which has been given, well that you each here review within yourselves the experiences of the Revelation as related to your individual lives.

In this manner may you each attune yourselves to the more comprehensive understanding of the latter portion of same.

For the latter portion becomes again the invitation to all for all to partake of the life that is theirs, so living same in such a manner that each individual they contact in each experience of their associations may find every one different—and closer in accord with those teachings that are so a part of the Revelation; the body-Christ, the body-self, that may be one with Him.

Ready for questions.

Q-1. Explain Rev. 19:9-10. To whom is John talking here? Is it Peter?

A-1. That which is represented by Peter. What did Peter represent? That as had been given, "Flesh and blood hath not revealed this unto thee, but my father in heaven."

All then who have taken, who do take that which had been given as the example, as the pattern, as the manner of expression, as the acknowledgement of the activities within self, are in that position—that they have touched, do touch as it were the knowledge of God in that His ways, His laws, His love are not only a part of their individual lives but are by them manifested in their daily life, their daily conversation as one to another.

Yes, then—to the Peter in every experience of the body, the mind, the soul.

Q-2. Explain the symbols of the white horse and rider in Rev. 19. Is this the Christ?

A-2. This is the Christ in that it, as the horse, in the experiences of the awakening is the symbol of the messenger; and this is Christ, Jesus, the messenger.

Q-3. Explain what is meant by the first and second resurrections.

A-3. The first is of those who have not tasted death in the sense of the dread of same. The second is of those who have GAINED the understanding that in Him there IS no death.

Q-4. What is the meaning of one thousand years that Satan is bound?

A-4. Is banished. That, as there are the activities of the forty and four thousand—in the same manner that the prayer of ten just should save a city, the deeds, the prayers of the faithful will allow that period when the incarnation of those only that are in the Lord shall rule the earth, and the period is as a thousand years.

Thus is Satan bound, thus is Satan banished from the earth. The desire to do evil is only of him. And when there are—as the symbols—those only whose desire and purpose of their heart is to glorify the Father, these will be those periods when this shall come to pass.

Be YE *ALL* DETERMINED within thy minds, thy hearts, thy purposes, to be of that number!

Q-5. In Rev. 21—What is the meaning of "a new heaven and a new earth: for the first heaven and the first earth were passed away; and there was no more sea"?

A-5. When the foundations of the earth are broken up by those very disturbances. Can the mind of man comprehend no desire to sin, no purpose but that the glory of the Son may be manifested in his life? Is this not a new heaven, a new earth? For the former things would have passed away. For as the desires, the purposes, the aims are to bring about the whole change physically, so does it create in the experience of each soul a new vision, a new comprehension.

For as has been given, it hath not entered the heart of man to know the glories that have been prepared, that are a part of the experiences of those that love ONLY the Lord and His ways.

Q-6. Please explain second through fourth verse of Chapter 21—the new Jerusalem and no more death.

A-6. Those then that are come into the new life, the new understanding, the new regeneration, there IS then the new Jerusalem. For as has been given, the place is not as a place alone but as a condition, as an experience of the soul.

Jerusalem has figuratively, symbolically, meant the holy place, the holy city—for there, the ark of the covenant, the ark of the covenant in the minds, the hearts, the understandings, the comprehensions of those who have put away the earthly desires and become as the NEW purposes in their experience, become the new Jerusalem, the new undertakings, the new desires.

Q-7. What is meant by the second death in Rev. 21:8?

A-7. Those that have passed into the understanding and then fall away, become minded of the earthly desires for self-exaltation, know the second death.

Q-8. What is meant by the Holy Jerusalem [in] Rev. 21:12?

A-8. As indicated, that purpose, that estate to which there is the attaining of those who through the purifying—as has been indicated in the earlier portion—now come to the holy purpose—as the Holy Jerusalem; the Holy of Holies becomes the dwelling as it were of those.

Q-9. What is meant by the twelve gates?

A-9. The twelve manners, the twelve ways, the twelve openings, the twelve experiences of the physical to all, and those that have all been purified in purpose for the activities with same.

Q-10. What is the significance of the twelve angels?

A-10. The twelve purposes as represented by the activities of the openings to the bodily forces for their activities in the experiences of expression in the phases of the activities of the individual.

Q-11. Please explain the twelve names which represent the twelve tribes of the children of Israel.

A-11. The same as the twelve gates, the twelve angels, the twelve ways, the twelve understandings; or the approach to ISRAEL, the seeker—all seeking not then as the expression of self but as *one* in the Holy One!

Q-12. Rev. 21:15. Please interpret—What is the golden reed to measure the city? and what is the significance of the stones of the new Jerusalem and their colors?

A-12. The new understanding, the reed to measure the city, the abilities of each. Not unto all is it given to be ministers, not unto all to be interpreters, not unto all to be this or that; but measured according to that whereunto they have purposed in their hearts. Though all are as one, remember it has been given that the purpose of the heart is to know YOURSELF to BE yourself and yet one with God even as Jesus, even as is represented in God the Father, Christ the Son, and the Holy Spirit; each knowing themselves to be themselves yet ONE!

So the measurements for those that make the vibrations within themselves that become attuned to the new purpose, the new desire, the new hopes, the new Revelation, the new understandings to do the will of the Father with the will of that made perfect in the Christ.

Q-13. Rev. 22:1. Please interpret: "And he showed me a pure river of water of life, clear as crystal proceeding out of the throne of God and of the Lamb."

A-13. As the river, the water, the life represents the active flow of the purpose of the souls of men made pure in same. Then they flow with that purpose from the throne of God itself, made pure in the blood of the Lamb—which is in Jesus, the Christ, to those who seek to know His ways.

Q-14. Rev. 22:2. What is meant by the tree of life with its twelve kinds of fruit that yielded her fruit every month and the leaves of the tree for the healing of the nations?

A-14. That as the tree planted by the water of life; that is, as the sturdiness of the purpose of the individual in its sureness in the Christ; and the leaves represent the activities that are as for the healing of all that the individual activities may contact, even in material life. And that it is CONTINUOUS, as by the month, as for the purpose, as for the activities.

Q-15. Rev. 22:10,11. "Seal not the sayings of the prophecy," etc., and "He that is unjust, let him be unjust still; and he which is filthy be filthy still," etc.

A-15. As that period approaches when there shall be those influences of the power of those incarnated in the activities of the earth, then the purposes become set as in that indicated by the activities of each being in that to which they have then given themselves.

Q-16. Just how should this material be presented so as to be the most helpful and readable? Comment on the following:

A-16. Rather than commenting (for these touch upon the same), we would give this: First let there be not one but ALL who would purpose, who have purposed to be among that number that are called of God to give to those that seek the interpretation, compare and prepare the messages that have been given; and then choose ye they that would write, and let them—yea, by day and night—find themselves even as John, moved only by the spirit of truth. Thus preparing the message.

THEN when prepared, in one SITTING read the whole TO your source of information and receive the rejections or acceptations!

We are through for the present.

281-38

This psychic reading given by Edgar Cayce at his home on Arctic Crescent, Virginia Beach, Va., this 27th day of October, 1937, in accordance with request made by the Glad Helpers—3:15 to 3:35 P.M. Present: Edgar Cayce; Gertrude Cayce, Conductor; Gladys Davis, Steno; Florence and Edith Edmonds, Esther Wynne, Hannah Miller, Helen Ellington, Margaret Wilkins, Ruth LeNoir, Myrtle Demaio, Alice Harris, Ruth Denney, and Hugh Lynn Cayce.

Mrs. C: You will give at this time a discourse on the endocrine glands of the human organism, discussing their functions in relation to physical body and their relations to the mental and spiritual forces.

Mr. C: Yes, we have the activity of the endocrine system, as may be described from this body here. A discourse, to be of help or aid, may not be finished under fifteen or twenty series; for this is the system whereby or in which dispositions, characters, natures and races all have their source.

Little of course is as yet known or recorded as to the activities of same. For these are being discovered, or rediscovered by man in his search for the anatomical structure of the human body; and are continuing to be found. Hence, as is the natural thing, they are not present in a dead body.

Hence those influences or opportunities that have been given to man under varied circumstances from the study of the anatomical structure in a way or means or manner in which they may be observed; namely, through the digestive system (and even about this very little is known). For only this one portion in the animal kingdom and in the history of medicine has been studied by observation.

So in the study of the glandular systems that work within the glands or the organs, or the active forces of a physical body, these become then only those that may be seen or observed as from an INDIVIDUAL activity; and thus are only RELATIVE—or may be correlated to others as they may be observed in that which is produced within same.

For as has been indicated in some manners, some activities, there is an activity within the system produced by anger, fear, mirth, joy, or any of those active forces, that produces through the glandular secretion those activities that flow into the whole of the system. Such an activity then is of this endocrine system, and only has been observed in very remote manners, or just here and there. Only the more recently has this activity received that consideration from the specialist in ANY activity in the relationships to the human body.

And as has been indicated by those who are possibly leading the whole of the revolutionary activities as related to these, in making for the visibility even of the circulatory system, there is to be considered ever the whole activity; not as separating them one from another but the whole anatomical structure must be considered EVER as a whole.

Then we would give—to be as brief as possible in this short period, though for you to be aware or gain much it will take eight to ten to fifteen such periods for a really INSTRUCTIVE influence:

What are the activities of the glands? Most every organ of the body may be considered a gland, or at least there must be within the functioning activity of each portion—as the eye, the ear, the nose, the brain itself, the neck, the trachea, the bronchi, the lungs, the heart, the liver, the spleen, the pancreas—that which enables it to perform its duty in taking FROM the system that which enables it to REPRODUCE itself! That is the functioning of the glands!

Not as a whole only, but as individual as well as the whole.

Hence there is then in the system that activity of the soul, that is the gift of the Creator to man. It may be easily seen, then, how very closely the glands are associated with reproduction, degeneration, regeneration; and this throughout—not only the physical forces of the body but the mental body and the soul body.

The glandular forces then are ever akin to the sources from which, through which, the soul dwells within the body.

As an illustration—for this may be very brief for this particular period, but that you may grasp an inkling even of what you have begun:

Let us consider the Race question. Why in the mixture of races is there in the third and then the tenth generation a reverting to first principles? (Remember, we are speaking only from the physical reaction.)

Because that period is required for the cycle of activity in the glandular force of reproduction to reassert itself. How is it given in our Word? That the sins of the fathers are visited unto the children of the third and fourth generation, even to the tenth. This is not saying that the results are seen only in the bodily functions of the descendants, as is ordinarily implied; but that the essence of the message is given to the individual respecting the activity of which he may or must eventually be well aware in his own being. That is, what effect does it have upon you to even get mad, to laugh, to cry, to be sorrowful? All of these activities affect not only yourself, your relationships to your fellow man, but your next experience in the earth!

This is indicated in this particular body which lies here, through which the information is being given—you call him Cayce; John would be better!

There are those very influences as used or manifested in those periods of activity in indulgences, as we have indicated, which have magnified such activity of the glandular system. Hence in the present actions as related to the physical forces of the body these make for a continual warring—against those influences or activities within the system.

This same reverting to first causes may be seen in others, when there has been the self-indulgence in any manner. Hence as you may see about you, and which is coming to pass: Why is the race of the people in America growing taller and taller? The exercising of the glandular forces as related to the activity that produces within the system the extension of the physical structural forces of the body! Fast rather than thinking! The glories of self rather than the glories of God!

Monstrosities or giants or such active forces are the results from the glandular secretions produced in the system—and these show themselves again and again.

This does not necessitate, as you may see from viewing of same, that the parents of such be monstrosities themselves, but that they have in their union made possible the expression of that which HAS made for the extravagant use of the individual's influence in his own experiences in the earth!

Then we find the endocrine system—not glands but system—is that which is disseminated throughout the whole of the body, as related to the physical forces of same; and may be studied or may be followed in their relationship not only to the physical structural forces of the body but to what we call hereditary and environmental forces and how they may be expected to react upon the system.

And if these are considered in their proper relationships at those periods during conception and during those formative periods, the application of these may be made in such a way and manner as to make—as the Romans did—a beautiful, lovely body; yet the life may be as of Satan itself!

We are through for the present.

281-46

This psychic reading given by Edgar Cayce at his home on Arctic Crescent, Virginia Beach, Va., this 25th day of September, 1940, in accordance with request by those present—3:40 to 4:00 P.M., EST. Present: Edgar Cayce; Gertrude Cayce, Conductor; Gladys Davis, Steno; Esther Wynne, Florence Edmonds, Hannah Miller, Frances Y. Morrow, Helen Godfrey, Sallie Jones, and Hugh Lynn Cayce.

Mrs. C: You will have before you the members of the Glad Helpers gathered here. You will give at this time the first of a series of discourses on the endocrine system in the human body, presenting this information in such a way as will aid us in understanding the functions of each of the seven major glandular centers in relation to other glands in the system; heredity, temperament, character, environment, physical, mental and spiritual growth and expression. You will answer the questions, as I ask them.

Mr. C: Yes, we have the group as gathered here; their purposes, their desires. In giving that as may be understandable in the study of man—man then as the inception and conception into that FROM the purpose, desire, and its relationships to the universe and universal consciousness—it will be well to follow, in the first, what the happenings are in conception; the growth and the determining factors as to that growth—spiritually, mentally, physically—by and through the word of that Creator.

Man was given the ability to create through self a channel through which the manifestations of spirit might be made manifest in a material world. As is observed in such, there needs be first that of desire, purpose. It is known as a fact that this may be wholly of the carnal or animal nature on the part of even one, and yet conception may take place; and the end of that physical activity is written in that purpose and desire.

Then it is evident that there is the ideal, as well as the partial or whole carnal force, that may be manifested or exercised in and through such activities—as to bring a channel of mental, spiritual and material expression in the earth.

The ideal manner, first, is that there may be a channel through which the spirit of truth, hope, divine knowledge and purpose, may be made manifest. What then, ye may ask, are the spiritual, mental and physical variations that may take place under the physical activities for varied expressions?

It may be seen that from the same source, even at the same period of conception, there may come quite varied expressions or characteristics in the INDIVIDUAL expression manifested.

Desire, first, creates certain forces about which there is a physical nucleus that is the pattern of the universe; with a number. Thence it is given by some sages that each entity, each expression in a material experience has its number. Yet the more often there is the "guess" or mistake as to what physically caused there to be a number for an individual entity. There may be all the variations possible represented in thy digits from one to nine. This means the variations of the positive and negative influences or the neurones or electrons, or forces that form that vibration upon which that individual entity WILL or DOES vibrate at its period or source of conception. And each relationship of its vibration to the universe is relative, according to its number, in relationships to influences and environs, heredity as well as those influences which are a part of its conscious experience.

Thus the greater unison of purpose, of desire, at a period of conception brings the more universal consciousness—or being—for a perfect or equalized vibration for that conception.

As an illustration of such (that this may be wholly—or in part, by some—understood): When Hannah desired that there be an expression that God, the Universal Consciousness, had not forgotten that there were prayers and alms offered, was there wholly the lack of selfishness? or was there the shadow of jealousy?

Then we find there was the promise of the dedication and the purposes, that this expression would be wholly given to the Lord, ever. Yet it brought into being an entity, though dedicated as few—yea, as none other individually—to the Lord, unable of himself to give that in expression which would keep his own offspring in the SAME vibration!

Thus we see the RELATIVE relationships of the electrons, the neurones, the positive and negative forces brought into being at the period when there begins the OPPORTUNITY of conception.

Then, when such takes place—no matter as to what may be the vibrations that are set by the union of body, of mind and of purpose or spirit at such a period (for, to be sure, these are as varied as the individual)—there remains the IDEAL manner.

But—ye are asking—what physically takes place? Is it a physical activity of a gland, an impulse, a heartbeat, that becomes an influence for activity through the body so conceived?

The cord that is eventually known or classified as the pineal is the first movement that takes place of a physical nature through the act of conception; determining eventually—as we shall see—not only the physical stature of the individual entity but the MENTAL capacity also, and the spiritual attributes.

We would rest for the period.

281-47

This psychic reading given by Edgar Cayce at his home on Arctic Crescent, Virginia Beach, Va., this 2nd day of October, 1940, in accordance with request made by those present—3:30 to 3:50 P.M. Present: Edgar Cayce, Gertrude Cayce, Conductor; Gladys Davis, Steno; Esther Wynne, Florence Edmonds, Frances Y. Morrow, Helen Ellington, Ruth LeNoir, Helen Godfrey, Sallie Jones, and Mae Verhoeven.

Mrs. C: You will have before you the members of the Glad Helpers gathered here. You will continue with the discourse on the endocrine system in the human body.

Mr. C: Yes.

As the nucleus forms, there begins that activity which becomes the motivating force of the mental, the physical and the spiritual influences as related to GROWTH.

It has been indicated, by the sage, the manner of growth in the womb is not understood by man; yet here ye may find a concept of that development.

That gland [pineal?], a nucleus extending in the shape or form of a moving atom, gathers from its surroundings physical nourishment; and from the mind of the body it takes its PHYSICAL characteristics, or the molding as it were of its features as related to the external expression of same.

Then as the mind of the bearer binds those forces that are its natures in itself, its purposes, its desires, its hopes, its fears, these begin gradually to extend themselves through the nucleus; so that as the shape or form begins to find expression, there are also the channels through which the growth of the spiritual being gives its expression.

It is centered first, then about that known as the cranial center; next the ninth dorsal, or that which is the motivative force to other portions through the umbilical cord, that begins then in the third week to give material manifestations in physical development.

Then the centers of the heart, liver and kidney areas begin their expression.

Thus we have first the pineal, the aerial [See 281-53, A-5; 281-55, A-1, 2], the adrenals, the thymus—or the pump gland of the heart itself.

Each organ as it materializes in its development forms its own nucleus for the production of that which enables it in itself, from its own glandular system, to reproduce itself.

With the production of itself, the blood system begins its flow—then—in the second month of conception.

Then there begins the growth of the glands that form eyes, ears, nasal passages; and those areas begin their formations.

The seeking here is for that area, that center, in which the system makes its relative relationships or associations with spiritual, mental and physical being.

These areas indicated, that have come through growth into being in relation to the mental, spiritual and physical attitude of the mother, are constantly dependent upon that one from which the body draws its PHYSICAL sustenance; but purpose, desire and hope are through the mental. Thus these centers are opposite the umbilical cord, or those areas through which ALL messages of desire, or of the mental nature, pass; not only to the brain in its reflexes but along the cords to the pineal—that has been and is the extenuation of its first cause.

In those glands that are eventually known as the genital, or in the lyden, and the inner centers of the thyroid through and from which the exterior forces are indicated in their activity, there begins then the formation of the superficial circulation; that leads or connects between its spiritual import, its mental purpose, and its physical development—for their coordination.

Thus we find, as indicated in the bodily expressions, there comes in these areas—or from those centers of the areas given—the disturbances of a physical nature to which the young are more susceptible; which are of a glandular nature, finding expressions in the various forms in the physical to the superficial and the deeper circulation, between the cerebrospinal and sympathetic, or to the organs that are under the direction of same. We refer to such as measles, mumps, conditions of throat, the head and eyes. All of these are glandular centers.

That is why in portions of the Scripture the extenuating activities that take place in the spiritual being are described by the expressions through those body centers.

These follow through, throughout the periods of gestation, and are dependent still upon the environs, the mental attributes and activities, the purposes and aims of that individual BEARING the entity.

Thus it comes into the material world with that held to by THAT parent, with the CHARACTERISTICS that are the sum of spiritual, mental AND material purposes of the FIRST cause, as combined with its age and era or period of development.

We rest here.

281-48

This psychic reading given by Edgar Cayce at his home on Arctic Crescent, Virginia Beach, Va., this 16th day of October, 1940, in accordance with request by those present—3:20 to 4:00 P.M., EST. Present: Edgar Cayce; Gertrude Cayce, Conductor; Gladys Davis, Steno; Florence Edmonds, Esther Wynne, Hannah Miller, Frances Y. Morrow, Helen Ellington, Helen Godfrey, Mae Verhoeven, Sallie Jones, Louise Dill, and Gladis Hardin.

Mrs. C: You will have before you the members of the Glad Helpers gathered here. You will continue with the discourse on the endocrine system of the human body.

Mr. C: Yes, we have the group as gathered here; and their study of the endocrine system.

It has been indicated as to what takes place at the time of conception, and the manner, and the influences which regulate activities spiritually, mentally, physically, through the period of gestation. It will possibly be well to illustrate same; that there may be drawn, by those studying same, the experience as in the life of individuals.

We begin then with the seers or sages of old, from that period indicated as to how influences affected the offspring:

When Abraham and Sarah were given the promise of an heir through which the nations of the earth would be blessed, there were many years of preparation of these individuals, of the physical, mental and spiritual natures. Again and again it is indicated as to how they each in their material concept (watch the words here, please, if you would understand) attempted to offer a plan, or way, through which this material blessing from a spiritual source might be made manifest.

Hence we find as to how the material or mental self—misunderstanding, misconstruing the spiritual promises—offered or EFFECTED channels through which quite a different individual entity was made manifest; and through same brought confusion, distress, disturbance one to another in the material manifestations.

Yet, when the last promise was given, that even in their old age there would be given an heir, we find that when Sarah thus conceived there was the development of a body physically, mentally and spiritually so well balanced as to be almost etheric in his relationships to the world about him, when the material manifestation had grown to maturity.

Here we find, then, that mind and matter are coordinated into bringing a channel for spiritual activity that is not exceeded in any of the characters depicted in Holy Writ.

What, then, were the characteristics, the activity of the glandular system as related to that individual entity? We find that there was a perfect coordination in and through the whole period of gestation, and the fulfilling of the time according to the law set in motion by the divine influence that was the directing force of both parents through the period.

We find also that throughout the period of gestation the activities about the entity, the mother, were such as to INFLUENCE the entity yet unborn, in patience to a degree not manifested in any other of the patriarchs. While the physical conditions made manifest in the body during the growth into manhood were affected by MATERIAL laws, there was not the changing or deviating whatsoever from the spiritual through the mental.

Hence we have that illustration of what may be termed the individual ideally conceived, ideally cherished and nourished through the periods of gestation. As to the care afterward—these vary, as we shall see from other illustrations.

What, then, were the developments of that ideally conceived entity as related to the study here of the endocrine system?

First—the individual was one conceived in promise; with the desire, the purpose, the hope—in the act OF conception—to bring forth that which had BEEN promised. Hence the ideal attitude of both parents in that individual case.

Hence as given, first the pineal, the cranial, the thymus; then the aerial, then the gradual development of those influences which brought a goodly child; one subject to the care of both parents—by natural tendencies from conception; bringing into materialization that one worthy of being accepted and of RECEIVING the promise beyond MANY of those who were of the seed of Abraham.

Then we have that illustration in the sons of Isaac, when there were those periods in which there was to be the fulfilling of the promise to Isaac and Rebekah. We find that their MINDS differed as to the nature or character of channel through which there would come this promise; when, as we understand, there must be the cooperation spiritually, mentally, in order for the physical result to be the same. HERE we find a different situation taking place at the time of conception, for BOTH attitudes found expression. Hence twins were found to be the result of this long preparation, and yet two minds, two opinions, two ideas, two ideals. Hence we find that HERE it became necessary that even the DIVINE indicate to the mother that channel which was to be the ruler, or that one upon whom would be bestowed the rightful heritage through which the greater blessings were to be indicated to the world, to humanity, to mankind as a whole.

Hence we find two natures, two characteristics—physically, mentally, spiritually. Here we find what might be termed a perfect channel again, and with same a testing—not only of the parents themselves but of the individuals that were begotten under those conditions in which the promise was as clear to them as it had been to Abraham.

What, then, were the physical and mental attitudes which contributed to this condition which existed in that period, and that may be used as an illustration of those ideas being presented here for the study of man, his nature, his characteristics, his spirituality, his weakness in physical being?

Here we find, as indicated, there was NOT a union of purpose in those periods of conception. Hence we find both characteristics, or both purposes of the individuals, were made materially manifest.

What then, ye may well ask, made this difference in the characteristics of the individuals; conceived of the same parents, under the environ or the law from the body of the one; with such a different characteristic made manifest as they grew to maturity?

As indicated, the first cause—that purpose with which the individuals performed the act for conception to take place, or under which it did take place. THAT is the First Cause! And the growth of that conceived under the same environ, through the same circulation, through the same impulse, was such that—when gestation was finished—one was of the nature of characteristic of the mother, the other was of the nature of indifference with the determination of the father; one smooth as the mother, the other hairy, red, as the father in maturity; and their characteristics made manifest were just those examples of the variations. Though conceived at once, born together, they were far separated in their purposes, their aims, their hopes; one holding to that which made body, mind and soul coordinant; the other satisfying, gratifying the appetites of the physical and mental without coordinating same through its spiritual relationships to the progenitor or those conditions and environs from which they each drew their desires, their hopes, their wishes.

Do ye think that one received a different instruction from the other? Each received the same, yet their reaction, their choice of that in the environment made physical characteristics that varied in their activity.

Why were the characteristics such that one desired or loved the chase, the hunt or the like, while the other chose rather the home, the mother, the environ about same? Were these depicted in the very physiognomy of each individual? When they had reached that period when the CHOICES were made, these were manifested. But when did they begin? What gland developed this characteristic in one and not in the other? The cranial and the thymus receiving the varied vibration, one brought harmony—not fear, but harmony—with caution; the other brought just the opposite, by this "stepping up" in the rate of vibration. Or, if we were to study these by numbers, we would find one a three, the other a five; yet conceived together.

What do we mean here by the vibration of the number? One had the nucleus, the structure about same, three to one of its spiritual import; the other five to one of the material import, see?

Hence we find there the various forms or manners in which there is illustrated those characteristics that made for individual activity, that PROMPTED the carrying on of that through which the channel of hope might be made manifest.

Let's change these then to those illustrations of quite varied forms, in which more of the characteristics became manifested of the environmental nature; for the illustrations we have just used show how the characteristics of the individuals responded to the environment as each grew to maturity and became active in relationships and dealings with others.

Then, with Jacob and Rachel we have the material love, and those natures in which the characteristics of material love were athwarted. Yet, in the very conception of same—though under stress (for there is held here by the mother the desire to outshine, as it might be poorly said)—we find a goodly child, one with all the attributes of the spiritual-minded individual; partaking of both the father and the mother in the seeking for a channel through which God might be manifested in the earth. And yet the entity had those physical attributes that brought into the experience of individuals those things that were reflected in the mind, in the movements and activities of the mother throughout the periods of gestation—when the entity had grown to manhood.

Also from the same attitude taken by those parents when the second son, Benjamin, was conceived—what were the varying characteristics here? The material love was just as great, the satisfying of material desire was completely fulfilled; yet it lacked that desire to BRING such as was wholly a channel through which the SPIRITUAL was to be made manifest. But it was a channel that EVENTUALLY brought the material made manifest in Saul, an incarnation of Benjamin.

Hence we find the varied characteristics illustrated not only by the attitude of the pair as the channel being made manifest, but the attitude of that channel which was given from the beginning.

Now, conceive first what the variations are in the sexes, as given in the beginning in the creating of same; one to be a channel of material and mental satisfaction to the other; the other to be a channel, a manner, through which there was to be the alleviation of desire when spiritualized in the purpose toward the mate.

Hence we may find again and again here, in the Word, that which IS the connection between man and his Maker; that finds its final concept in the manner which John presents to the elect, in which all the varied attributes of the human development—in body, in mind, in spirit, with each phase of man's development—are also chosen as channels through which expressions of same are given.

We would rest with the illustrations; for there are others that need to be given.

We are through for the present.

GLAND	CHURCH	LORD'S PRAYER	PLANETS	ANCIENT 4 ELEMENTS	4 BEASTS	OPENING SEALS	COLORS
PITUITARY	LAODICEA	HEAVEN	JUPITER			SILENCE	VIOLET
PINEAL	PHILADELPHIA	NAME	MERCURY			UPHEAVALS (EARTHQUAKE)	INDIGO
THYROID	SARDIS	WILL	URANUS			SOULS SLAIN	GRAY (BLUE)
THYMUS	THYATIRA	EVIL	VENUS	AIR	EAGLE	PALE HORSE	GREEN
SOLAR PLEXUS	PERGAMOS	DEBTS	MARS	FIRE	LION	RED HORSE	YELLOW
LYDEN	SMYRNA	TEMPTATION	NEPTUNE	WATER	MAN	BLACK HORSE	ORANGE
GONADS	EPHESUS	BREAD	SATURN	EARTH	CALF	WHITE HORSE	RED

281-49

This psychic reading given by Edgar Cayce at his home on Arctic Crescent, Virginia Beach, Va., this 23rd day of October, 1940, in accordance with request by those present—3:30 to 3:50 P.M. EST. Present: Edgar Cayce; Gertrude Cayce, Conductor; Gladys Davis, Steno; Florence Edmonds, Esther Wynne, Hannah Miller, Frances Y. Morrow, Helen Ellington, Ruth LeNoir, Helen Godfrey, Mae Verhoeven, Louise X. Dill, and Sallie Jones.

Mrs. C: You will have before you the members of the Glad Helpers gathered here. You will continue with the discourse on the endocrine system of the human body.

Mr. C: Yes, we have the group as gathered here, and their study of the endocrine system.

In that which has been given there is the attempt to show the necessary coordination of the mental with the physical and spiritual; or, to be exact, the coordinating of the mental with the spiritual that so alters the characteristics, the purposes, the hopes of the individual entity materialized and manifested. That entity, however, is altered by choices made under its own impulse.

But to further demonstrate or illustrate those phases of the emotions, and that necessary in the union of purpose for the channels, we find that—as indicated—other illustrations are needed.

From the patriarchs there may be taken others—as first indicated in Samson; and also that which has been referred to in those relationships borne by Kish and Methulabah [?], when there were the preparations for the individual entity that was to be king over that chosen people. We find that the preparation of the parents, mentally and physically, was such that there was an elongation of activity in the endocrine system of the pineal; so that the stature of the entity then was of a different type, a different nature, and the mental and spiritual so balanced and coordinated that through the experience of the entity there was a physical and mental development equaled and surpassed by few. Yet the APPLICATION of the entity OF those opportunities was personal; so that what was individually personified of the mental and spiritual of the entity's sojourn was then of self in its LATTER analysis.

But the activities of the glands—what has this to do with those activities or choices that the entity or individual makes after the periods of gestation are completed, either during the period when the entity is under the direction or counsel of the parents, or tutors or friends and associates? What have the glands to do with the choices the individual makes? This depends upon whether or not the activity has been such that there is kept the coordinating of the glands of the body as related TO the activity of the organs being directed.

Then, it is not that the entire life experience is laid out for an individual when there has been received that imprint as of the first breath, or the spirit entering the body as prepared for activity in the material world. For, again, choice is left to the individual, and the personality—as to whether it is the laudation of the ego or cooperation with its fellow men, or as a consecration to the service of the Creative Forces in its material environs.

All of these are to be taken into consideration, then; just as they are indicated in the study that first prompted this search for the BEGINNINGS of individuality and personality in an entity entering and becoming active in the material complacency of a changing world.

Further illustrations we may find, of both a physical and a mental nature.

When Manoah sought with his whole desire and purpose that there might be the blight taken from his associations among his fellows, he with his companion, prayed oft; and then the visitation came.

Here we find a consideration also to be taken, when one studies even the anatomical structure of the channel for expression of body, mind and soul. In the material world, in the anatomy books that have been written by some, attempted by many, there is considered only the physical channel, and not the mental and spiritual attributes and activities. But if ye are studying these in the light that they are to be applied in the interpreting of Revelation, then the mental and spiritual must also be taken into consideration.

The prayer of Manoah and his companion was answered by the visitation of a heavenly figure, in the form of a man; which was not conceivable by the husband—yet when satisfied of same, and the wife—Mahoa [?]—conceived, the entity physically—PHYSICALLY—was the greater tower of strength. Yet as indicated that strength lay in the hair of the head of the individual. What GLAND caused that activity of such a physical nature, as to be the determining factor in that development?

As is indicated, the thyroid is within the body so placed as to have that influence. There are only a few of these that are not within the organs themselves.

It has been given at first that as each organ develops in the foetus there is the development of the gland within itself to give it the ability to REPRODUCE itself. Yet there are those outside, or they are centers from and through which pass the emotions, the activities from the organs of other portions of the body; and become so influenced as to produce a definite PHYSICAL effect.

If they produce the definite mental effect, if they produce through same definite spiritual attributes or abilities, and if these are coordinated by the individual into personality—what are the results?

Here this is illustrated in Samson—a lad who grew to manhood with the unusual strength and power, the ability to cope with exterior forces and influences that were beyond the understanding and comprehension of his associates. Yet his ability to say no to the opposite sex was nil—his ability not to be influenced by the opposite sex was nil—because of the desire for the gratification of those activities which were of a glandular nature within the body.

What are the lessons to be gained or understood, then, from the illustrations here given?

We will begin, then, with the various glands that act independent of the organs, and yet AFFECT them through THEIR glandular force or source that lies within the functioning of the organ itself.

We are through for the present.

281-51

This psychic reading given by Edgar Cayce at his home on Arctic Crescent, Virginia Beach, Va., this 15th day of January, 1941, in accordance with request made by those present—3:30 to 4:10 P.M. Present: Edgar Cayce; Hugh Lynn Cayce, Conductor; Gladys Davis, Steno; Florence Edmonds, Ruth LeNoir, Helen Ellington, Frances Y. Morrow, Louise B. Chisholm, Esther Wynne, Sallie Jones, Helen Godfrey, Hannah Miller, and Mae Verhoeven.

HLC: You will have before you the Glad Helpers Prayer Group, members of which are present in this room, and their study of the endocrine system in the human body. You will continue with the discourse on this subject.

Mr. C: Yes, we have the group as gathered here; as a group, as individuals; and the information which has been indicated through this channel. In continuing with the subject, and as we come to the application of that which has been indicated, let that which is given here and now NOT become confusing. For, it will require deep meditation upon such, that ye may get the correct insight; which ye will not be able to put into words at first, and will KNOW when ye know, but by the experience of coordinating physical, mental and spiritual attributes into one.

For, as given, few have conceived of—or attempted to analyze—the effect created in a physical body through the MENTAL impressions received, or conceded that there is an activity spiritually that may go on in active force within the human body.

For so oft we see contradictory effects produced in the activities of the individuality and personality of persons.

Also it has been and is hard for individuals to conceive of Adam sinning in a material world—as a man, a son, made by the hands of God.

Neither is it easy to understand the illustrations used from the life of Kish, who conceived through righteous desire a son, a channel chosen for a manifestation of material power in a material world; given through the choice of the Maker Himself, and yet the INDIVIDUAL in his personal relationships defied even that which had been prophesied by himself!

Few can conceive of the body through which the Prince of Peace manifested—the Son, the first and the last Adam—as having been a channel for material desire, when considered as a body so purified as to bear that perfect One.

Yet, all of these facts are demonstrated in the life of each individual.

There has long been sought, by a few, the interpretation of the seven centers; and many have in various stages of awareness, or development, placed the association or connection between physical, mental and spiritual in varied portions of the body. Some have interpreted as of the mind, motivated by impulse; and thus called the center from which mind acts.

This is only relatively so, as will be understood by those who analyze those conditions presented through these interpretations; for in fact the body, the mind and the soul are ONE, in the material manifestation. Yet in analyzing them, as given through the Revelation by John, they are active in the various influences that are a part of each living organism conceived in the forces making up that known as man; that power able to conceive—in mind—of God, and to demonstrate same in relationships to others; that in mind able to conceive of manners for the destruction of its fellow man, little realizing that it is *self* being destroyed by that very activity!

Then, why are there such contradictions within those very influences? As is said, in the heart love finds its way. Love is conceived as of God, as of all-pleasant, as all-giving; given in that great expression—indicating to what power it may arise—"God so loved the world as to give His only begotten son; that through Him we might have eternal life."

Yet the other side, or the reverse of love, is suffering, hate, malice, injustice. It is the reverse. Why?

What is that about man's activity in body, as an individual, that causes such?

This has been indicated through those patterns which have been used as illustrations of what took place in the UNION of bodies that through desire, hope, conceived or prepared in conception a channel through which all this contradiction might be made manifest.

Is the First Cause, then, that the separation of God in the desire for companionship with Himself, that as created or brought into a material manifestation the reverse of love, of hope, of patience, of all the attributes that are the spirit of activity, the moving influence or force?

This we see manifested in a physical body through the glandular system—as the activity of conception, the dividing of the activity of the gland itself, that brings conception.

Thus, this is the first of the centers from which arises all that is movement, to bring into being both the face and the preface—or the back, or the reverse—in the experience. It carries with it, what? That MIND! For, remember, ever, the pattern is ever the same—Mind the builder!

Conceived, then the first movement is along that center or gland which either fades or becomes a channel along which there may move the power and might to find expression through the very activities of the organs of the body itself.

Then the next is the pineal, through which the brain forces make manifest—either in its determining factor there of becoming mighty in stature physically or dwarfed; as may be understood by the face, as may be said, that is held to by the INDIVIDUAL separation and COMBINATION of the activity of the glands in that period of conception. Hence there arises the race condition or contour, or the figure of that beheld by that choice in its activity as it has separated itself from the first cause, or first premise; by the very will of the Father-God in the beginning.

Then there is the third, that is ever of the feeding or building nature—or the basic cord through which during the period of gestation there is fed the imaginations, as well as the latent response of the body to those conditions external—or that center from which there is drawn the growth in the physical.

Then there becomes the first indication of individuality being established in that movement which has come about in its growth, its evolvement; or the gland of the solar plexus, or that YE misinterpret and call the adrenals—as they act with the emotions and the growth and unfoldment of the body itself.

There begins then the gland—the heart—through which courses begin to flow; and then the gland—the liver—its counterpart; and then the spleen (as a balance); the thyroid—as the outer individual begins to show activities for self-protection, or the first laws of nature as would be made manifest in the material associations.

Then there are the general, or the whole of the activities through the system, as in the thymus, all of the centers of activity through which spirit first moves from the lyden—the center of the spiritual forces; the brain, or the highest force individually or personally; then the others in their order as they control themselves.

Then within each of the organs themselves (though they each are, in the main, glands) the functioning is stimulated by the activity of each organ's ability to assimilate that needed from the environs, as well as from that upon which it is fed, to grow INTO that direction given BY the mental purpose, the mental desire of the PERSONALITY—AS it, as an individual, makes itself manifest in a material environ.

Hence we find—as has been interpreted for those who would interpret—the seven centers, the seven churches, the seven activities to which an individual physical activity is prompted.

We would rest for the present.

281-52

This psychic reading given by Edgar Cayce at his home on Arctic Crescent, Virginia Beach, Va., this 5th day of February, 1941, in accordance with request by those present—3:30 to 3:40 P.M. EST. Present: Edgar Cayce; Hugh Lynn Cayce, Conductor; Gladys Davis, Steno; Florence Edmonds, Hannah Miller, Frances Y. Morrow, Ruth LeNoir, Helen Godfrey, and Mae Verhoeven.

HLC: You will have before you the Glad Helpers Prayer Group, members of which are present in this room. You will consider their work and study on the endocrine system of the human body, and continue the discourse on this subject.

Mr. C: Yes, we have the work of the Glad Helpers Prayer Group, members present in this room, and their study of the endocrine system as indicated through this channel.

As we find, with the information that has been given, now there should be rather those agreements—by the study of that given; and thus from same form the questions as MIGHT be expressed in "Is it false or is it true?" Else, the group may become burdened with knowledge and have little of wisdom—in making application of such knowledge as to become helpful or beneficial to them.

For, in their study and in the work of the prayer group, this must be a practical thing; that it may be used by them as individuals in aiding others to dismiss error from their consciousness, and in its place to put not merely the wishful thinking but activities of such a nature as to be helpful in same.

Let the approach be made by not other than the question, then, "Is it true or false?"

We are through for the present.

(Extract from 2436-1—a baby a few months old, born prematurely, who has not been able to see. Nothing wrong can be found on examination, but the child just does not see:)

A more perfect understanding of the condition might be gained best from the interpreting of the life experiences of the entity (through a life reading), as in relationship to those responsible for the entity's physical entrance into the present experience...

As we have indicated, and as indicated by some—in the period of conception, the activities and the functioning of various portions of a developing body are guided through that unity of purpose in the coming into being of the channel for the expression of a soul-entity. Those influences that direct even in the physical coordination of the senses are of the spiritual-mental import.

It may be considered from a purely physical angle that those conditions apparent through the stages of gestation, birth, and bodily development, have their physical reactions in the body in the present. However, when there is taken into consideration the normalcy of all other functionings of this organism, or entity, we find that this phase—the period of conception—must also be considered—if there would be brought to the body at this time, in this experience, the material or physical benefits toward the restoration of vision.

Taken from *The Gang Age* by Paul Hanly Furfey, Ph.D.
(Found in the Norfolk Public Library)
Page 13—Footnote

Modern research on the ductless glands has thrown considerable light on the causes of these phenomena. For a long time the ductless glands were a mystery to the physiologist. It is now known that they secrete substances called hormones or autacoids which are absorbed by the blood. These autacoids have remarkable effects on the organism. For instance, the autacoid secreted by the thyroid gland has been isolated and is known as thyroxin. It has been experimentally demonstrated that thyroxin has a profound influence on metabolism. If an animal is deprived of its supply of thyroxin through removal of the thyroid gland it shows a thickening and swelling of the skin, low body temperature and increased sugar tolerance. It becomes slow and sluggish and metabolism is diminished. In short it presents the typical picture of myxodema. But if thyroxin is administered either hypodermically or by mouth these symptoms disappear.

It is now pretty generally admitted that the striking physical and mental changes at adolescence are due to the activity of an autacoid substance secreted by the cells of Leydig in the gonads, the so-called "interstitial" cells. The autacoid in question has never been isolated; but it is known that whenever the Leydig cells atrophy through destructive tumors, through the activity of X-rays or in cryptorchism the characteristic changes of adolescence fail to appear.

The other ductless glands also seem to play some part in this phenomenon. It is known that the thyroid has an influence; for in myxodema spoken of above the individual does not develop characteristically at adolescence. The same is to be said of the anterior lobe of the pituitary gland. Evidence in regard to the pineal gland is conflicting, but the weight of authority inclines to the view that this gland has also a positive influence. The same may be said of the cortex of the adrenal gland. There is some experimental evidence that the thymus has an opposite effect and that its removal tends to hasten adolescence. Others report removal of the thymus without any noticeable post-operative change. *It will be seen that the whole subject of the influence of the ductless glands on personality is at present hopelessly complicated; but research workers are constantly bringing to light new facts and the next few years will see many puzzling questions answered.*

(Paul Hanly Furfey, Ph.D.—instructor in sociology in the Catholic University of America; printed in U.S.A. by the Ferris Printing Company; Copyright 1926 by The Macmillan Company)

281-53

This psychic reading given by Edgar Cayce at his home on Arctic Crescent, Virginia Beach, Va., this 2nd day of April, 1941, in accordance with request made by those present—3:55 to 4:20 P.M. Present: Edgar Cayce, Hugh Lynn Cayce, Conductor; Gladys Davis, Steno; Florence Edmonds, Esther Wynne, Frances Y. Morrow, Hannah Miller, Ruth LeNoir, Helen Ellington, Gladis Hardin, Sallie Jones, and Mae Verhoeven.

HLC: You will have before you the Glad Helpers Prayer Group, members of which are present in this room. You will consider their work and study on the endocrine system of the human body, answering the questions they submit, as I ask them.

Mr. C: Yes, we have the group gathered here; as a group and as individuals, also their work and study of the endocrine system in the human body, with the information which has been indicated through this channel—that was to be analyzed in the mind of each.

Ready for questions.

Q-1. Are the following statements true or false? Comment on each as I read it: The life force rises directly from the Leydig gland through the gonads, thence to pineal, and then to the other centers.

A-1. This is correct; though, to be sure, as it rises and is distributed through the other centers it returns to the solar plexus area for its impulse through the system.

For the moment, let's consider the variation here in this life force—or as respecting this life force. The question is asked not in relation to the life alone as manifested in the human body, but as to the process through which coordination is attained or gained in and through meditation, see?

Hence physically, as we have indicated, there is first the nucleus—or the union of the first activities; and then the pineal as the long thread activity to the center of the brain, see? Then from there, as development progresses, there are those activities through reflexes to the growth or the developing of the body.

Interpret that variation, then, as being indicated here. One life force is the body-growth, as just described. The other is the impulse that arises, from the life center, in meditation.

Q-2. As the life force passes through the glands it illuminates them.

A-2. In meditation, yes. In the life growth, yes and no; it illuminates them to their own activity in life growth.

Q-3. The Leydig gland is the same as that we have called the lyden, and is located in the gonads.

A-3. It is in and above, or the activity passes through the gonads. Lyden is the meaning—or the seal, see? while Leydig is the name of the individual who indicated this was the activity. You can call it either of these that you want to.

Q-4. The life force crosses the solar plexus each time it passes to another center.

A-4. In growth, yes. In meditation, yes and no; if there remains the balance as of the attunement, yes.

When we are considering these various phases, the questions should be prepared so that they would not crisscross, or so that there would not be a confusion or a misinterpretation as to what is meant.

You see, what takes place in the developing body, or in life growth (which we have used as the demonstration, or have illustrated), may be different from that which takes place as one attempts to meditate and to distribute the life force in order to aid another—or to control the influence as in healing, or to attain to an attunement in self for a deeper or better understanding. These questions or statements are such that they will be confusing to some; but if they are asked properly there will not be confusion.

Q-5. The solar plexus is the aerial gland.

A-5. No. By the term aerial we mean that impulse or activity that flows in an upward, lifting, raising or rising movement. It is an activity in itself, you see; not as a gland but as an activity UPON glands as it flows in, through, from or to the various centers of activity in the system itself. It is a function. Let's illustrate—possibly this will give an interpretation such that you may understand:

In your radio you have what you call an aerial for communications that are without any visible connection. This is not a part of that making up the framework, yet it is necessary for certain characters of reception or for the better distribution of that which takes place in the instrument as related to communication itself.

So in the physical body the aerial activity is the flow through the pineal, to and through all the centers. It aids the individual, or is an effective activity for the individual who may consciously attempt to attune, coordinate, or to bring about perfect accord, or to keep a balance in that attempting to be reached or attained through the process.

As the process begins in the physical body, it is along the pineal; or it is the same movement that is the controlling or attuning influence from the mother with the developing forces of the body through the period of gestation.

That is the manner, or the process, or the way in which the impressions are made. So, if there is beauty about the body of the mother through such periods, there are those influences to bring about accord. It may be indicated in contour of face. It may be indicated in the process of change in the activity of the thyroid as related to all the forces—even to the color of hair or eyes, or the skin's activity; the nails, or more toes than should be—or less, or such activities. Or, the influences existent through such processes might make for a lacking of something in the body itself, pathologically; by the attempt to create a normal balance without the necessary influences being available.

All of this is what we have referred to as the aerial activity, see?

HLC: I see.

Mr. C: Don't say you see if you don't see! You only had a portion of it! Let's illustrate it in this way, so you will comprehend:

Understand the processes of activity through which there are the needs of the aerial in reception. For, of course, it is a matter of vibration in the body, as well as that illustrated in the physical condition. Thus there are activities about a body that is supplying the needs physically and mentally for a developing body, that become a part of the process, see?

Q-6. The entity preparing to be born into the earth has an influence upon the mother in building its own body.

A-6. No. That would be the same as saying that an atom had an influence upon that to which it could be attracted! See the variation?

As in the realms outside of the material body, we have influences that are sympathetic one to another and we have influences that have an antipathy one for another—as in fire and water, yet they are much alike. There are other forces that are active in the same manner, or that are of the same nature.

But in the physical world there is builded a body, by the process of a physical law, see? Now: There is builded also a mental body, see?

God breathed into man the breath of life and he became the *living* soul.

Then, with the first breath of the infant there comes into being in the flesh a soul—that has been attracted, that has been called for, by all the influences and activities that have gone to make up the process throughout the period of gestation, see?

Many souls are seeking to enter, but not all are attracted. Some may be repelled. Some are attracted and then suddenly repelled, so that the life in the earth is only a few days. Oft the passing of such a soul is accredited to, and IS because of disease, neglect or the like, but STILL there was the attraction, was there not?

Hence to say that the body is in any way builded by an entity from the other side is incorrect. BUT those mental and physical forces that ARE builded ARE those influences needed FOR that soul that does enter!

Q-7. The entity desiring to enter governs the change in sex, which may occur as late as the third month.

A-7. It may occur even nineteen years after the body is born! So, it doesn't change in that direction!

Q-8. The physical development of the child is wholly dependent upon the mother from whom it draws physical sustenance, but its purpose, desire and hope are built up or influenced by the minds of all concerned.

A-8. That's the first question you've asked correctly. CORRECT!

We are through for the present.

(Extract from reading 2475-1—3/27/41—regarding experiments in Yoga exercises and breathing:)

These exercises are excellent, yet it is necessary that special preparation be made—or that a perfect understanding be had by the body as to what takes place when such exercises are used.

For, BREATH is the basis of the living organism's activity. Thus, such exercises may be beneficial or detrimental in their effect upon a body...

It would be very well for the body to study very carefully the information which we have given through these sources as respecting Meditation...

...in the physical body there ARE those influences, then, through which each of these phases of an entity may or does become an active influence.

There may be brought about an awareness of this by the exercising of the mind, through the manner of directing the breathing.

For, in the body there is that center in which the soul is expressive, creative in its nature—the Leydig center.

By this breathing, this may be made to expand—as it moves along the path that is taken in its first inception, at conception, and opens the seven centers of the body that radiate or are active upon the organisms of the body.

This in its direction may be held or made to be a helpful influence for specific conditions, at times—by those who have taught, or who through experience have found as it were the key, or that which one may do and yet must not do; owing to whatever preparation has been made or may be made by the body for the use of this ability, this expression through the body-forces.

As this life-force is expanded, it moves first from the Leydig center through the adrenals, in what may be termed an upward trend, to the pineal and to the centers in control of the emotions—or reflexes through the nerve forces of the body.

Thus an entity puts itself, through such an activity, into association or in conjunction with all it has EVER been or may be. For, it loosens the physical consciousness to the universal consciousness.

To allow self in a universal state to be controlled, or to be dominated, may become harmful.

But to know, to feel, to comprehend as to WHO or as to WHAT is the directing influence when the self-consciousness has been released and the real ego allowed to rise to expression, is to be in that state of the universal consciousness—which is indicated in this body here, Edgar Cayce, through which there is given this interpretation...

So, in analyzing all this—first study the variations of what has been the body-temperament, in thought, in food. For, the body-physical becomes that which it assimilates from material nature. The body-mental becomes that it assimilates from both the physical-mental and the spiritual-mental. The soul is ALL of that the entity is, has been or may be.

Then, WHO and WHAT would the entity have to direct self in such experiences?

To be loosed without a governor, or a director, may easily become harmful.

But as we would give, from here, let not such a director be that of an entity. Rather so surround self with the universal consciousness of the CHRIST, as to be directed by that influence as may be committed to thee.

Thus the entity may use constructively that which has been attained...

Thus ye may constructively use that ability of spiritual attunement, which is the birthright of each soul; ye may use it as a helpful influence in thy experiences in the earth.

But make haste SLOWLY! Prepare the body. Prepare the mind, before ye attempt to loosen it in such measures or manners that it may be taken hold upon by those influences which constantly seek expressions of self rather than of a living, constructive influence of a CRUCIFIED Savior.

Then, crucify desire in self; that ye may be awakened to the real abilities of helpfulness that lie within thy grasp.

. . . without preparation, desires of EVERY nature may become so accentuated as to destroy—or to overexercise as to bring detrimental forces; unless the desire and purpose is acknowledged and set IN the influence of self as to its direction—when loosened by the kundaline activities through the body...

. . . this opening of the centers or the raising of the life force may be brought about by certain characters of breathing—for, as indicated, the breath is power in itself; and this power may be directed to certain portions of the body. But for what purpose? As yet it has been only to see what will happen!

Remember what curiosity did to the cat!

Remember what curiosity did to Galileo, and what it did to Watt—but they used it in quite different directions in each case!

281-54

This psychic reading given by Edgar Cayce at the office of the Association, Arctic Crescent, Virginia Beach, Va., this 28th day of May, 1941, 3:30 to 3:45 P.M., in accordance with request by those present: Edgar Cayce; Gertrude Cayce, Conductor; Gladys Davis, Steno; Florence Edmonds, Esther Wynne, Frances Y. Morrow, Hannah Miller, and Ruth LeNoir.

Mrs. C: You will have before you the Glad Helpers Prayer Group, members of which are present in this room. You will consider their work and study on the endocrine system of the human body, answering the questions they submit, as I ask them.

Mr. C: Yes, we have the group as gathered here, as a group and as individuals; also their work and study on the endocrine system.

As we have indicated—much study, much meditation is needed here. Much has been given. As it is better understood, papers may be prepared on same which would prove not only interesting but most beneficial.

Continue with the study of same.

Ready for questions.

Q-1. Are the following statements true or false: First—Saul, the son of righteous Kish, in the latter part of his life chose evil. It was the exercising of his own choice rather than environmental or hereditary conditions.

A-1. Correct.

Q-2. God made the mineral, vegetable and animal kingdoms, then out of these He made man and breathed into him the breath of life. Adam, who at that period was devoid of any of the spiritualized cells of the physical body, had a stronger urge to revert to physical desires.

A-2. Yes and no. Consider that, whether it is mineral, vegetable or animal, these are spiritualized in that ability of using, doing, being all that the Creator had given them to do.

Hence man was given that which is NOT a part of mineral, vegetable or animal kingdoms; though man, by man, is considered of the animal kingdom. WILL—with the environmental forces and the spiritual negative in the serpent— acceded to desire, to become and to experience IN that kingdom of influence. This brought the acceptance, by man's own will.

Q-3. The mother of Jesus in being a channel for material desires was making practical her spiritual activities.

A-3. Correct.

Q-4. It would be well for prospective parents to learn the lessons illustrated by the lives of Samuel, Saul, Samson, Joseph, Jesus, etc.

A-4. It would be well.

Q-5. Instruction regarding the endocrine glands should be given to the parents of coming generations.

A-5. Correct.

Q-6. It is the spiritual activity within the body of the parents, or the lack of it that determines the influence predominant in the life of their child.

A-6. This is true.

Q-7. Anger causes poisons to be secreted from the glands. Joy has the opposite effect.

The adrenal glands are principally involved, reacting through the solar plexus to all parts of the body.

A-7. The adrenals principally, but ALL of the glands are involved; as: A nursing mother would find that anger would affect the mammary glands. One nursing would find the digestive glands affected. The liver, the kidneys and ALL glands are affected; though it is correct that the reaction is PRINCIPALLY through the adrenals.

Q-8. As the shape or form of the embryo begins to find expression, the growth of the spiritual being gives it expression through the channels of the aerial.

A-8. It gives EXPRESSION through the channels of the aerial, but arises from the lyden [Leydig]—to be sure.

Q-9. Medical science calls the glands at the base of the brain Pituitary and 3rd eye Pineal. Why have these names been reversed? Please explain.

A-9. Their activity indicates that, from the angles of this study, these should be reversed.

Q-10. Meaning we should reverse ours, or that medical science should?

A-10. To understand what is being given, reverse them! We are not telling medical science what to do! We are telling YOU what to do!

We are through for the present.

281-55

This psychic reading given by Edgar Cayce at the office of the Association, Arctic Crescent, Virginia Beach, Va., this 7th day of June, 1941, in accordance with request by those present—3:40 to 4:05 P.M., EST. Present: Edgar Cayce; Gertrude Cayce, Conductor; Gladys Davis, Steno; Beverly Simmons, Ruth Denney, and Mae Verhoeven.

Mrs. C: You will have before you the Glad Helpers Prayer Group, members of which are present in this room. You will consider their work and study on the endocrine system of the human body, answering the questions they submit, as I ask them.

Mr. C: Yes, we have the work of the Glad Helpers, and their work on the endocrine system—as a group, as individuals, and those present in this room.

In answering questions, it is well that all members of the group, as well as those present, analyze their own experiences in the light of that which has been, may be or will be given respecting the manners in which they each may use such information as a helpful influence—first in their OWN experience, and then in assisting others to understand their purposes, their desires—physically, mentally, spiritually—in human relationships.

Ready for questions.

Q-1. Are the following statements true or false? Inception is the aerial activity to the nucleus.

A-1. This is correct, if there is the understanding that there is the physical, the mental AND the spiritual aspect also.

Q-2. Conception is the physical activity.

A-2. Not necessarily. For, aerial activity produces conception. It is that movement by which the parts of the activity become one. THAT is conception.

Q-3. In giving that as may be understandable in the study of man, it is necessary to understand that purpose for which an entity decided to enter the earth plane from the first creation of that entity.

A-3. This is too far-reaching to be answered yes or no. For, each experience of a soul-entity in materiality is part of the whole experience of the entity. Each inception, each conception upon which the soul depends for its period of manifestation is as but a moment, a day, a year in the activity of the ENTITY itself. Thus it could not be said that an individual conception is a beginning. It is a part of a whole—from those activities first conceived in mind—and there is no time in spirit, see?

Q-4. There may be wholly the carnal or animal nature on the part of both and yet conception may take place.

A-4. Correct. But there is also the physical law that is active under such conditions. There are also laws of the mental and the spiritual being that are also active. As it were, it is an individual using a life-giving and a death-dealing influence without happening to be destroyed.

Q-5. Comment on the following: Considered from the physical—when conception takes place only the physical body is limited.

A-5. And this is relatively so. For, when conception takes place there is also to be considered the form or manner in which the environmental conditions are to influence the relative physical stature, the relative physical beauty, the relative physical activity as to whether it is to become male or female—by the motivative force of the nucleus about which the positive and negative forces are vibrating. This is not determined at conception but is a development—the sex, see?

Q-6. Considered from the mental, when conception takes place the mental capacity is limited to the highest positive count of the soul number.

A-6. Yes and no. For, again, there are those relative relationships with the environmental forces. For, it is or has been conceded that in the Grecian experience the beauty and the stature and the symmetrical figure were all wrought by the environment. So, also, the environment of the mental force may be such as to bring those vibrations that may alter or attune, or confuse or hinder, that mental expansion. For, within the nucleus at conception is the pattern of all that is possible. And remember, man—the soul of man, the body of man, the mind of man—is nearer to limitlessness than anything in creation.

Hence those who consider the manner of being channels through which souls may enter are taking hold upon God-Force itself; and it is not the same as an animal, insect or any of the rest of creation—which is limited always.

This statement would be true, then, of ANY conception below man.

Q-7. Considered from the spiritual—when conception takes place the spiritual attributes are limited to the highest positive count of the soul number.

A-7. Here you are accrediting again those conditions to material things, and yet you are dealing with the infinite. Then, this is not true.

Q-8. Conception can only take place when the spiritual ideal set by both is met.

A-8. TRUE conception, SPIRITUAL conception, MENTAL conception only takes place under such; but, as we have just stated above, physical conception may take place from purely carnal influences!

Q-9. Conception can take place when the spiritual ideal set by one is met.

A-9. Conception may take place under ANY circumstances—physical, mental or spiritual!

Q-10. When twins are conceived the ideal of each parent is expressed.

A-10. This may or may not be true.

Q-11. When triplets or more are conceived it is the result of confusing ideals in each parent.

A-11. Remember, it is physical first, mental next, and spiritual next. All are dependent one upon the other.

Q-12. An individual entity is attracted to the soul number which is determined at conception.

A-12. Again you are confusing signs for reality. Yes, it may be; but how many twos are there in your mind? How many of ANY number, or how many combinations of same? It is true that there are certain set numbers, but as to the CAPACITY of that number—how many times may there be threes, fives, eights, nines? These are limitless! So are the abilities, spiritual, of an entity's conception in activity.

Q-13. The changing of the positive and negative forces by the mind of the mother determines the entity that enters.

A-13. Yes and no.

Q-14. An entity only has a soul number when in the earth plane.

A-14. Yes.

Q-15. Through other planetary sojourns an entity has the opportunity to change its rate of vibration so as to be attracted in the earth plane under another soul number.

A-15. Each planetary influence vibrates at a different rate of vibration. An entity entering that influence enters that vibration; not necessary that he change, but it is the grace of God that he may! It is part of the universal consciousness, the universal law.

Q-16. Numbers are indications of abilities, as the astrological influence indicates urges.

A-16. Correct from a physical standpoint only. These have nothing to do with WILL, that is the controlling factor of an individual entity or soul. They are merely signs! Do not dwell upon signs and become a sign reader, and believe in signs and not in the TRUTH!

Q-17. The number is parallel to the incarnation, which is relative to the universal consciousness.

A-17. Yes and no.

We are through for the present.

281-57

This psychic reading given by Edgar Cayce at the office of the Association, Arctic Crescent, Virginia Beach, Va., this 27th day of August, 1941, in accordance with request made by those present–4:00 to 4:20 P.M., EDST. Present: Edgar Cayce; Gertrude Cayce, conductor; Gladys Davis, steno; Hannah Miller, Frances Y. Morrow, Florence Edmonds, Ruth LeNoir, Almeda Newman, and Beulah Emmet.

Mrs. C: You will have before you the Glad Helpers Prayer Group, members of which are present in this room. You will consider their work and study on the endocrine system of the human body, and continue the discourse on this subject; answering the questions that may be submitted, as I ask them:

Mr. C: Yes, we have the work of the prayer group; its purposes, its aims and desires, and the studies thus far made of the endocrine system. In continuing a discourse, or in giving information regarding same, it would be well—before too much INFORMATION becomes burdensome—that what has already been given be better understood; either by the attempts of individuals to discuss same or by the compilers setting in order those activities that are related to the physical, the mental and spiritual development.

As may be easily indicated, some of the activities of the glands relate to the purely physical functioning; yet the physical functioning in a life-giving body must of its very nature be empowered with mind and spirit.

Ye have interpreted, and have data indicating what, where, when there are the various stations or centers in the body-function physically, and how these also are analyzed as to their activity in a physical sense, and how they each are related to the mental body, and the relation its relative activity bears with the spiritual forces of the body.

Thus this group should be able to answer—to self, at least—that question which has not been answered since man began to think: Where is the dwelling place of the soul in the physical body? What is the connection or center through which the mind and the soul function, that makes one individual a devil and another a saint?

These should be the studies. Then, they may be applied to that purpose for which this group came into being; aiding seekers to find health, understanding and prosperity in their own environs.

Then, find the answers to these in that ye have attained, in that which has been given. Ye comprehend that though there may be the complete development to manhood or womanhood, the foetus in its activities, the gland of reproduction becomes the source from and through which impulse acts. Thus it is the source of propagation throughout the experience.

Ye have gained that the first movement of same physically reaches out and becomes the brain, through which the pineal in its activity brings its physical development; and that it is related to the mind of the body and the environs of the body supplying physical activities to that developing physical entity. Ye know that it reverts then to the brain of the nervous system, to the solar plexus center, and then reflexes through its own MENTAL activity to the physical forces of the still developing body. Ye know that when such a body has developed, when gestation has been completed and it becomes an entity in itself—because of its center through which all physical and mental impulse has passed—it is then cut asunder—and yet functions on. Why? How?

These are not merely pathological questions, but mental and spiritual also.

We are through for the present.

281-58

This psychic reading given by Edgar Cayce at the office of the Association, Arctic Crescent, Virginia Beach, Va., this 1st day of October, 1941, in accordance with request made by those present—3:50 to 4:00 P.M., EST: Edgar Cayce; Gertrude Cayce, Conductor; Gladys Davis, Steno; Esther Wynne, Florence Edmonds, Frances Y. Morrow, Hannah Miller, Ruth LeNoir, Mae Verhoeven, Sallie Jones, and others.

Mrs. C: You will have before you the Glad Helpers Prayer Group, members of which are present in this room, and their study of the endocrine system of the human body. You will answer the questions they submit, as I ask them.

Mr. C: Yes, we have the group as gathered here, as a group, as individuals, and their study of the endocrine system. Ready for questions.

Q-1. Please consider the outlines, copy of which I hold in my hand, and make such corrections and additions that may be necessary.

A-1. These—corrections or the activities—are not to be from here. This is the work of the group as individuals, from that they have gained that has proven helpful in their OWN minds and may prove helpful in others'.

Q-2. Please give a discourse on each of the seven major glandular centers, as I call them, that will help us and others to have a better understanding of their functions physically and mentally during the adolescent period, the adult period and the changing period; also mentally and spiritually during meditation, opening of the door, the baptism of the Holy Spirit: First—Pituitary.

A-2. This, as has been indicated, is the way along the system. (This is going backward—we should begin with the first cause, if an understanding is to be maintained!) These, they pass along the way; that has to do with the correlating of physical, mental and spiritual understanding. It is the growth of body and mind, the opening of which is the arousing in the adolescent to the disputations that become the conflicting influences in the experience of the individual entity.

It is the door, as interpreted by some, through which physically all of the reflex actions respond through the various forces of the nerve system.

It is that to and through which the mental activities come that produce the influences in the imaginative system as well as the racial prejudices as termed the predominating influences—or the blood force itself.

In the spiritual, it is that to which the singleness in the adult brings the awakening to its capabilities, its possibilities, its ultimate hope and desire.

It is that which in the change period brings the physical influence in which there is the correlating by experience, through the changing influences in body as related to its OWN findings and its individual intent and purpose. Or, as may be termed, it is physically the ripening of the fruit of the experience of the body; as to whether it has been material-mindedness or of spiritual import.

In the mental it is that which gives judgment and understanding, tolerance AND relationships to the determining factors. Hence we find some grow old gracefully, some tolerantly, some fussily and some very meanly. ALL of these, then, are the expressions of that which has been the dominant force that began from its first active influence that passed from its innate to the animate, to its full completion in the individual experience of the entity.

This is the influence also, or the activities spoken of, as the door upon and through which the old men may dream dreams, the young men may see visions. All of these are the expressions of this activity in its relationships, correlated with other influences and glands that are of the physical as well as the mental natures in the body.

We are through for the present.

PITUITARY BODY (*Gray's Anatomy*)

Function: Extracts give a substance which causes constriction of the blood vessels with rise of arterial blood-pressure. This substance seems to have a stimulating effect on most of the smooth muscles, acting directly upon the muscle causing contraction. It also increases the secretion of the urine; of the mammary glands when in functional activity; and of the cerebrospinal fluid. Many authors regard the pars nervosa and the pars intermedia as the posterior lobe.

The pars anterior exercises a stimulating effect on the growth of the skeleton and probably on connective tissues in general.

Enlargement of the hypophysis and the cavity of the sella turcica are found in the rare disease ACROMEGALY, which is characterized by gradual enlargement of the face, hands, and feet, with headache and often a peculiar type of blindness. The blindness is due to the pressure of the enlarging hypophysis on the optic chiasma.

THE DUCTLESS GLANDS *(Gray's Anatomy)*

Certain organs very similar to secreting glands, but differing in one essential particular, viz., they do not possess any ducts by which their secretion is discharged...that is to say they are capable of forming, from materials brought to them, INTERNAL SECRETION in the blood, substances which have a certain influence upon the nutritive and other changes going on in the body. This secretion is carried into the blood stream, either directly by the veins or indirectly through the medium of the lymphatics.

These glands include the THYROID, the PARATHYROIDS and the THYMUS; the PITUITARY BODY and the PINEAL BODY; the chromaphil and cortical systems to which belong the SUPRARENALS, the PARAGANGLIA and AORTIC GLANDS, the GLOMUS CAROTICUM and perhaps the GLOMUS COCCYGEUM. The SPLEEN is usually included in this list and sometimes the LYMPH and HEMOLYMPH NODES described with the lymphatic system. Other glands as the liver, pancreas and sexual glands give off internal secretions, as do the gastric and intestinal mucous membranes.

281-63

This psychic reading given by Edgar Cayce at the office of the Association, Arctic Crescent, Virginia Beach, Va., this 6th day of March, 1943, in accordance with request made by those present, 4:00 to 4:35 P.M., EST. Present: Edgar Cayce; Gertrude Cayce, Conductor; Gladys Davis, Steno; Ruth Denney, Helen Ellington; Jane Williams; Beverly Simmons; Grace Premo, and Mae Verhoeven.

Mrs. C: You will have before you the enquiring minds of those present in this room who are studying the Book of Revelation in relation to the human body; also the information already compiled and that which may be acquired, including the chart which I hold in my hand. These individuals seek an understanding of all the attributes and influences that go to make up a living, moving, human body. You will answer the questions they submit, as I ask them.

Mr. C: Yes, we have the enquiring minds of those present in this room, those seen and unseen; the information that has been given respecting the application of the study of Revelation in reference to the human body.

Ready for questions.

Q-1. Comment on the chart, give corrections and value of it as a key to this study.

A-1. As interpreted in the minds of those who have put the chart together, this in the main is very good. As to the varied centers, their reactions and activities, these—to be sure—become more individual. But as we have indicated, and as will be the experience of individuals in the study of this chart, these will necessarily respond to that consciousness or awareness that has been attained by the student—or the individual entity. And these should be a helpful influence in the minds of those as they attempt to apply same in their own experience and relationships.

To be sure, as given, and as may be the experience of those as they study the outline indicated from the chart—there will be times when individuals will interpret correctly. There will be times when there will be doubts—until a practical application of same is made in the experience of the individual entity.

Q-2. What attribute dominates the X and Y chromosomes found in the spermatozoa and ovum?

A-2. This is dependent upon purpose and attitude of individual entities that produce or bring about the uniting of same. If this is from those conditions that have had those activities which cause any deteriorating effect, it produces then that value of the cycle about the center of the positive and negative forces. What produces same? Attitude!

Q-3. What influence dominates the activity of each of the 3 distinct divisions in the cell that produces the sperm?

A-3. The life experience of the individual entity, as a whole; as related to the spiritual ideal of that entity—which may be indicated in that He gave, "Ye do not gather grapes from thistles."

Q-4. The ovum?

A-4. The same.

Q-5. Why are the divisions unequal in the breaking-down process of the cell producing ovum?

A-5. That is the activity of the negative and positive forces as related one to another. Just as in the current in electrical energies the electrons by activity are broken down, as dissipation takes place; production of the cell in its unity, if there is activity upon same by an ideal or purpose in the act itself, then there becomes variations in its centers about which the vibration begins.

Q-6. What influence does the individuality of each of the polar bodies have on fertilization of the ovum, and development in the nucleus?

A-6. Each supplies that individuality which in its union produces a personality. This then would come to this: What is personality and individuality, as related to the sex relationship in the act itself? These determine, then, much of that activity that is the dominating influence in that brought about, by the contact of or the piercing of the ovum.

Q-7. How are the chromosomes from each of the polar bodies used in cooperation with the 24 from the sperm and 24 from the ovum to bring into manifestation the 3 types of cell layers—ectoderm, entoderm, mesoderm—in development of embryo?

A-7. These are as the factors in that of anatomical rebuilding of influences or force upon the body produced. These each, then, have their relationship to each layer as related to that which brings about the individuality or the sex activity of the body, in the activity of the ovum in this relationship.

Q-8. What power does the centrosome have, and what is it relative to in a living, human body?

A-8. The emotions as related to the CENTRAL forces in eventual activity within the lyden gland itself, or that ability to reproduce within its own self.

Q-9. How many genes are contained in the chromosome, and what is their relative activity to various portions of the human body?

A-9. These are varied in their activity in the body-building force, by the relationship of the individual entity that has the controlling force upon the developing of the foetus in its activity, see? For, as the first activity is the reaching out by the very force of the numbers of the cellular force in the various layer in that activity, these bring their relative relationships upon each center from and through which impulses arise in the body forces themselves. One is active through emotions, one upon the reflexes, one upon the centralization—or coordination of the reflexes with this activity in itself.

Q-10. Why are the Y chromosomes found in some of the spermatozoa and are lacking in all ova and their polar bodies?

A-10. This is the variation in the very nature or character in the spermatozoa and the ovum activity itself. These are the natures of this. For, one was created first and the other came out FROM same.

Q-11. What is the difference in quality between an ovum fertilized by a sperm containing an X chromosome and one containing a Y chromosome?

A-11. The ability of the reflexes, as just indicated, as to the nature or the activities of same in their relationships to one another.

Q-12. Is our chart valuable in tracing disease from result to cause? Please give an example using chart.

A-12. This as a tracing of heredity in disease may be valuable. As for that of other natures, not so good. These would give, as by the very nature of the chart activity, how the activity of the chromosome upon the ovum shows whether the body would be susceptible to one or another character of disease.

Q-13. Please give a pattern outlining how the 12 major divisions of the body are set up through the endocrine system in the nucleus.

A-13. This has been given, as to how they pass from one influence to another, in the manner in which the mother in its application of thought, of food, of mind, carries those activities to the various centers making the body-building, the nerve and blood building, the emotions, and the very natures to which the pattern will be formed in its relationship to that with which contact is made.

For, oft—as may be demonstrated in individualities—there are those who are geniuses and yet are so very close to the border that an emotional shock may make a demon of a genius. There are those activities in which a spiritualized cell, by environment, may make of the demon a saint.

Q-14. Would the history of the Jewish race from Abraham to Jesus parallel the development of the embryo from conception to birth?

A-14. Rather would the history of man from Noah to Abraham; while that from Abraham to Christ would be the mental unfoldment of the body. For, that which leads to the Christ is the mind. And the mind's unfoldment may be that indicated from Abraham to the Christ.

Q-15. Please give others we may parallel.

A-15. Such activities as just indicated give the parallel or pattern through which it may be indicated at the birth of an individual entity as to the direction it will take.

Q-16. Please give definite direction to Ruth Denney, present in this room, for future study and fuller understanding.

A-16. As indicated, knowledge without the practical ability to apply same may become sin. For, it is knowledge misapplied that was the fall—or the confusion—in Eve.

In the application and study, then, of all influences that go to make up the developments—as the entity may find, as indicated to the entity in that just stated, the unfoldment of the mind as may be paralleled by the history of the communication of spirit, or God, with individual entities from Abraham to Christ, may be seen in thine own children. For, this is the manner to make same practical—that knowledge ye have gained in not only watching but aiding in the unfoldment of their minds. Do not put off questions asked too long to be answered. And have an answer when the question is asked.

We are through for the present.

281-63
Supplement

THE REVELATION—Chart prepared by Helen Ellington and Gladys Davis, based on their study of 281 series, *Bible Dictionary* (Smith's) [1885 edition, Holman and Co.], meditation, etc. (See page 68, Q-1.)

281-29, A-32; Rev. 7, Rdg. 10/28/36-A-32:
281-30, A-6; Rev. 7, Gen. 49, Rdg. 2/17/37-A-6:

4 Corners of the Earth (Body-Jacob) (Influences)
12 Tribes: 12 Major Divisions:

SPIRITUAL (Hail-Water-Sea):
3 Attributes:
Light .... Zabulon .... Digestive
Soul (Love) .... Joseph .... Covering
Will .... Benjamin .... Bone Structure

MENTAL (Fire-Heat):
3 Attributes:
Desire .... Simeon .... Organs
Choice .... Levi .... Glands
Conscience .... Issachar .... Membranes

HEREDITY (Air-Blood):
3 Attributes:
Life (Sensation) .... Aser .... Lymph
Opportunity .... Nephthalim .... Nerves
Power .... Manasses .... Elimination

ENVIRONMENT (Earth-Physical):
3 Attributes:
Preservation .... Juda .... Assimilation
(To Mental
Material-Spiritual)
Perpetuation .... Reuben .... Blood Circulation
(Keeping Alive)
Attraction .... Gad .... Cells
(Construction)

EXPLANATION OF ABOVE CHART

Spiritual is the life, Mind is the builder, Physical is the result. The body is a physical pattern of the spiritual. Consequently, each major division of the Body must be complete in itself. No one organ can be a major division as it is only a result or a channel through which the three major divisions work; namely, Cells, Blood Circulation, Assimilation.

Without either the Construction by Attraction of Cells, the Keeping Alive by Perpetuation of the Blood Circulation, the influences to the Mental Material-Spiritual by Preservation of the Assimilation, a Physical Body could not—and would cease to—exist. It could not Attract other Cells so as to Perpetuate its own kind and Preserve the Mental-Spiritual Influences inherited from the beginning, and thus rise to the next step—the Power of overcoming, through Elimination of the dross.

When reaching that Power, all the Nerves of the Body become aware of greater Opportunity to have Life. The Nervous System gives us so many opportunities to express, to choose, Life. Without the Nerves everything would be sort of Dead. (See Dan, the Serpent—left out of the 12 Tribes because he represents Death; and through rising to the Power and the Opportunity of Life we do not find Death as an Attribute of the Body. The Serpent-Satan cannot express in flesh save through the Environment we give him.)

Lymph means "water." Water means spirit, that from which all things sprang. Consequently, Lymph means Life—we have just come to the realization that our heritage is Life eternal. (An interesting point here is that the Lymph vessels with the lacteals form the absorbent system for Assimilated fats, and it is the only channel of Assimilation that does not empty into the liver. Remember, the liver, and kidneys are the positive and negative poles of the Physical Body.)

Consequently, we rise to the MENTAL influence, realizing that Mind is the Builder and we must do something about it; hence our conscience becomes Active. Conscience is the nearest dwelling place in our bodies of the holy of holies, the spirit of the Master. Thus it must be represented in the Physical by the Membranes that are skin-like tissue covering parts of the body, lining cavitles and canals which communicate with the external air, lining cavities which have no external communication. (It is interesting to note here that if a certain kind of membrane fluid is secreted in excess, one has a dropsical "water" condition. Probably one dries up and dies if there is too little secretion.)

Then, having been pricked by Conscience, one has a Choice to make through the seven spiritual centers, the 7 glands about which so little is known in the Physical. (See chart of the 7 Churches, and Rev. 1 to 7.)

We can choose to express through the Glands and open the 7 spiritual centers, or we can Choose to leave them closed and just be Physical. We are always making the Choice, consciously or unconsciously.

Choice is governed greatly by Desire; and Desire would attract Organs through which to function in the Physical Body. It was Desire that caused man to come into a Physical Body, and the Organs have to function in order to manifest or express Desire.

Choosing and Desiring then to go upward toward our Source, we come to the SPIRITUAL Influence, with its Attributes. In order to attain stability and be able to STAND in the presence of the Most High, we must exercise Will; that factor which can make us strong, positive, and upright. Consequently, we have selected Bone Structure as the representation in the Physical for such a strong Attribute.

The Soul could not express very well in the earth without a Covering; so it gradually took onto itself a Physical Body. Hence in the present Body our Soul shines through or is expressed through our center Covering. (See similarity here to our MENTAL Attribute of Conscience, represented in the skin-like Coverings called Membranes.)

The highest SPIRITUAL Attribute is Light. The first creation was Light. If our Soul continues to follow the Light, we will get back to our Source. The first thing a Body does when it is born into Light (Physical) is to start Digesting. Consequently, we have put the Digestive System as the representation of Light in the Physical Body. We must properly Digest all the Attributes; that is, spiritualize them, and return them to their Source in Spirit. Then we each will be as a complete Cell (Corpuscle) in the Body of God (Spirit), throbbing, pulsing, CREATING, CO-WORKING with the Whole, yet realizing ourselves to be INDIVIDUAL.

So, before Creation there was Spirit. The Spirit comes down through Influences, through the Attributes, into the Physical Body; and returns, starting from the Cells to build through the Physical to the Spirit again. With this picture we see exactly what was meant in Group #1 Reading on Spirit when it said Spirit was the beginning and the end of all steps for a soul's development, in the earth. Also we understand the Spirit of Jesus Christ saying in the vision to John, "I am Alpha and Omega, the beginning and the end, the first and the last."

Notice the SPIRITUAL Attribute of Soul being represented in the Physical by the Tribe of Joseph, who became Jesus, the Christ. The meaning of the name Joseph is "he will increase," and he is the purest character known to history except Jesus. Read the story of Joseph and his brothers with the Chart in mind, fitting each one into his place. Notice how closely allied with Benjamin the brother Joseph is, and how beloved Benjamin is. The Soul without the Will would be lost indeed. Joseph was the eleventh son of Jacob (Body) but the first son of Rachel. Probably this means something, and also Rachel—which we have to figure out.

Benjamin (fortune) was the twelfth son of Jacob (Body) and the second son of Rachel. There's the weakness and the strength in the 2. The Soul and Will united makes the Triune of strength. Benjamin had the affection of his brothers, and received their favors as a matter of course, and was not very positive, but a quiet, gentle spirit. The Will without the Soul couldn't do very much. The TRIBE of Benjamin was always of least consequence. The tribe was almost destroyed for violating the rights of hospitality (Judges 19:20), 600 only escaping to the rock Rimmon—which they held for four months against their enemies (Judges 20:47). The Benjamites seized the "daughters of Shiloh" and preserved a tribe from extinction (Judges 21:19) "at an annual feast of the Lord." The first deliverer of Israel (from Moab) in the time of the judges, was Ehud, a Benjamite. The first king of Israel was Saul, a Benjamite; and Saul (Paul), the apostle, was also of this tribe. It is interesting to note also that in Jerusalem (temple body) there is a Gate called Benjamin.

Also it is interesting to notice that when Jacob (body) blesses or gives the message to his sons, he calls them in order of their birth: but in Revelation, according to the Spirit, they are given their place according to spiritual merit.

Simeon and Levi, being Desire and Choice, must certainly be closely united. Simeon (harkening) and Levi (to adhere) killed a whole tribe because of wrong they considered done to their only sister, Dinah (Genesis 34).

Here it might be worth while to note that there are 12 Openings in the Body of Man, and 13 in the Body of Woman. Perhaps this Dinah (acquitted) caused so much trouble in the beginning. Nothing is recorded as to what became of Dinah. She was a 13th child of Jacob (Body)—the only daughter.

Simeon was the 2nd son of Jacob (Body). Here's the weakness of 2 again, and only becomes strong with the Choice added to Desire. The only great name of the tribe on record is the widow Judith, the heroine of the apocryphal Book of Judith, where she appears as an ideal type of piety, beauty, courage and chastity. There were 18 cities given to Simeon, including the famous well of Beersheba. A part of the tribe (500 men) took possession of a district in Mount Seir, where they were still living after the return from Captivity (I Chronicles 4:42, 43).

Levi, 3rd son of Jacob. Levi's descendants, among whom were Moses and Aaron, were made the ministers of religion and the representatives of the national faith. Jacob prophesied that Levi should be scattered among his brothers, which was fulfilled in the distribution of the tribe among the 48 Levitical cities, which were scattered throughout the whole country. The tribe displaced the earlier priesthood of the first-born as representatives of the holiness of the people. They guarded the ark, and were reckoned separately as the host (of the Lord), and were not counted in the army. (See GLANDS under this in Chart—spiritual centers). Their special duties were the daily sacrifice, and the work about the tabernacle (and Temple), in a certain appointed order (Numbers 3, 4, 7). (See division in *Bible Dictionary* of the tribe into 3 separate branches according to their functions [Exodus 6:16-25].) So MUCH is given about this tribe that seems to have a peculiar significance to the Body-Physical-Spiritual, and Jacob's saying "I will divide them in Jacob (body), and scatter them in Israel (seekers)."

Issachar (hire), 9th son of Jacob, 5th son of Leah. He is not mentioned again as a person, only as a tribe. (Interesting, considering this to be Conscience.) Its land was and is now the richest in Palestine. We are left to suppose that the tribe fell into idolatry, because there is nothing recorded in favor of its religious history. In the order of march in the desert, Issachar's place was on the east of the tabernacle, with Juda and Zabulon. Notice "A strong-boned he-ass, couching down between two hedgerows," apparently the missing link—or connecting link—between the Preservation of the Physical (Juda) and the Light of the Spiritual (Zabulon). Since Conscience is not very tangible in the Physical Body, it is easy to see why the tribe apparently passed out of existence.

Aser, 8th son of Jacob, 4th son of Bilhah. The boundaries of the tribe are extremely difficult to trace. (Imagine trying to trace life in a Physical Body, or measure the 8th step—after the 7th gland-seal is opened.) It is only known that the boundaries were North of Carmel (Park—fruitful field), on the Great Sea (7 glandular centers leading to Spiritual). Notice the description in anatomy as to how the lymph ducts carry the "water" of the blood. The land (tribe of Aser) contained some of the richest soil in Palestine, and minerals. Anna, who lived in the temple, watching for the coming of Christ, was of this tribe.

Nephthalim (wrestled), 5th son of Jacob, 2nd of Bilhah. There is not a word said about him personally in the Scriptures. See Exodus, Twelve Tribes. Evidently Nephthalim used his Opportunity to become all "Nerves," that is, "Impulses," instead of actualities or personal recognition. Notice, "Nephthalim IS a hind let loose; he giveth goodly words." Jesus said, "Father, thy word is truth." So perhaps the Nerves give the words of truth the Opportunity to register and be carried to all parts of the Body.

Manasses: There is no reason given for depriving Manasses of his birthright, as there was in the case of his grand-uncle Esau. On leaving Egypt at the Exodus this was the least of the 12 tribes, but later increased so that he is honored with a first mention before Ephraim. The division of the tribe is one of the singular facts in the history of the Israelites (seekers) and seems to be at variance with the national feeling and laws. Some of this tribe were warriors and made extensive conquests. There is no account of this tribe separate from Ephraim, and it is likely that the two neighbors were spoken of as one people. It is interesting here to note that we have Manasses corresponding with Elimination in the Body; and evidently Manasses takes the place of Dan (Satan-Death), Eliminates Death and becomes Powerful.

It is also interesting here to notice that Ephraim was given the birthright, yet Manasses is one of the 12 divisions of the body mentioned in Rev. Consequently, Ephraim must have to do with that 13th element again, or the Opening of the Woman—which becomes so necessary to the tribe of Manasses, in order to become Powerful through united strength to Eliminate Satan (Dan Serpent), or to undo the harm caused when "the Sons of God looked upon the Daughters of Men," etc. Consequently, Woman spiritualized—as in Mary, the Mother of the Lord—gives Power to man and strength to overcome.

Ephraim means "double fruitfulness"; he was the 2nd son of Joseph by his wife Asenath. Again the weakness of 2 unless made strong in the Triune. Joshua the son of Nun was of the tribe of Ephraim. Joseph disliked the idea of Jacob blessing Ephraim above his older brother Manasseh, yet Joseph himself chose the tribe of Ephraim for his channel of reappearance as Joshua. There was the earthly Power objecting to the spiritual Power; or man saying "Let me sit on the right hand," etc., not realizing yet it has to be merited. The portion of Ephraim in Canaan (lower country, bowed down) was elevated, hilly, and having the plain of Sharon, a narrow strip on the West, Esdraelon on the North, and the Jordan valley on the East, in the center of the country. It was 55 miles from East to West and 70 miles from North to South. The whole was called Mt. Ephraim. It had the "precious things of the earth, and the fullness thereof," as blessed by Moses. The finest and most fruitful of all the land. Afterward called Samaria. Its wealth and importance were increased by the presence of the Ark of the Covenant and the Tabernacle at Shiloh within its borders. The people were jealous, and at enmity with the tribe of Judah from the time of David. If this does mean the Woman, can't you see the jealousy and warring with Juda through the gradual giving away of the Power into the hands of Juda for the Preservation? Very few attempts to conquer Ephraim were ever made, and Shalmaneser (see explanation below) only succeeded through the internal divisions of the kingdom of Samaria (watch mountain). Samaria is mentioned along with Shechem. (See Shechem Samaria).

Ahlmaneser (reverential towards fire), King of Assyria, took Samaria after a siege of 3 years, and carried Hoshea captive beyond the Euphrates, ending the kingdom of Israel. Notice the Fire under the MENTAL Influence. When Samaria (city on a hill, watch-mountain) is overcome, we rise to the MENTAL Influence with its attributes and are able to conquer the 12 major divisions of the body (12 tribes) through Mind over Matter.

Judah (praise Jehovah), 4th son of Jacob by Leah (see 4 influences to body of man from his Source throughout). Judah was a leader in family matters from his youth up, and more is known of him than any other save Joseph. Reuben advised the brothers to throw Joseph into a pit, and Judah proposed the sale to the traders, both acting honorably to themselves, wishing to save the life of Joseph (Preservation, you see). Judah went before Jacob (Body) into Egypt (mystery). In the beginning the Soul has to Assimilate before it could build up a Body. Jacob (Body) honors Judah (Preservation) first in his blessings. It was from the line of Judah and Tamar that Jesus came. Here again we see a Woman playing such an important part in the PRESERVING of the strain. See Genesis 38. Nothing is given as to where Tamar came from, or from what family; yet what she did was counted to her for righteousness.

Reuben (behold, a son), 1st son of Jacob and Leah. The tribe of Reuben was located, at their own request, on the East side of Jordan, and against the wishes of Moses. (Numbers 32:19.) Notice Jordan means "the descender," the watering place; largest river in Palestine. Notice how Perpetuation and Blood Circulation fit in with this, when we consider that the Blood in the Physical is the pattern of Water in the Spiritual—that from whence all comes. The children of Israel passed over Jordan, and were Perpetuated.

Gad (troop), Jacob's 7th son, 1st born of Ailpah, brother to Aser (Life). The country given to the tribe was the center of the east of Jordan (notice Reuben's choice, above). The most beautiful district in Syria (high); a high range of purple tinted mountains, cut down by deep ravines, partially clothed with forests of oak, sycamores, beech, figs, evergreen shrubs, etc. The climate is fine and soil fertile, affording the best pasturage. Notice the similarity between the location of Gad in the "center" and the glands of reproduction in the Body—the seat of the "tree of life," the Opportunity to retrace one's steps through Attracting and Constructing Spiritual Cells that will overcome the "troop" that has been Attracted by undesirables or non-essentials throughout the ages. It is noteworthy that the tribe of Gad was carried into captivity, and its cities inhabited by Ammonites (sons of my relatives). The Ammonites were descended from Lot. Women of the Ammonites were in Solomon's house. The last mention of them is in 1 Macc. v. 5, 30-43. Solomon means wisdom. So with Wisdom we will start spiritualizing our Cells and by the law of Attraction return to that from whence we came.

Zabulon is the Light, the haven in the Sea (Spiritual), from which we first began to Digest outside things and add all these Attributes. "Zabulon shall dwell at the haven of the sea; and he shall be for an haven of ships; and his border shall be unto Zidon." Zidon means "fishing." The Jews never conquered the city, and so far failed of the promise. It is one great garden, filled with every kind of fruit-bearing trees, nourished by streams from Lebanon (white)—the white mountains of Palestine, on the north of the country given to the Israelites. Zabulon means "dwelling"; it is a city without foundation, a house not made with hands, whose Maker and Finisher is God.

See Matthew 4:13-14; reading 1462-1—Gates of Zubar (?) in Temple Beautiful, Temple of Sacrifice in Egypt; later became in other languages known as Zabulon. The LIGHT of those activities made for greater purifying, enlightenment, in other lands.

See reading 281-63, 3/6/43, which precedes this.

The Book of

THE REVELATION

WITH THE EDGAR CAYCE READINGS
AS GIVEN FOR EACH CHAPTER

THE REVELATION

Chapter 1

1. The Revelation of Jesus Christ, which God gave unto him, to shew unto his servants things which must shortly come to pass; and he sent and signified it by his angel unto his servant John:

2. Who bare record of the word of God, and of the testimony of Jesus Christ, and of all things that he saw.

3. Blessed is he that readeth, and they that hear the words of this prophecy, and keep those things which are written therein: for the time is at hand.

4. John to the seven churches which are in Asia: Grace be unto you, and peace, from him which is, and which was, and which is to come; and from the seven Spirits which are before His throne;

5. And from Jesus Christ, who is the faithful witness, and the firstbegotten of the dead, and the prince of the kings of the earth. Unto him that loved us, and washed us from our sins in his own blood,

6. And hath made us kings and priests unto God and his Father; to him be glory and dominion for ever and ever. Amen.

7. Behold, he cometh with clouds; and every eye shall see him, and they also which pierced him: and all kindreds of the earth shall wail because of him. Even so, Amen.

8. I am Alpha and Omega, the beginning and the ending, saith the Lord, which is, and which was, and which is to come, the Almighty.

9. I John, who also am your brother, and companion in tribulation, and in the kingdom and patience of Jesus Christ, was in the isle that is called Patmos, for the word of God, and for the testimony of Jesus Christ.

Mr. C: Yes, we have the text written in the Revelation, as recorded in the King James version of same.

In making this worthwhile in the experience of individuals who are seeking for the light, for the revelation that may be theirs as promised in the promises of same, it would be well that there be considered first the conditions which surrounded the writer, the apostle, the beloved, the last of those chosen; writing to a persecuted people, many despairing, many fallen away, yet, many seeking to hold to that which had been delivered to them through the efforts and activities of those upon whom the spirit had fallen by the very indwelling and the manifestations that had become the common knowledge of all.

Remember, then, that Peter—chosen as the rock, chosen to open the doors of that known today as the church—had said to this companion, "I will endeavor to keep thee in remembrance; even after my demise I will return to you."

The beloved, then, was banished to the isle, and was in meditation, in prayer, in communion with those saints who were in that position to see, to comprehend the greater needs of those that would carry on. 281-16

Chapter 1 continued

10. I was in the Spirit on the Lord's Day, and heard behind me a great voice, as of a trumpet.

11. Saying, I am Alpha and Omega, the first and the last; and, What thou seest, write in a book, and send it unto the seven churches which are in Asia, unto Ephesus, and unto Smyrna, and unto Pergamos, and unto Thyatira, and unto Sardis, and unto Philadelphia, and unto Laodicea.

12. And I turned to see the voice that spake with me. And being turned, I saw seven golden candlesticks;

13. And in the midst of the seven candlesticks one like unto the Son of man, clothed with a garment down to the foot, and girt about the paps with a golden girdle.

14. His head and his hairs were white like wool, as white as snow; and his eyes were as a flame of fire;

15. And his feet like unto fine brass, as if they burned in a furnace; and his voice as the sound of many waters.

16. And he had in his right hand seven stars; and out of his mouth went a sharp two-edged sword; and his countenance was as the sun shineth in his strength.

17. And when I saw him, I fell at his feet as dead. And he laid his right hand upon me, saying unto me, Fear not; I am the first and the last:

18. I am he that liveth, and was dead; and, behold, I am alive for evermore, Amen; and have the keys of hell and of death.

19. Write the things which thou hast seen, and the things which are, and the things which shall be hereafter;

20. The mystery of the seven stars which thou sawest in my right hand, and the seven golden candlesticks. The seven stars are the angels of the seven churches; and the seven candlesticks which thou sawest are the seven churches.

And, as given in the beginning, "I was in the Spirit on the Lord's day, and beheld, and heard, and saw, and was told to *write.*"

Why, then, ye ask now, was this written (this vision) in such a manner that is hard to be interpreted, save in the experience of every soul who seeks to know, to walk in, a closer communion with Him?

For the visions, the experiences, the names, the churches, the places, the dragons, the cities, all are but emblems of those forces that may war within the individual in its journey through the material, or from the entering into the material manifestation to the entering into the glory, or the awakening in the spirit, in the inter-between, in the borderland, in the shadow.

Hence we find, as the churches are named, they are as the forces that are known as the senses, that must be spiritualized by the will of the individual made one in the very activities in a material world. 281-16

Q-1. Are we correct in interpreting the seven churches as symbols of seven spiritual centers in the physical body?

A-1. Correct.

Q-2. Do we have these correctly placed? As each is called, comment on each in relation to an individual's development and experiences in connection with these centers. Gonads—Ephesus; Lyden—Smyrna; Solar Plexus—Pergamos; Thymus—Thyatira; Thyroid—Sardis; Pineal—Philadelphia; Pituitary—Laodicea.

A-2. Rather than the commenting, it is well that these are correctly placed, but each individual's *experience* in the application of that gained by each in his or her experience will be different. To give an interpretation that the opening or activity through a certain center raises or means or applies this or that, then would become rote. But know the way, then each may apply same as his or her environment, ability, experience, gives the opportunity. For know, in all and through all, the activity of self is only as a channel—and God giveth the understanding, the increase, to such; and in the manner as is best fitted for the individual. It is not then as a formula, that there are to be certain activities and certain results. These are true in the sense that they each represent or present the opportunity for the opening to the understanding of the individual, but the application is as to the individual. For, as has been given, man is free-willed. And only when this is entirely given, and actively given, to the will of the Father may it be even as the life of the Christ. 281-29

Q-3. Do the seven angels govern in order the major glandular centers of the physical body?

A-3. In their order, as they have been set. 281-31

And the elders and the Lamb are the emblems, are the shadows of those acceptances or rejections that are made in the experiences of the individual.

As we find, in the various manners and forms that are presented as the vision or visions proceed, every force that is manifest is of one source; but the soul, the will of the individual, either makes such into a coordinating or cooperating influence in bringing about more and more manifestations in the material world of those experiences that are seen from the spiritual conditions, or the opposite.

Why, then, is it presented, ye ask, in the form of symbols? Why is there used those varied activities? These are for those that were, or will be, or may become, through the seeking, those initiated into an understanding of the glories that may be theirs if they will but put into work, into activity, that they know in the present.

In seeking, then, do individuals find from the beginning that there is presented, in every line, in every form, that good and bad (as termed) that arises from their activity, in what they do about that knowledge they have respecting the law, the love, the mercy, the understanding of the wherefore of the Lamb's advent into the world that they, through His ensample set, may present themselves before that throne even as He, becoming—as given—heirs, joint heirs with Him, as the sons of God, to that *everlasting* glory that may be had in Him.

Then, seek to know to what self is lacking, even as given in the first four chapters (as divided in the present).

What is lacking in self? Are ye cold? Are ye hot? Have ye been negligent of the knowledge that is thine? Are ye stiff-necked? Are ye adulterous in thought, in act, in the very glories that are thine?

Then, again—may ye not have had through the varied experiences those presentations before the throne, even as the elders twenty and four that are represented by the figures within thine own head, that which is shown in the physical forces of self? Has it not been given to thee, or has not the message come as the rider of the pale, the black, the white, or the red horses that are the figures of the messages that have come to thee in thine varied experiences? Or, art thou among the figures represented in the Babylon, or in the rivers of blood, or in the trees of life?

These we see, then, represent *self;* self's body-physical, self's body-mental, self's body-spiritual; with the attributes of the body-physical, attributes of the body-mental, attributes of the body-spiritual, and they are *one* in thee—even as the Father, the Son and the Holy Spirit is one in Him.

Then, dost thou seek to enter into the glories of the Father? Whosoever will may come, may take of the water of life freely—even as flows from the throne of the Lamb. For, the very leaves of the trees are for the healing of the nations, and—if ye will accept—the blood cleanses from all unrighteousness. How? From what? Saves self from what? To what are ye called? To know that only from the falling away of self may ye be saved. Unto the glorifying of self in Him may ye be saved.

Then, whosoever will, come! 281-16

In considering then the studies that have been made with this group, in the understanding of the Revelation as given by the beloved of Him: These as we find have been well, and as you each become conscious in your own experience of the movement *of* the influences *through* the body upon the various stages of awareness, there comes a determination, a desire, a longing for the greater light. To him, to her that is faithful, there shall be given a *crown* of light. And His Name shall be above every name: For ye that have seen the light know in whom thou hast believed, and know that in thine own body, thine own mind, there is set the temple of the living God, and that it may function in thy dealings with thy fellow man in such measures that ye become as rivers of light, as fountains of knowledge, as mountains of strengths, as the pastures for the hungry, as the rest for the weary, as the strength for the weak. Keep the faith. 281-28

Q-1. Please discuss more fully the relation of colors to the seven major glandular centers. Do the colors vary for each center with different individuals, or may definite colors be associated with each center?

A-1. Both. For to each—remember, to study each of these in the light not only of what has just been given but that as is a practical experience in the material world—as is known, vibration is the essence or the basis of color. As color and vibration then become to the consciousness along the various centers in an individual's experience in meditation made aware, they come to mean definite experiences. Just as anger is red, or as something depressing is blue; yet in their shades, their tones, their activities, to each they begin with the use of same in the experience to mean those various stages. For instance, while red is anger, rosy to most souls means delight and joy—yet to others, as they are formed in their transmission from center to center, come to mean or to express what *manner* of joy; whether that as would arise from a material, a mental or a spiritual experience. Just as may be seen in the common interpretation of white, but with all manner of rays from same begins or comes to mean that above the aura of all in its vibration from the body and from the activity of the mental experience when the various centers are vibrating to color.

Q-2. If so, give color for: (1) Gonads (2) Lyden (3) Solar Plexus (4) Thymus (5) Thyroid (6) Pineal (7) Pituitary.

A-2. These come from the leaden, going on through to the highest—to that as is the halo. To each they become the various forces as active throughout, and will go in the regular order of the prism. 281-30

CHURCH	VIRTUE	FAULTS	SEAL	VISION	SPIRITUAL CENTERS/ GLANDS	LORD'S PRAYER
EPHESUS	PATIENCE	LEFT FIRST LOVE	1	WHITE HORSE	GONADS (Desire)	BREAD

Chapter 2

1. Unto the angel of the church of Ephesus write; These things saith he that holdeth the seven stars in his right hand, who walketh in the midst of the seven golden candlesticks;

2. I know thy works, and thy labour, and thy patience, and how thou canst not bear them which are evil: and thou hast tried them which say they are apostles, and are not, and hast found them liars;

3. And hast borne, and hast patience, and for my name's sake hast laboured, and hast not fainted.

4. Nevertheless I have somewhat against thee, because thou hast left thy first love.

5. Remember therefore from whence thou art fallen, and repent, and do the first works; or else I will come unto thee quickly, and will remove thy candlestick out of his place, except thou repent.

6. But this thou hast, that thou hatest the deeds of the Nicolaitans, which I also hate.

7. He that hath an ear, let him hear what the Spirit saith unto the churches; To him that overcometh will I give to eat of the tree of life, which is in the midst of the paradise of God.

CHURCH	VIRTUE	FAULTS	SEAL	VISION	SPIRITUAL CENTERS/ GLANDS	LORD'S PRAYER
SMYRNA	SUFFERING	INSINCERITY	2	BLACK HORSE	LYDEN	TEMP-TATION

Chapter 2 continued

8. And unto the angel of the church in Smyrna write; These things saith the first and the last, which was dead, and is alive;

9. I know thy works, and tribulations, and poverty, (but thou art rich) and I know the blasphemy of them which say they are Jews, and are not, but are the synagogue of Satan.

10. Fear none of those things which thou shalt suffer: behold, the devil shall cast some of you into prison, that ye may be tried; and ye shall have tribulation ten days: be thou faithful unto death, and I will give thee a crown of life.

11. He that hath an ear, let him hear what the Spirit saith unto the churches; He that overcometh shall not be hurt of the second death.

CHURCH	VIRTUE	FAULTS	SEAL	VISION	SPIRITUAL CENTERS/ GLANDS	LORD'S PRAYER
PERGAMOS	FAITHFUL	STUMBLING BLOCK	3	RED HORSE	ADRENAL/ SOLAR PLEXUS	DEBTS

Chapter 2 continued

12. And to the angel of the church in Pergamos write; These things saith he which hath the sharp sword with two edges;

13. I know thy works, and where thou dwellest, even where Satan's seat is: and thou holdest fast my name, and hast not denied my faith, even in those days wherein Antipas was my faithful martyr, who was slain among you, where Satan dwelleth.

14. But I have a few things against thee, because thou hast there them that hold the doctrine of Balaam, who taught Balak to cast a stumbling block before the children of Israel, to eat things sacrificed unto idols, and to commit fornication.

15. So hast thou also them that hold the doctrine of the Nicolaitans, which things I hate.

16. Repent; or else I will come unto thee quickly, and will fight against them with the sword of my mouth.

17. He that hath an ear, let him hear what the Spirit saith unto the churches; To him that overcometh will I give to eat of the hidden manna, and will give him a white stone, and in the stone a new name written, which no man knoweth saving he that receiveth it.

Q-1. Please interpret the 2nd Chapter, 17th verse of Revelation. "To him that overcometh will I give to eat of the hidden manna, and will give him a white stone, and in the stone a new name written, which no man knoweth saving he that receiveth it."

A-1. In giving the interpretation of this particular portion of the Revelation, it must all be kept in mind that, as has been indicated, while many of the references—or all—refer to the physical body as the pattern, there is that as may be said to be the literal and the spiritual and the metaphysical interpretation of almost all portions of the Scripture, and especially of the Revelation as given by John.

Yet all of these to be true, to be practical, to be applicable in the experiences of individuals, must coordinate; or be as one, even as the Father, the Son and the Holy Spirit.

In the interpretation of the Name, then: Each entity, each soul, is known—in all the experiences through its activities—as a name to designate it from another. It is not only then a material convenience, but it implies— as has been given, unless it is for material gain—a definite period in the evolution of the experience of the entity in the material plane.

Then as each entity under a given name makes its correlating of that it does about the Creative Forces in its experience, it is coming under those influences that are being fed by the manna—which is a representation of the universality as well as the stability of purposes in the Creative Forces as manifested to a group or a nation of peoples.

So it becomes that as the Master gave, "Ye shall not live by bread alone but by every word that proceedeth from the mouth of the Father."

That indeed is the holy manna which each entity, each soul in each experience must make a part of its mental and spiritual self. Thus it becomes as is indicated, in that the name—as in each experience—bears a relative relationship to the development of the individual entity in each experience.

Then in the end, or in those periods as indicated, it is when each entity, each soul has so manifested, so acted in its relationships as to become then as the new name; white, clear, known only to him that hath overcome. Overcome what? The world, even as He.

For what meaneth a name? John, Jane, Peter, Andrew, Bartholomew, Thaddeus, Rhoda, Hannah? All of these have not only the attunement of a vibration but of color, harmony; and all those relative relationships as one to another.

Then as has been asked, and has been indicated in another portion of Revelation, all those that bear the mark, those that have the name, those that have the stone—these are representatives then of the same experience in the various phases of an individual experience for its activity.

Then the interpretation is that they *have* overcome, they *have* the new name, they *have* the manna, they *have* the understanding, they *have* their relationships as secure in the blood of the Lamb! 281-31

CHURCH	VIRTUE	FAULTS	SEAL	VISION	SPIRITUAL CENTERS/ GLANDS	LORD'S PRAYER
THYATIRA	CHARITY	FORNICATION	4	PALE HORSE	THYMUS	EVIL

Chapter 2 continued

18. And unto the angel of the church in Thyatira write; These things saith the Son of God, who hath his eyes like unto a flame of fire, and his feet are like fine brass;

19. I know thy works, and charity, and service, and faith, and thy patience, and thy works; and the last to be more than the first.

20. Notwithstanding I have a few things against thee, because thou sufferest that woman Jezebel, which calleth herself a prophetess, to teach and to seduce my servants to commit fornication and to eat things sacrificed unto idols.

21. And I gave her space to repent of her fornication; and she repented not.

22. Behold, I will cast her into a bed, and them that commit adultery with her into great tribulation, except they repent of their deeds.

23. And I will kill her children with death; and all the churches shall know that I am he which searcheth the reins and hearts: and I will give unto every one of you according to your works.

24. But unto you I say, and unto the rest in Thyatira, as many as have not this doctrine, and which have not known the depths of Satan, as they speak; I will put upon you none other burden.

25. But that which ye have already, hold fast till I come.

26. And he that overcometh, and keepeth my works unto the end, to him will I give power over the nations:

27. And he shall rule them with a rod of iron; as the vessels of a potter shall they be broken to shivers: even as I received of my Father.

28. And I will give him the morning star.

29. He that hath an ear, let him hear what the Spirit saith unto the churches.

Q-6. Is this the period of the great tribulation spoken of in Revelation, or just the beginning, and if so just how can we help ourselves and others to walk more closely with God?

A-6. The great tribulation and periods of tribulation, as given, are the experiences of every soul, every entity. They arise from influences created by man through activity in the sphere of any sojourn. Man may become, with the people of the universe, ruler of any of the various spheres through which the soul passes in its experiences. Hence, as the cycles pass, as the cycles are passing, when there *is* come a time, a period of readjusting in the spheres (as well as in the little earth, the little soul)—seek, then, as known, to present self spotless before that throne; even as *all* are commanded to be circumspect, in thought, in act, to that which is held by self as that necessary for the closer walk with Him. In that manner only may each atom (as man is an atom, or corpuscle, in the body of the Father) become a helpmeet with Him in bringing that to pass that all may be one with Him. 281-16

CHURCH	VIRTUE	FAULTS	SEAL	VISION	SPIRITUAL CENTERS/ GLANDS	LORD'S PRAYER
SARDIS	FEW NOT DEFILED	IMPERFECT	5	SOULS OF PERFECT SLAIN	THYROID	WILL

Chapter 3

1. And unto the angel of the church in Sardis write; These things saith he that hath the seven Spirits of God, and the seven stars; I know thy works, that thou hast a name that thou livest, and art dead.

2. Be watchful, and strengthen the things which remain, that are ready to die: for I have not found thy works perfect before God.

3. Remember therefore how thou hast received and heard, and hold fast, and repent. If therefore thou shalt not watch, I will come on thee as a thief, and thou shalt not know what hour I will come upon thee.

4. Thou hast a few names even in Sardis which have not defiled their garments; and they shall walk with me in white: for they are worthy.

5. He that overcometh, the same shall be clothed in white raiment; and I will not blot out his name out of the book of life, but I will confess his name before my Father, and before his angels.

6. He that hath an ear, let him hear what the Spirit saith unto the churches.

Q-3. Do the seven angels govern in order the major glandular centers of the physical body?

A-3. In their order, as they have been set. 281-31

CHURCH	VIRTUE	FAULTS	SEAL	VISION	SPIRITUAL CENTERS/ GLANDS	LORD'S PRAYER
PHILA-DELPHIA	OPEN DOOR	NO FAULTS	6	EARTHQUAKE	PINEAL	NAME

Chapter 3 continued

7. And to the angel of the church in Philadelphia write; These things saith he that is holy, he that is true, he that hath the key of David, he that openeth an d no man shutteth; and shutteth, and no man openeth;

8. I know thy works; behold, I have set before thee an open door, and no man can shut it; for thou hast a little strength, and hast kept my word, and hast not denied my name.

9. Behold, I will make them of the synagogue of Satan which say they are Jews, and are not, but do lie; behold, I will make them to come and worship before thy feet, and to know that I have loved thee.

10. Because thou hast kept the word of my patience, I also will keep thee from the hour of temptation, which shall come upon all the world, to try them that swell upon the earth.

11. Behold, I come quickly; hold that fast which thou hast, that no man take thy crown.

12. Him that overcometh will I make a pillar in the temple of my God, and he shall go no more out: and I will write upon him the name of my God, and the name of the city of my God, which is new Jerusalem, which cometh down out of heaven from my God: and I will write upon him my new name.

13. He that hath an ear, let him hear what the Spirit saith unto the churches.

Q-6. Are we correct in interpreting the four beasts as the four fundamental physical natures (desires) of man which must be overcome? Give us more light on each of these.

A-6. Correct. In all of these, let this be understood: These are symbolized; they are as in these representing the elemental forces—as the body is of the earth, is of the elements. For as has so oft been given, and as may be found in man, every element or every influence that is outside of man is found in the *living* man—not a dead one but a *living* man! For the *living* force is that *of* which all that is *was* brought into being. Hence all the influences, all the forces, all the activities are in that. And in man, man's experience, there never has been, never will be found in material activity an instrument, an action, that is not shown as a replica or expression or manifestation of that in a living man; whether it be in this, that or the other of the forces of nature, of activity. For when such is active, unless found in man—or an answer to something within, it would not be cognizable by man.

Q-7. Do we have these four beasts placed correctly in relation to the centers in the body and the ancient elementals? Air—Eagle—Thymus?

A-7. These are relatively, yes. Relatively correct.

Q-8. Fire—Lion—Solar Plexus?

A-8. Correct.

Q-9. Water—Man—Lyden?

A-9. Yes.

Q-10. Earth—Calf—Gonads?

A-10. Yes. 281-29

CHURCH	VIRTUE	FAULTS	SEAL	VISION	SPIRITUAL CENTERS/ GLANDS	LORD'S PRAYER
LAODICEA		LUKEWARM	7	SILENCE	PITUITARY	FATHER

Chapter 3 continued

14. And unto the angel of the church of the Laodiceans write; These things saith the Amen, the faithful and true witness, the beginning of the creation of God;

15. I know thy works, that thou art neither cold nor hot: I would thou wert cold or hot.

16. So then because thou art lukewarm, and neither cold not hot, I will spew thee out of my mouth.

17. Because thou sayest, I am rich, and increased with goods, and have need of nothing; and knowest not that thou art wretched, and miserable, and poor, and blind, and naked.

18. I counsel thee to buy of me gold tried in the fire, that thou mayest be rich; and white raiment, that thou mayest be clothed, and that the shame of thy nakedness do not appear; and anoint thine eyes with eyesalve, that thou mayest see.

19. As many as I love, I rebuke and chasten: be zealous therefore, and repent.

20. Behold, I stand at the door, and knock: if any man hear my voice, and open the door, I will come in to him, and will sup with him, and he with me.

21. To him that overcometh will I grant to sit with me in my throne, even as I also overcame, and am set down with my Father in his throne.

22. He that hath an ear, let him hear what the Spirit saith unto the churches.

GLANDS	BEASTS	ELEMENTS
THYMUS	EAGLE	AIR
ADRENAL	LION	FIRE
LYDEN	MAN	WATER
GONADS	CALF	EARTH

Chapter 4

1. After this I looked, and behold, a door was opened in heaven: and the first voice which I heard was as it were of a trumpet talking with me; which said, Come up hither, and I will shew thee things which must be hereafter.
2. And immediately I was in the Spirit: and, behold, a throne was set in heaven, and one sat on the throne.
3. And he that sat was to look upon like a jasper and a sardine stone: and there was a rainbow round about the throne, in sight like unto an emerald.
4. And round about the throne were four and twenty seats: and upon the seats I saw four and twenty elders sitting, clothed in white raiment; and they had on their heads crowns of gold.
5. And out of the throne proceeded lightnings and thunderings and voices: and there were seven lamps of fire burning before the throne, which are the seven Spirits of God.
6. And before the throne there was a sea of glass like unto crystal: and in the midst of the throne, and round about the throne, were four beasts full of eyes before and behind.
7. And the first beast was like a lion, and the second beast like a calf, and the third beast had a face as a man, and the fourth beast was like a flying eagle.
8. And the four beasts had each of them six wings about him; and they were full of eyes within: and they rest not day and night, saying, Holy, holy, holy, Lord God Almighty, which was, and is, and is to come.
9. And when those beasts give glory and honour and thanks to him that sat on the throne, who liveth for ever and ever,
10. The four and twenty elders fall down before him that sat on the throne, and worship him that liveth for ever and ever, and cast their crowns before the throne, saying,
11. Thou art worthy, O Lord, to receive glory and honour and power: for thou hast created all things, and for thy pleasure they are and were created.

Q-3. Which is the highest gland in the body—the pineal or the pituitary?

A-3. The pituitary!

Q-4. Are we correct in interpreting the twenty-four elders as the twenty-four cranial nerves of the head especially related to the five senses?

A-4. Correct.

Q-5. Is the frequent reference to the throne indicating the head in which are found the higher gland centers?

A-5. Correct.

Q-31. What is meant by the seven lamps of fire burning before the throne, described as the seven spirits of God—Ch. 4:5?

A-31. Those influences or forces which in their activity in the natures of man are without, that stand ever before the throne of grace—or God, to become the messengers, the aiders, the destructions of hindrances; as the ways between man's approach to—as was represented in the ways of dividing man's knowledge of or between—good and evil. Hence they work ever as those influences or forces that stand between, as it were; being the helpful influences that become as the powers of activity in the very nature or force of man. 281-29

Q-7. What is meant by the four beasts?

A-7. As given, the four destructive influences that make the greater desire for the carnal forces, that rise as the beasts within self to destroy. Even as man, in his desire to make for companionship, brought those elements within self's own experience. These must be met. Even as the dragon represents the one that separated self so far as to fight with, to destroy with, those that would make of themselves a kingdom of their own. 281-16

Q-9. Voice from four horns before the throne.

A-9. As indicated by the horns of the altar, as indicated by the four forces in nature, as indicated by the four influences in the experiences of the individual soul which cry then in the voice raised as a sweet incense, or as the essence of the purifying that has come to the individual entity or soul to arise before the Throne of Him who is Lord of Lords and King of Kings, for His love as given, as shown in that as accomplished in the raising of self in the Christ, the Son, in Jesus. 281-31

Chapter 5

1. And I saw in the right hand of him that sat on the throne a book written within and on the back side, sealed with seven seals.

2. And I saw a strong angel proclaiming with a loud voice, Who is worthy to open the book, and to loose the seals thereof?

3. And no man in heaven, nor in earth, neither under the earth, was able to open the book, neither to look thereon.

4. And I wept much, because no man was found worthy to open and to read the book, neither to look thereon.

5. And one of the elders saith unto me, Weep not: behold, the Lion of the tribe of Juda, the Root of David, hath prevailed to open the book, and to loose the seven seals thereof.

6. And I beheld, and, lo, in the midst of the throne and of the four beasts, and in the midst of the elders, stood a Lamb as it had been slain, having seven horns and seven eyes, which are the seven Spirits of God sent forth into all the earth.

7. And he came and took the book out of the right hand of him that sat upon the throne.

8. And when he had taken the book, the four beasts and four and twenty elders fell down before the Lamb, having every one of them harps, and golden vials full of odours, which are the prayers of saints.

9. And they sung a new song, saying, Thou art worthy to take the book, and to open the seals thereof: for thou wast slain, and hast redeemed us to God by thy blood out of every kindred, and tongue, and people, and nation;

10. And hast made us unto our God kings and priests: and we shall reign on the earth.

11. And I beheld, and I heard the voice of many angels round about the throne, and the beasts, and the elders: and the number of them was ten thousand times ten thousand, and thousands of thousands;

12. Saying with a loud voice, Worthy is the Lamb that was slain, to receive power, and riches, and wisdom, and strength, and honour, and glory, and blessing.

13. And every creature which is in heaven, and on the earth, and under the earth, and such as are in the sea, and all that are in them heard I saying, Blessing, and honour, and glory, and power, be unto him that sitteth upon the throne, and unto the Lamb for ever and ever.

14. And the four beasts said, Amen. And the four and twenty elders fell down and worshipped him that liveth for ever and ever.

Q-11. Is the book with the seven seals the human body with the seven spiritual centers?

A-11. This is correct.

Q-12. Do we have the opening of the seals correctly placed in our chart? As each is called, give advice that will help us in properly opening these centers.

A-12. [Interrupting] First, let's give as this: Do not attempt to open any of the centers of the book until self has been tried in the balance of self's own conscious relationship to the Creative Forces and not found wanting by the spiritual answer in self to that rather as is seen in the manner in which the book itself becomes as that in the whole body which may be assimilated by the body, when taken properly. In these then there has been set as *ye* have in thine outline. These are well. *Do not* misuse them!

Q-13. Gonads—White Horse?

A-13. Yes.

Q-14. Lyden—Black Horse?

A-14.Yes.

Q-15. Solar Plexus—Red Horse?

A-15. Yes.

Q-16. Thymus—Pale Horse?

A-16. Yes. For a reference to these, let each in your study of these, as in relation to the centers themselves, consider the effect of the color itself upon thine own body as ye attempt to apply same by either concentration, dedication or meditating upon these. For as has been given, color is but vibration. Vibration is movement. Movement is activity of a positive and negative force. Is the activity of self as in relationship to these then positive? Proceed.

Q-17. Thyroid—Souls slain for Word of God?

A-17. Correct.

Q-18. What color here?

A-18. Gray.

Q-19. Pineal—Upheavals?

A-19. Correct, but this would have to be *relatively* so. For these are at those periods when, in the colors that these arise to—which are of the purple, they become rather such that there *must* be the *disseminating* or the giving away of the egoism of self. Consider as an example in thy study of same, the servant Moses. For these become as may be found even for and from that record as ye have, the stumbling block at Meribah.

Q-20. Pituitary—Silence?

A-20. Silence, golden; the forces upon which the greater expression has been set of all the influences of might and power as may be seen in man's experience—*Silence* if ye would hear the Voice of thy Maker!

Q-21. Do the planets as placed in our chart have proper relation and significance? Pituitary—Jupiter; Pineal—Mercury; Thyroid—Uranus; Thymus—Venus; Solar Plexus—Mars; Lyden—Neptune; Gonads—Saturn?

A-21. These are very well done. These vary, to be sure, according to the variation of an *experience.* For these are the variable forces in the very nature of man himself, for he partakes of all and from all the influences and forces. For remember as has been given, it is not that the planets rule the man; rather has man, as man of God, ruled the planets! For he's a portion of same.

Then, these are as we have given; only relative. Relatively, these are correct. At times these are represented by others. It is here the application of these influences in the experience of the individual rather than there being set, as it were, a blanket to cover each and every individual.

Q-22. Does the outline of the Lord's Prayer as placed on our chart have any bearing on the opening of the centers?

A-22. Here is indicated the manner in which it was given as to the purpose for which it was given; not as an *only* way but as a way that would answer for those that sought to be—as others—seekers for *a* way, *an* understanding, to the relationships to the Creative Forces. It bears in relationships to this, then, the proper place.

Q-23. Pituitary—Heaven?

A-23. Correct. In all of its activities these open, for the upward lift of the thoughts of man as in relationships to that which becomes—how has it been given?—"He is alpha, omega, the beginning and the end." Hence as we find in its relationships to man, it becomes then the beginnings, the endings, of all things.

Q-24. Pineal—Name?

A-24. Relatively, yes.

Q-25. Thyroid—Will?

A-25. Correct.

Q-26. Thymus—Evil?

A-26. Correct.

Q-27. Solar Plexus—Debts?

A-27. Yes.

Q-28. Lyden—Temptation?

A-28. Correct.

Q-29. Gonads—Bread?

A-29. Right.

281-29

SEALS	EXPERIENCES OR SOUNDS AT OPENING	GLAND	PRAYER
7	SILENCE	PITUITARY	FATHER
6	EARTHQUAKE	PINEAL	NAME
5	SOULS OF FAITHFUL SLAIN	THYROID	WILL
4	PALE HORSE	THYMUS	EVIL
3	RED HORSE	ADRENAL	DEBTS
2	BLACK HORSE	LYDEN	TEMPTATION
1	WHITE HORSE	GONADS	BREAD

Chapter 6

1. And I saw when the Lamb opened one of the seals, and I heard as it we re the noise of thunder, one of the four beasts saying, Come and see.

2. And I saw, and behold a white horse: and he that sat on him had a bow; and a crown was given unto him: and he went forth conquering, and to conquer.

3. And when he had opened the second seal, I heard the second beast say, Come and see.

4. And there went out another horse that was red: and power was given to him that sat thereon to take peace from the earth, and that they should kill one another; and there was given unto him a great sword.

5. And when he had opened the third seal, I heard the third beast say, Come and see. And I beheld, and lo a black horse; and he that sat on him had a pair of balances in his hand.

6. And I heard a voice in the midst of the four beasts say, A measure of wheat for a penny, and three measures of barley for a penny; and see thou hurt not the oil and the wine.

7. And when he had opened the fourth seal, I heard the voice of the fourth beast say, Come and see.

8. And I looked, and behold a pale horse: and his name that sat on him was Death, and Hell followed with him. And power was given unto them over the fourth part of the earth, to kill with sword, and with hunger, and with death, and with the beasts of the earth.

9. And when he had opened the fifth seal, I saw under the altar the souls of them that were slain for the word of God, and for the testimony which they held:

10. And they cried with a loud voice, saying, How long, O Lord, holy and true, dost thou not judge and avenge our blood on them that dwell on the earth?

Q-30. How should the Lord's Prayer be used in this connection?

A-30. As in feeling, as it were, the flow of the meanings of each portion of same throughout the body-physical. For as there is the response to the mental representations of all of these in the *mental* body, it may build into the physical body in the manner as He, thy Lord, thy Brother, so well expressed in, "I have bread ye know not of."

281-29

Q-3. What is the significance of the color of the four horses associated with four lower centers; pale horse for Thymus; red for Solar Plexus; black for Lyden; white for Gonads?

A-3. That comes as has just been given as the illustration of same from the *emotions* or physical forces that ride forth to their expression in the higher forces of the activity.

Q-4. Please explain what was meant in reading of Oct. 28, regarding the "relative" connection of Name in the Lord's Prayer with the Pineal gland?

A-4. This might occupy a whole period of several hours, if the full conclusion were to be given; but each must reach this. There is a Name to each soul. For He hath called His own *by name!* What name? All the names that may have been as a material experience through an earthly sojourn, or all the names that may have been through the experience of an entity in that environ or those relative associations of Venus, Mars, Jupiter, Uranus, Saturn, Sun, Moon, or what! Or a Name that is above *every* name!

Then as has been indicated this becomes relative, as is signified in the indication as given to the number, which is of John's own. But as has been given, every influence—you see—is *relative!* Hence the name is relative to that which is accomplished by the soul in its sojourn throughout its whole experience; whether in those environs about this individual sphere or another—this individual sphere meaning thine own sun, thine own planets with all of their attributes (does an earth mind comprehend such?) and it carried through with what is its *relative* force to that which has been or is the activity of the entity-soul (not a body now at all!) toward Constructive Force or God, or God's infinitive force to that integral activity of the soul in its sojourn. Hence it becomes *relative.* And for the finite mind to say Jane, John, Joe, James or Jude would mean only as the *vibrations* of those bring the *relative* force or influence to which, through which an entity's sojourns have brought the concrete experience in any one given or definite period of activity!

Was one named John by chance? Was one named Joe or Llewellyn by chance? No; they are relative! While it may be truly in the material plane relative because you have a rich aunt by that name, or relative because an uncle might be named that—but these carry then the vibrations of same; and in the end the name is the sum total of what the soul-entity in all of its vibratory forces has borne toward the Creative Force itself.

Hence each soul has a definite influence upon the experiences through which it may be passing. This ye have illustrated in thine own secret organizations, in thy papal activities in the religious associations, and in each vibration. For when ye have set a vibration by the activity of thy *soul's* force, ye are then either in parallel, in direct accord, or in opposition to constructive force—whatever may be the position or activity of the soul in infinity. For ye *are* gods! But you are becoming devils or real gods!

281-30

Chapter 6 continued

11. And white robes were given unto every one of them; and it was said unto them, that they should rest yet for a little season, until their fellow servants also and their brethren, that should be killed as they were, should be fulfilled.

12. And I beheld when he had opened the sixth seal, and, lo, there was a great earthquake; and the sun became black as sackcloth of hair, and the moon became as blood;

13. And the stars of heaven fell unto the earth, even as a fig tree casteth her untimely figs, when she is shaken of a mighty wind.

14. And the heaven departed as a scroll when it is rolled together; and every mountain and island were moved out of their places.

15. And the kings of the earth, and the great men, and the rich men, and the chief captains, and the mighty men, and every bondman, and every free man, hid themselves in the dens and in the rocks of the mountains;

16. And said to the mountains and rocks, Fall on us, and hide us from the face of him that sitteth on the throne, and from the wrath of the Lamb:

17. For the great day of his wrath is come; and who shall be able to stand?

MAJOR DIVISIONS OF THE PHYSICAL BODY				
THOSE OF CONSTRUCTION	BONES	MUSCLES	LIGAMENTS	SKIN
THOSE THAT KEEP ALIVE	LUNGS	HEART	BLOOD	LIVER
THOSE THAT INFLUENCE THAT OF THE PHYSICAL, MENTAL, AND SPIRITUAL	CENTRAL NERVOUS SYSTEM; CEREBROSPINAL; SYMPATHETIC NERVOUS SYSTEM; DUCTLESS GLANDS			

Chapter 7

1. And after these things I saw four angels standing on the four corners of the earth, holding the four winds of the earth, that the wind should not blow on the earth, nor on the sea, nor on any tree.

2. And I saw another angel ascending from the east, having the seal of the living God: and he cried with a loud voice to the four angels, to whom it was given to hurt the earth and the sea,

3. Saying, Hurt not the earth, neither the sea, nor the trees, till we have sealed the servants of our God in their foreheads.

4. And I heard the number of them which were sealed: and there were sealed a hundred and forty and four thousand of all the tribes of the children of Israel.

5. Of the tribe of Juda were sealed twelve thousand. Of the tribe of Reuben were sealed twelve thousand. Of the tribe of Gad were sealed twelve thousand.

6. Of the tribe of Aser were sealed twelve thousand. Of the tribe of Nephthalim were sealed twelve thousand. Of the tribe of Manasses were sealed twelve thousand.

7. Of the tribe of Simeon were sealed twelve thousand. Of the tribe of Levi were sealed twelve thousand. Of the tribe of Issachar were sealed twelve thousand.

8. Of the tribe of Zabulon were sealed twelve thousand. Of the tribe of Joseph were sealed twelve thousand. Of the tribe of Benjamin were sealed twelve thousand.

9. After this I beheld, and, lo, a great multitude, which no man could number, of all nations, and kindreds, and people, and tongues, stood before the throne, and before the Lamb, clothed with white robes, and palms in their hands;

10. And cried with a loud voice, saying, Salvation to our God which sitteth upon the throne, and unto the Lamb.

11. And all the angels stood round about the throne, and about the elders and the four beasts, and fell before the throne on their faces, and worshipped God,

Q-32. What is meant by the angels at the four corners of the earth as given in Ch. 7?
A-32. These are only as from the body-forces ever. There are those four influences or forces in the natures of man from his source; as in environment, heredity as of the earth and as of the mental and spiritual. These are as the four corners that become represented here as the very natures or forces to which all approaches to all these influences are made in the very nature of man.

Q-33. Are we correct in interpreting the 144,000 who were sealed as being spiritualized cellular structure of the twelve major divisions of the body?
A-33. Correct. And this is as of a man, and the name of same.

Q-34. Are the zodiacal divisions of the body proper and do they have any relation to this?
A-34. Only relatively. For this is as we have given again and again in reference to same; for as they have been set as the zodiacal signs, correct. As they have moved in their orb or their sphere about the earth, these have just recently passed and have become—as has been indicated—a very different nature to them 281-29

Q-5. What was meant in the reading of Oct. 28, in connection with 144,000 who were sealed as being spiritualized cellular structure of the twelve major divisions of the body, when the reading gave, "Correct, and this is as of a man, and the name of same." Please explain.
A-5. Just as has been illustrated or given, as to the relative force of the vibratory forces of the individual; which is shown in an individual soul or entity by its name and its activity in all the influences or environs through which it passes in that which is a shadow in man (active, living) to those influences that are relative to the infinitive position of a soul's activity in a universe.

Q-6. In connection with the symbols of Revelation, what are the twelve major divisions of the body?
A-6. Those that are of the general construction and those that are of the keeping alive physical, and those that are in keeping with the influences to the mental, to the material, to the spiritual; and the illustrations are shown in the bodily forces that are opened for those activities in a material plane. 281-30

Q-35. Is the multitude before the throne as described in Ch. 7 the rest of the cellular structure in process of spiritualization?
A-35. This is correct. 281-29

Q-3. Do the seven angels govern in order the major glandular centers of the physical body?
A-3. In their order, as they have been set. 281-31

Q-7. What is meant by the four beasts?
A-7. As given, the four destructive influences that make the greater desire for the carnal forces, that rise as the beasts within self to destroy. Even as man, in his desire to make for companionship, brought those elements within self's own experience. These must be met. Even as the dragon represents the one that separated self so far as to fight with, to destroy with, those that would make of themselves a kingdom of their own. 281-16

Chapter 7 continued

12. Saying, Amen: Blessing, and glory, and wisdom, and thanksgiving, and honour, and power, and might, be unto our God for ever and ever. Amen.
13. And one of the elders answered, saying unto me, What are these which are arrayed in white robes? and whence came they?
14. And I said unto him, Sir, thou knowest. And he said to me, These are they which came out of great tribulation, and have washed their robes, and made them white in the blood of the Lamb.
15. Therefore are they before the throne of God, and serve him day and night in his temple: and he that sitteth on the throne shall dwell among them.
16. They shall hunger no more, neither thirst any more; neither shall the sun light on them, nor any heat.
17. For the Lamb which is in the midst of the throne shall feed them, and shall lead them unto living fountains of waters: and God shall wipe away all tears from their eyes.

Q-6. Is this the period of the great tribulation spoken of in Revelation, or just the beginning, and if so just how can we help ourselves and others to walk more closely with God?

A-6. The great tribulation and periods of tribulation, as given, are the experiences of every soul, every entity. They arise from influences created by man through activity in the sphere of any sojourn. Man may become, with the people of the universe, ruler of any of the various spheres through which the soul passes in its experiences. Hence, as the cycles pass, as the cycles are passing, when there *is* come a time, a period of readjusting in the spheres (as well as in the little earth, the little soul)—seek, then, as known, to present self spotless before that throne; even as *all* are commanded to be circumspect, in thought, in act, to that which is held by self as that necessary for the closer walk with Him. In that manner only may each atom (as man is an atom, or corpuscle, in the body of the Father) become a helpmeet with Him in bringing that to pass that all may be one with Him. 281-16

Chapter 8

1. And when he had opened the seventh seal, there was silence in he aven about the space of half an hour.

2. And I saw the seven angels which stood before God; and to them were given seven trumpets.

3. And another angel came and stood at the altar, having a golden censer; and there was given unto him much incense, that he should offer it with the prayers of all saints upon the golden altar which was before the throne.

4. And the smoke of the incense, which came with the prayers of the saints, ascended up before God out of the angel's hand.

5. And the angel took the censer, and filled it with fire of the altar, and cast it into the earth: and there were voices, and thunderings, and lightnings, and an earthquake.

6. And the seven angels which had the seven trumpets prepared themselves to sound.

7. The first angel sounded, and there followed hail and fire mingled with blood, and they were cast upon the earth: and the third part of trees was burnt up, and all green grass was burnt up.

8. And the second angel sounded, and as it were a great mountain burning with fire was cast into the sea: and the third part of the sea became blood;

9. And the third part of the creatures which were in the sea, and had life, died; and the third part of the ships were destroyed.

10. And the third angel sounded, and there fell a great star from heaven, burning as it were a lamp, and it fell upon the third part of the rivers, and upon the fountains of waters;

11. And the name of the star is called Wormwood: and the third part of the waters became wormwood; and many men died of the waters, because they were made bitter.

12. And the fourth angel sounded, and the third part of the sun was smitten, and the third part of the moon, and the third part of the stars; so as the third part of them was darkened, and the day shone not for a third part of it, and the night likewise.

13. And I beheld, and heard an angel flying through the midst of heaven, saying with a loud voice, Woe, woe, woe, to the inhabiters of the earth by reason of the other voices of the trumpet of the three angels, which are yet to sound.

Q-36. Are we correct in interpreting the sounding of the seven angels as the experience during physical purification?

A-36. Correct. 281-29

Q-7. What is meant by the symbol of the angel with the golden censer and incense described in Rev. 8:3-5?

A-7. As the influence is visualized in the experience of each soul by the name as implied in "angel," or the good that goes out from the individual soul in its relationships to the influences or forces about same, so is it called or given as the angel with the censer of the activities that emanate from each individual. And as has been given in other illustrations, that ye ARE—that of good—rises ever as an incense, sweet before the throne of mercy. Or to take the back track, as it were, and take the angel with the censer, with the incense that is before the image of a soul seeking to become one with the Creative Forces or God—that which has been kind, gentle, patient, merciful, long-suffering in self's experience during a day, rises before the throne of the mercy seat within self to that of an incense of satisfaction. Why? Hate, unkindness, harshness, all such become as base in thine own experience, and as usual one condemns self by saying, "Why can't I do this or that?" And, "What is the use?" Well—and the censer is broken! 281-30

Q-4. Please explain the meaning of some of the symbols in the sounding of the seven angels: (1) Hail and Fire, blood and one-third of earth burned. What is the earth in this connection?

A-4. As has been intimated or given in the first interpretations of what the elements represent, that are apparent or a portion of the First Cause; as the Earth, Air, Water and the like. These are then as has just been given, ever to represent or be symbolical of the same influences or forces throughout; else we may become confused as to their place. Earth—that as we represent as being in a state of transition, or as earthy. Not necessarily lowly or unduly a condition that would belie development. But as Fire is purifying, as Hail is the crystallization of the Water, the Air and the temperaments, so all of these then represent those as figuratives of that as may be purified by the fires of Nature; as may be represented by the earth when they are met and conquered and used for the development—as in the Hail and the like becoming purifying in their natures for the crystallization and the oneness of the individual's purposes and desires.

For to go back just a bit, that we may ever keep what is the purpose of the Revelation: Was it for the purpose of confusing, of being mysterious? (This has been gone over before, to be sure.) Rather was it not to present it that each entity, each soul, might find within itself that which answers to that within, that makes the real answer to that as was before stated, "My Spirit beareth witness with thy spirit"? And until the answer is in accord, in attune, is there the consciousness of the prompting of the ability in a manifested material world to make same practical?

Then as the progress is made, as the understanding comes more and more, *never, NEVER* does it make the manifested individual entity other than the more humble, the more meek, the more long-suffering, the more patient. Of this ye may be sure.

Then in all of the experiences of the opening of the centers as are represented, and those vibrations that find expression in the various temperaments of individual souls, these come not as justifications in *self* but justification in the Lamb of God!

Q-5. (2) Mountain of fire in sea, sea becomes blood.

A-5. Again as the body elements that become conflicting one with another, which shows the overcoming within the individual activities of the influences that are constantly warring within.

How has it been said? "O today there is life and death, good and evil—Choose thou." This may be said to be symbolical then of these conflicting forces within the influences that are ever present, or as given by another, "The Spirit is willing, the flesh is weak." These are symbolical then, one interpreting the other. 281-31

Q-8. Do the seven angels described in Rev. 8-9 represent spiritual forces governing the various dimensional planes through which souls pass between incarnations on the earth? Please explain.

A-8. This is a very good interpretation. Yes. While this explanation becomes a portion of another group's study and activity in the lesson just being approached on *happiness*, it may be best explained in this; as to how this must indeed be interpreted in the experience of each soul, whether considered in a material plane in which there is found the real essence of happiness or that in the interim when ye are looked over, or when the promises become more and more as has been interpreted from that given by others—to be absent from the body-physical is to be present in the grace and glory and presence of divinity; or to be those influences that make for an activity in an influence without self.

Now ye are studying yourself! Do not confuse the interpretation with that outside of thyself, but happiness is love of something outside of self! It may never be obtained, may never be known by loving only things within self or self's own domain!

Then the expression that has been given by an entity in a sojourn in the earth becomes as a portion of that activity as has been given, "He hath given His angels charge concerning thee, lest at any time ye dash thy foot against a stone."

Hence we find that in the expression then of those interims where there are the guiding influences of that we have loved, we have love—for this becomes then very definite.

If ye have loved self-glory, if ye have loved the honor of the people more than those thoughts of the mental and spiritual and moral welfare, what manner of angels will direct thee between thy interims?

Think on the study then of self, in thy body—but let it all become as has been *so oft* given:

Study to show thyself approved unto God, the God in self, the God in thine own consciousness—that *is* creative in its essence; rightly divining and dividing the words of truth and light; keeping self unspotted from the world. And ye become lights to those that sit in darkness, to those that wander.

Though ye may be reviled, revile not again. Though ye may be spoken of harshly, smile—SMILE! For it is upon the river of life that smiles are made. Not grins! No Cheshire cat activities bring other than those that are of the earth, of such natures that create in the minds and the experiences those things that become repulsive. But the smile of understanding cheers on the hearts of those who are discouraged who are disheartened. It costs so little! It does thee so much good, and lifts the burdens of so many! 281-30

Q-2. Continuing with the references to the seven angels described in Rev. 8-9, are we correct in interpreting the sounding of these seven angels as the influence of spiritual development in these other planes becoming through the vibrating centers of the physical body during the process of purification?

A-2. Correct. But these are always interpreted in individual experiences as the true sound, true tone.

Now, this is not to confuse but rather to clarify for those who are studying these, in the relationships to what takes place as the various centers in the body are opened, that are represented by the Spirit's activative forces upon same; that these may be the more perfectly understood:

Just as the individual who has by practical application gained the correct pitch, correct tone in a musical composition. This may be as a soul-expression or a mechanical expression; and only when it is in the true accord, as from the soul, is it perfectly understood. See?

Q-6. (3) Great star falls from heaven. What are the one-third part of the rivers and fountains that it falls upon?

A-6. The star signifies simply the coming of the influence from without to the influences from within, as is signified by "His Star have we seen." Then this becomes that as falls upon the 3rd, or that is a 3rd portion of the bodily activities—and as interpreted in the experience of the individual, ye have made so many steps as it were along the way.

Q-7. One-third part of sun smitten and one-third of stars.

A-7. These are symbolical and represent in the experience of the individual that of life and heat, beauty and that as given in another portion, "The stars declare the glory of God, the firmament showeth His handiwork." These then represent in the experiences the vibrations of the emotions that are being aroused, as has just been given. Again less and less then is it of self, and more and more unto the glory of the Father.

Q-8. Star from heaven, Key to bottomless pit. What are the locusts as described in this sounding? King Apollyon in this connection?

A-8. As has been given as to how each of these vibratory forces arises from the lower portion, or as has been put in another setting—that which represents in the bodily forces the most uncomely, or that from the depths of the bottomless pit, or from out the presence of God, again has the spirit of man arisen to the glory of the star as in the Son (not sun, but Son), to those glories that become as the natures of the bodily forces, and every influence as comes through the earthly natures becomes lost in that beauty in the Son. 281-31

Chapter 9

1. And the fifth angel sounded, and I saw a star fall from heaven unto the earth: and to him was given the key of the bottomless pit.

2. And he opened the bottomless pit; and there arose a smoke out of the pit, as the smoke of a great furnace; and the sun and the air were darkened by reason of the smoke of the pit.

3. And there came out of the smoke locusts upon the earth: and unto them was given power, as the scorpions of the earth have power.

4. And it was commanded them that they should not hurt the grass of the earth, neither any green thing, neither any tree; but only those men which have not the seal of God in their foreheads.

5. And to them it was given that they should not kill them but that they should be tormented five months: and their torment was as the torment of a scorpion, when he striketh a man.

6. And in those days shall men seek death, and shall not find it; and shall desire to die, and death shall flee from them.

7. And the shapes of the locusts were like unto horses prepared unto battle; and on their heads were as it were crowns like gold, and their faces were as the faces of men.

8. And they had hair as the hair of women, and their teeth were as the teeth of lions.

9. And they had breastplates, as it were breastplates of iron; and the sound of their wings was as the sound of chariots of many horses running to battle.

10. And they had tails like unto scorpions, and there were stings in their tails: and their power was to hurt men five months.

11. And they had a king over them, which is the angel of the bottomless pit, whose name in the Hebrew tongue is Abaddon, but in the Greek tongue hath his name Apollyon.

12. One woe is past; and, behold, there come two woes more hereafter.

13. And the sixth angel sounded, and I heard a voice from the four horns of the golden altar which is before God,

14. Saying to the sixth angel which had the trumpet, Loose the four angels which are bound in the great river Euphrates.

15. And the four angels were loosed, which were prepared for an hour, and a day, and a month, and a year, for to slay the third part of men.

16. And the number of the army of the horsemen were two hundred thousand thousand: and I heard the number of them.

Q-6. (3) Great star falls from heaven. What are the one-third part of the rivers and fountains that it falls upon?

A-6. The star signifies simply the coming of the influence from without to the influences from within, as is signified by "His Star have we seen." Then this becomes that as falls upon the 3rd, or that is a 3rd portion of the bodily activities—and as interpreted in the experience of the individual, ye have made so many steps as it were along the way.

Q-8. Star from heaven, Key to bottomless pit. What are the locusts as described in this sounding? King Apollyon in this connection?

A-8. As has been given as to how each of these vibratory forces arises from the lower portion, or as has been put in another setting—that which represents in the bodily forces the most uncomely, or that from the depths of the bottomless pit, or from out the presence of God, again has the spirit of man arisen to the glory of the star as in the Son (not sun, but Son), to those glories that become as the natures of the bodily forces, and every influence as comes through the earthly natures becomes lost in that beauty in the Son.

Q-9. Voice from four horns before the throne.

A-9. As indicated by the horns of the altar, as indicated by the four forces in nature, as indicated by the four influences in the experiences of the individual soul which cry then in the voice raised as a sweet incense, or as the essence of the purifying that has come to the individual entity or soul to arise before the Throne of Him who is Lord of Lords and King of Kings, for His love as given, as shown in that as accomplished in the raising of self in the Christ, the Son, in Jesus. 281-31

Q-1. What is meant by the four angels bound in the river Euphrates in connection with the sounding of the sixth angel [Gen. 2:14; Rev. 9:14; 16:12]?

A-1. As has been given, each reference in the Revelation is to some portion of the body as in its relative position to the emotions physical, mental, material; and their activities through portions of the system, as places that represent conditions in some phase of manifestation or development of the entity. Or the whole (to be put in another way and manner) is an experience of man as known to those who were being spoken to by the writer.

Then we find, as in the beginning, the Euphrates—or *the good river* [Frat], or *the river* of the fiat [covenant Gen. 15:18]—is being represented as being sounded now for the beginnings of the changes which have been effected by the activities of those who have preceded, who have acted upon the various influences or forces by the opening of centers and the emotions and the understandings and the conditions of the individual entity.

Hence it represents now, as it were, to the individual—that ye now begin again to make practical or applicable, mentally, spiritually, materially, with that which has been thus far attained.

Q-2. What are the four angels that are bound in the river Euphrates?

A-2. As has been indicated, the four influences that are as the Air, the Earth, the Fire, the Water; being influences now that are—as understood by the entity, the soul, the individual—as a portion of itself again.

Q-3. What is meant by the symbol of the Euphrates in relation to the body, if it may be connected?

Chapter 9 continued

17. And thus I saw the horses in the vision, and them that sat on them, having breastplates of fire, and of jacinth, and brimstone: and the heads of the horses were as the heads of lions; and out of their mouths issued fire and smoke and brimstone.

18. By these three was the third part of men killed, by the fire, and by the smoke, and by the brimstone, which issued out of their mouths.

19. For their power is in their mouth, and in their tails: for their tails were like unto serpents, and had heads, and with them they do hurt.

20. And the rest of the men which were not killed by these plagues yet repented not of the works of their hands, that they should not worship devils, and idols of gold, and silver, and brass, and stone, and of wood; which neither can see, nor hear, nor walk:

21. Neither repented they of their murders, nor of their sorceries, nor of their fornication, nor of their thefts.

A-3. As has just been given, it represents that as a boundary of its beginnings, or a beginning, or an end, from the material standpoint. 281-32

Q-4. What is meant by the symbols of the horsemen who were to kill one-third part of men, in connection with the sounding of the sixth angel?

A-4. That as a place, as a condition, an experience through which the influences are acted upon by the emotions in which the changes are wrought by the application of those very forces or conditions that have been spoken of in the experience of the individual, see?

Or, as put by another, "When I was a child I did as a child, when I was a man I did as a man," the same as in the beginning and the same as in the activities, or the same as in the relationships to all of these then as has been given heretofore—they must be as one, they must be compatible, they must be coordinant, they must be in the relative relationships one to another. These then become as destroying influences within the individual, a third portion of that which has been set as such a necessary force for a material body. How hath it been given throughout? The Father, the Son, the Holy Spirit—which is the third. They are all one, and yet a third. The same as the death of those influences or forces or activities within the emotional, the physical, the material forces. All of these then are as representatives of these, or the activities from the fourfold elements that are activative in the experience of each entity, each soul.

281-32

Q-5. Will we be punished by fire and brimstone?

A-5. That as builded by self; as those emblematical influences are shown through the experiences of the beloved in that builded, that created. For, each soul is a portion of creation—and builds that in a portion of its experience that it, through its physical-mental or spiritual-mental, has builded for itself. And each entity's heaven or hell must, through *some* experience, be that which it has builded for itself.

Is thy hell one that is filled with fire or brimstone? But know, each and every soul *is* tried so as by fire; purified, purged; for He, though He were the Son, learned obedience through the things which He suffered. Ye also are known even as ye do, and have done. 281-16

Chapter 10

1. And I saw another mighty angel come down from heaven, clothed with a cloud: and a rainbow was upon his head, and his face was as it were the sun, and his feet as pillars of fire:

2. And he had in his hand a little book open: and he set his right foot upon the sea, and his left foot on the earth,

3. And cried with a loud voice, as when a lion roareth: and when he had cried, seven thunders uttered their voices.

4. And when the seven thunders had uttered their voices, I was about to write: and I heard a voice from heaven saying unto me, Seal up those things which the seven thunders uttered, and write them not.

5. And the angel which I saw stand upon the sea and upon the earth lifted up his hand to heaven,

6. And sware by him that liveth for ever and ever, who created heaven, and the things that therein are, and the earth, and the things that therein are, and the sea and the things which are therein that there should be time no longer:

7. But in the days of the voice of the seventh angel, when he shall begin to sound, the mystery of God should be finished, as he hath declared to his servants the prophets.

8. And the voice which I heard from heaven spake unto me again, and said, Go and take the little book which is open in the hand of the angel which standeth upon the sea and upon the earth.

9. And I went unto the angel, and said unto him, Give me the little book. And he said unto me, Take it, and eat it up; and it shall make thy belly bitter, but it shall be in thy mouth sweet as honey.

10. And I took the little book out of the angel's hand, and ate it up; and it was in my mouth sweet as honey: and as soon as I had eaten it, my belly was bitter.

11. And he said unto me, Thou must prophesy again before many peoples, and nations, and tongues, and kings.

Q-5. Do we interpret correctly the angel described in Rev. 10, with the little book, as a guardian of the book of knowledge?

A-5. This is a very good interpretation; or we come to that point in the experience of each soul—know ye have passed through the experiences of attaining to the understanding of thine emotions, the understanding of the needs of thy physical body, the understanding of thy relationships to the spiritual forces; and know ye come to that which is to be—what will ye do with that knowledge?

It might be set or interpreted as the guardian force, for as is understood by each and every one that have studied in these influences or forces, all force, all power, all knowledge (constructive) is from a one source—is it not?

Then the guardian force is that ability to use or abuse that which has been combined in the book; or the book may be the *body*, see, as an illustration of that, as a parallel of that. Know ye have gained these, know ye are to use these in thine own experience.

Q-6. Is the little book described in Rev. 10—Power of Creative Thought?

A-6. As has just been given, it may be that of the whole influence or that of the body itself, or—yes—that of creative thought itself; for these are one.

Q-7. What is the significance of John eating it up and of the verse, "Thou must prophesy again before many peoples, and nations, and tongues, and kings"?

A-7. As illustrated in that as indicated, and as from the use of same. Know ye have it—what will ye do with it? It becomes part and parcel, by the eating up. It is very beautiful to look upon, very beautiful to be desired; but in the application of same at times very bitter.

As is seen in the very manner in which—How did the Son in the earth become as an intermediator between sinful man and an All-Wise, All-Merciful God? By going through or experiencing, or in giving to, through the very sufferings in the body, the right, the purpose, the aim to be in that position!

Now, man having attained same by this study must prophesy—apply—prophesy *is* apply—before many in many experiences, in many ways, in many environs, in many lands. All of these are a part and parcel of same. How did He put it as He gave, "I will bring to your remembrance *all* things, from the foundations of the world."

Then as it has been experienced by those who have taken hold of, who have combined the book (that is the book of Life), into the experience, it becomes within its body then a part and parcel of—and is to be expended in its relationships to the environs in that of prophecy, yes; in experiences before kings, yes; yea as beggars; yea as rulers; yea as those in authority; yea as those authoritative over.

Think of how this is shown in the life of the Master Himself; He that made man, yet under the authority and the will of man by the mere giving of self in the experience of passing through same. Not that these were needed other than that it might be fulfilled, what? Prophecy, as had been given in man's search for God.

Then as this has been found, as is illustrated here by John, in the taking of the book and in becoming these, each then must pass in its experience through the same sources.

281-32

Chapter 11

1. And there was given me a reed like unto a rod: and the angel stood, saying, Rise, and measure the temple of God, and the altar, and them that worship therein.

2. But the court which is without the temple leave out, and measure it not; for it is given unto the Gentiles; and the holy city shall they tread under foot forty and two months.

3. And I will give power unto my two witnesses, and they shall prophesy a thousand two hundred and three score days, clothed in sackcloth.

4. These are the two olive trees, and the two candlesticks standing before the God of the earth.

5. And if any man will hurt them, fire proceedeth out of their mouth, and devoureth their enemies; and if any man will hurt them, he must in this manner be killed.

6. These have power to shut heaven, that it rain not in the days of their prophecy; and have power over waters to turn them to blood, and to smite the earth with all plagues, as often as they will.

7. And when they shall have finished their testimony, the beast that ascendeth out of the bottomless pit shall make war against them, and shall overcome them, and kill them.

8. And their dead bodies shall lie in the street of the great city, which spiritually is called Sodom and Egypt, where also our Lord was crucified.

9. And they of the people and kindreds and tongues and nations shall see their dead bodies three days and a half, and shall not suffer their dead bodies to be put in graves.

10. And they that dwell upon the earth shall rejoice over them, and make merry, and shall send gifts one to another; because these two prophets tormented them that dwelt on the earth.

11. And after three days and a half the Spirit of life from God entered into them, and they stood upon their feet; and great fear fell upon them which saw them.

12. And they heard a great voice from heaven saying unto them, Come up hither. And they ascended up to heaven in a cloud; and their enemies beheld them.

13. And the same hour was there a great earthquake, and the tenth part of the city fell, and in the earthquake were slain of men seven thousand: and the remnant were affrighted, and gave glory to the God of heaven.

Q-8. What is meant by the symbol of the "reed like unto a rod" with which John was told to measure the temple? Rev. 11. Please explain.

A-8. How again has it been given by Him? "With what measure ye mete it shall be measured to thee again." Know that he had acceded to the point wherein he is to set the metes and bounds (John as an individual). Ye, your own souls as individuals, who will you put in your heaven? Ye of a denomination, ye of a certain creed, ye of a certain measurement, with what measure ye mete it is measured to thee again.

This then is an illustration that to each there is given, what? All power to set that as the metes and bounds of what heaven in itself shall be to those who would gather these, or those, or the self. What would be heaven to a soul that built it for its individual self? Heaven, yes—but alone!

Those that will measure then, those that will set metes and bounds—how has it been given oft? When ye name a name, or when ye give metes and bounds, ye forget that God's force, God's power is *Infinite!* and this is beyond the comprehension of the finite mind. Yet as is illustrated here to John, as is illustrated to thee, thou art given—with the understanding—as to what the metes and bounds shall be. As to the numbers as seen, as understood, these become as parts of its *own* understanding.

Q-9. Is the temple here the physical body?

A-9. Rather the *mental* in which is the pattern as of the tabernacle; or the holy mount—or that as set by a *unified* service of the body-mind, the body-physical, the body-spiritual; that vehicle that is without nails (as was the tabernacle as a pattern), not bound together, yet a covering, a place, an understanding for a *unified* activity with Creative Forces, or the power of God. The veil without, the holy within, and the holy of holies—knowing that there must be the cleansing, there must be the purifying, there must be the consecration. All of these are as patterns, they are as conditions, they are as experiences for each and every soul.

Q-10. Is the court referred to the body apart from the spiritual centers?

A-10. As indicated, rather is it as the environ without—the body-physical and mental within for its sacrificial forces, and then to the spiritual force within as to the holy of holies.

Q-11. Are the Gentiles here those not seeking spiritual development?

A-11. Rather do the Gentiles here refer to that without the court. Not necessarily not seeking, but—remember the measuring rod He hath set. These do not change because if thou art worthy, Christ-like in the material, ye are Christ-like in the broader sense in the mental—and how much greater in the spiritual! The same as in those who are very devout without—as a Catholic, as a Protestant—as of such and such creed or faith; how much smaller have they grown within! 281-32

Q-1. What is meant by the two witnesses mentioned in Rev. 11:3? Are they the mental and emotional bodies of the soul of man?

A-1. As has been made reference, now—the Book of Life has been eaten. It is in the mouth, sweet; in the belly (or the body), bitter.

This may be the interpretation then: the mental or the subconscious; but rather is it the *conscious PHYSICAL* lives, or the attributes and the consciousness in the *experience* of the soul in the attributes of a physical consciousness!

Do not confuse self; and many of you are wondering just what it is. Then, as has been so oft given, all of this was recognized by John. Hence all of this is given in form, ritual,

Chapter 11 continued

14. The second woe is past; and, behold, the third woe cometh quickly.

15. And the seventh angel sounded; and there were great voices in heaven, saying, The kingdoms of this world are become the kingdoms of our Lord, and of His Christ; and he shall reign for ever and ever.

16. And the four and twenty elders, which sat before God on their seats, fell upon their faces, and worshipped God.

17. Saying, We give thee thanks, O Lord God Almighty, which art, and wast, and art to come; because thou has taken to thee thy great power, and hast reigned.

18. And the nations were angry, and thy wrath is come, and the time of the dead, that they should be judged, and that thou shouldest give reward unto thy servants the prophets, and to the saints, and them that fear thy name, small and great; and shouldest destroy them which destroy the earth.

19. And the temple of God was opened in heaven, and there was seen in his temple the ark of his testament; and there were lightnings, and voices, and thunderings, and an earthquake, and great hail.

the emblems, what we may term numerology, astrology, and all the forms of the ancient wisdoms; yet it is represented by the activities of same upon a physical being.

As has so oft been given, an individual experience in the earth plane is motivated by that which arises from its sojourns in the influences of the consciousnesses outside of the physical being—or as ye would say astrologically the sojourn in the environ of Venus, Jupiter, Mars, Neptune, Saturn, Uranus, Sun, Moon, and the constellations and those effects upon same—emotionally from the *innate* forces; *and* by the *emotional* effect from sojourns in the earth. Both of these are witnesses.

As the Book of Life then is opened, there is seen the effect of that which now has been attained by the opening of the system, the body, the mind; all of those effects that have been created by the ability of the entity to, in the physical being, attune self to the consciousness of being at-one with the divine within.

Now we see those in the material world using these influences for self-exaltation, self-indulgence, self-glorification; and yet we see those using same for the glory, the understanding, the knowledge, the wisdom of the Father.

These then are the witnesses. The innate and the emotional; or the spiritual-mental, the physical-mental; the subconscious, the superconscious.

Q-2. Explain the symbol of the death of the two witnesses.

A-2. As is the symbol of—Does the individual, unless—Let's illustrate by what has been given: The Master gave, "Before the world was, I AM! Now if ye abide in me and I in the Father, then I will bring to thy remembrance ALL *THINGS*—from the foundations of the world!"

Yet these are as dead, or the only consciousness that arises from same is that which is fanned into life or activity by the application of the laws concerning same. Hence they are as dead, yet become alive again by remembrance, by the application of thought. In what? The light of that which has been attained by the entity or soul that has applied the former lessons in its experience. 281-33

Q-8. Star from heaven, Key to bottomless pit. What are the locusts as described in this sounding? King Apollyon in this connection?

A-8. As has been given as to how each of these vibratory forces arises from the lower portion, or as has been put in another setting—that which represents in the bodily forces the most uncomely, or that from the depths of the bottomless pit, or from out the presence of God, again has the spirit of man arisen to the glory of the star as in the Son (not sun, but Son), to those glories that become as the natures of the bodily forces, and every influence as comes through the earthly natures becomes lost in that beauty in the Son. 281-31

Q-3. What is meant by the "great city which is called Sodom and Egypt, where also our Lord was crucified"?

A-3. As has been so often given, all places—as Egypt or Sodom or the Crucifixion, or the Lord—are conditions, circumstances, experiences, as well as individual places. Then in the minds of those who would attempt or that would seek knowledge, they represent their own experiences. Thus these to the people represent—Egypt, the release from bondage; Gomorrah, as a reckoning with sin—as the Lord was crucified there. As has been given, there has never been an experience when His Christ-mass, His death, His birth, wasn't an experience of the age, the people. Though it may go

under many names, as an individual may be under many names, in many environs, there is one—ONE—that ever comes as is shown in that later given as to those who have the name in the hand, in the head or in the forehead and the like; that is, what is the intent and purpose. Just as the Savior of the world, as Lord, as Christ—what do these as names indicate? That which is as a help in a time of trouble alone? or that to glory in, in thy joy, thy gladness, thy happiness? How many, O how many have there been that have laughed with God, that have wept with Jesus, that have gloried with the Christ! or rather has it been, "My happiness and my joy is of myself"?

No condemnation; but rather is there the pattern pointed to as was set by Him. He was *all* things to *all* men; rejoiced with those that did rejoice; He wept with those that wept. He was glad, He was happy, He was sorry, He kept the faith. 281-33

Q-4. What is signified by the revival of these witnesses?

A-4. How hath He given? "If ye meditate on these things, I will bring to thy remembrance all things." The reviving, the renewing, by the abilities of the soul to take hold upon the witnesses of the life itself! And what is life? God!

Q-5. What is meant by the sounding of the seventh angel? How should time be interpreted as given?

A-5. Remember, as has been given to him that was given a measure, as a mete, as a rod to measure heaven—as to how large his heaven would be. All right! Then we have as to how much time—What is time? Is it a record merely of the events of self or of the glory of God? What is the extent of the glory of thy heaven or of thy God? This is as a reckoning. Yet as is shown by the indication of so many days, so many weeks, it is the *inclination* of the individual mind in materiality to set (as was said of John) metes and bounds; and we judge from—How many days or years have ye set? Nineteen thirty-seven [1937] is what? And thy Lord has been continuous! yet ye say only 1937!

281-33

Chapter 12

1. And there appeared a great wonder in heaven; a woman clothed with the sun, and the moon under her feet, and upon her head a crown of twelve stars.

2. And she being with child cried, travailing in birth, and pained to be delivered.

3. And there appeared another wonder in heaven; and behold a great red dragon, having seven heads and ten horns, and seven crowns upon his heads.

4. And his tail drew the third part of the stars of heaven, and did cast them to the earth; and the dragon stood before the woman which was ready to be delivered, for to devour her child as soon as it was born.

5. And she brought forth a man child, who was to rule all nations with a rod of iron; and her child was caught up unto God, and to his throne.

6. And the woman fled into the wilderness, where she hath a place prepared of God, that they should feed her there a thousand two hundred and threescore days.

7. And there was war in heaven: Michael and his angels fought against the dragon; and the dragon fought and his angels.

8. And prevailed not; neither was their place found any more in heaven.

9. And the great dragon was cast out, that old serpent, called the Devil, and Satan, which deceiveth the whole world; he was cast out into the earth, and his angels were cast out with him.

10. And I heard a loud voice saying in heaven, Now is come salvation, and strength, and the kingdom of our God, and the power of his Christ; for the accuser of our brethren is cast down, which accused them before our God day and night.

11. And they overcame him by the blood of the Lamb, and by the word of their testimony; and they loved not their lives unto the death.

12. Therefore rejoice, ye heavens, and ye that dwell in them. Woe to the inhabiters of the earth and of the sea for the devil is come down unto you, having great wrath, because he knoweth that he hath but a short time.

13. And when the dragon saw that he was cast unto the earth, he persecuted the woman which brought forth the man child.

14. And to the woman were given two wings of a great eagle, that she might fly into the wilderness, into her place, where she is nourished for a time, and times, and half a time, from the face of the serpent.

Q-6. In Rev. 12 we find the symbols of the Woman, Dragon and Child. Do these represent the part played by souls in the creation and fall of man? Please explain the reference of these symbols.

A-6. Rather is the reference given to show to the individual entity that from which or through which the soul in the earth has passed in its creation, its activity in the earthly sojourn, see?

For as we go on or interpret further we find: The war was in heaven, see? The woman—or the mother—earth; the source from which all materiality is to become a conscious thing—and these are brought forth.

Now, as is given, ye have reached to that understanding of thy perfection with God; how in materiality ye may attune the attributes of self.

Now from what have ye arisen? These are emblems, significant of that as given as the name of Satan, the Devil, the Dragon or the like, through which man's rebellious forces arise, even though he has attained to the Book even itself in his body! And these are the experiences then to be met. 281-33

Q-1. What is meant by the symbol of the child in Rev. 12?

A-1. That which is the outgrowth of the application of the Word, or the Book, upon self. For as the child it is born of application of the elements in the body (physical, mental and spiritual) of the individual. 281-34

Q-7. What is meant here by the war in heaven between Michael and the Devil?

A-7. As has just been given, as is understood by those here, there is first—as is the spiritual concept—the spiritual rebellion, before it takes mental or physical form. This warring is illustrated there by the war between the Lord of the Way and the Lord of Darkness—or the Lord of Rebellion. 281-33

Yes, we have the Glad Helpers Group, as a group, as individuals; and the study that has been made by same on Revelation. In adding to *some* of those things as have been applied, let each consider how and why that such application would be made by the Beloved in a message of the nature and character. First, the body of the Christ represented to the world a channel, a door, a mediation to the Father. Hence this then may become as the study of self in its relationship to the material world, the mental world, the spiritual world. And this is the manner that has been presented as the way through which each individual would make application of same, of the life of the Christ in his or her own experience. 281-29

Q-8. What is meant by the symbols of the wings of eagle given to the woman for escape and "the time and times and half a time"?

A-8. This is as the entrance into or the flight from materiality into those influences through which the body may rest within itself; as physical, or the mental flight, or that to the astral forces as about its various changes. It is figurative of the transitions from the various spheres of mental experience; by mind, the spiritual influences as arise—and are as the use of same. Remember, all of these should be then in accord with that ye have attained to, that the Book of Life is given thee. What is the Book of Life?

The record of God, of thee, thy soul within and the knowledge of same. 281-33

Chapter 12 continued

15. And the serpent cast out of his mouth water as a flood after the woman, that he might cause her to be carried away by the flood.

16. And the earth helped the woman, and the earth opened her mouth, and swallowed up the flood which the dragon cast out of his mouth.

17. And the dragon was wroth with the woman, and went to make war with the remnant of her seed, which keep the commandments of God, and have the testimony of Jesus Christ.

Q-2. Explain the flood as caused by the serpent to destroy the woman and the help given by the earth. Rev. 12:15-16.

A-2. The flood is the emotions upon the influences of the body in all of its relationships to the activities in its relationships to others; and destroys the baser forces—aided by the application in the earth; which represents the elements of material manifestations in the experiences of the individual.

For, how hath He given? The children of earth are wiser in their generation than the children of light, or from the very growth of what is the experience of the individual in the earth in its seeking for light. Or as He gave in the parable, for impunity's sake or for custom's sake, or for the help that the influence may bring, He will arise and give.

So in the experience of the individual, know that there constantly arises within the sojourn in the life or in an experience in the earth the flood of emotions that make for doubt, fears, tribulation, disturbances, anxieties. For the very same of that as becometh then impunity, the earth aids in the quieting of the influence as is illustrated here. 281-34

Chapter 13

1. And I stood upon the sand of the sea, and saw a beast rise up out of the sea, having seven heads and ten horns, and upon his horns ten crowns, and upon his heads the name of blasphemy.

2. And the beast which I saw was like unto a leopard, and his feet were as the feet of a bear, and his mouth as the mouth of a lion; and the dragon gave him his power, and his seat, and great authority.

3. And I saw one of his heads as it were wounded to death; and his deadly wound was healed; and all the world wondered after the beast.

4. And they worshipped the dragon which gave power unto the beast: and they worshipped the beast, saying, Who is like unto the beast? Who is able to make war with him?

5. And there was given unto him a mouth speaking great things and blasphemies; and power was given unto him to continue forty and two months.

6. And he opened his mouth in blasphemy against God, to blaspheme his name, and his tabernacle and them that dwell in heaven.

7. And it was given unto him to make war with the saints, and to overcome them: and power was given him over all kindreds, and tongues, and nations.

8. And all that dwell upon the earth shall worship him, whose names are not written in the book of life of the Lamb slain from the foundation of the world.

9. If any man have an ear, let him hear.

10. He that leadeth into captivity shall go into captivity; he that killeth with the sword must be killed with the sword. Here is the patience and the faith of the saints.

11. And I beheld another beast coming up out of the earth; and he had two horns like a lamb, and he spake as a dragon.

12. And he exerciseth all power of the first beast before him, and causeth the earth and them which dwell therein to worship the first beast, whose deadly wound was healed.

13. And he doeth great wonders, so that he maketh fire come down from heaven on the earth in the sight of men,

Q-3. Please explain the symbol of the beast like a leopard with seven heads and ten horns. Rev. 13.

A-3. As has been described in the Revelation as to how the influences of the knowledge as gained arise through the various forces and centers of the body. Now we find them visualized by John the revelator as representing the beast, or by the beast that makes for the fears as given in the minds of many by the representing of same in the forms as given, working as it were upon those very forces that have been aroused by the application in the seeking for the understanding of the book, or of the body, or of the relationship of the individual to the relationships borne by the individual. For it is all as individual, yet is applicable to every force or influence that is in the earth in an individual experience.

Q-4. Explain what is meant by those whose names are not written in the Book of Life.

A-4. Those not written are those who have climbed up some other way, or have only for impunity's sake or only for the momentary conscience's sake, as from the influence about them, acknowledged the Way. For as we see later more definitely given, whosoever *will* may take of the water of life.

But as has been given, there are those who from the first—as he that is last to be bound—had the import to do evil. Then those who have followed closely after the flesh, or the indulgences of the emotions of the body alone, without the considerations of others, without other than self's own interest—as is shown by the beast that is loosened—these are they whose names are not written, and these are they who are easily led about by every wind that bloweth, unstable as it were in those as represented in a portion or one of the churches; not hot, not cold, but allowing today, tomorrow, the circumstance of the moment to sway—without purpose, without direction, without the Name. For there is only given under heaven that Name whereby men may be saved, by their belief, their faith, their trust, their works in Him. Hence those who do them not, those who are seen about the individuals striving, are not to be by the individual lamented so much as that the individual loses his own way, but rather knowing that God, the merciful Father, the loving Father of the Christ, in His own time, His own way, will bring those necessary influences.

Be YE then, as is given, in the same association by the promptings of that ye have gained. Having tasted of the tree of life, the knowledge of God, make thyself and thy calling and thy election SURE in that ye faint not when ye see these troubles, these disturbances that are only of the earth-earthy, that only are the emotions of the desires of self's own show coming to pass in thine experience.

Q-5. Explain the symbol of the second beast with two horns, having the power to perform miracles. Rev. 13.

A-5. As has been given by Him, the power as attained by the study that has been shown in the first portions is to be applied, or may be applied unworthily—as is shown by the beast with two ways, two horns. Then here, how hath it been given? One Lord, one faith, one God, one baptism, one way! Yet in the experiences as ye watch about you there are constantly shown the influences by the very forces of the beast with the double-mindedness, as showing wonders in the earth yet they must come even as He hath given, "Though ye may have done this or that, though ye may have healed the sick, though ye may have cast out demons in my name, I know ye not; for ye have followed rather as the beast of self-aggrandizement, self-indulgence, self-glorification," even as the beast shown here.

Chapter 13 continued

14. And deceiveth them that dwell on the earth by the means of those miracles which he had power to do in the sight of the beast; saying to them that dwell on the earth, that they should make an image to the beast, which had the wound by a sword, and did live.

15. And he had power to give life unto the image of the beast, that the image of the beast should both speak, and cause that as many as would not worship the image of the beast should be killed.

16. And he causeth all, both small and great, rich and poor, free and bond, to receive a mark in their right hand, or in their foreheads:

17. And that no man might buy or sell, save he that had the mark, or the name of the beast, or the number of his name.

18. Here is wisdom. Let him that hath understanding count the number of the beast: for it is the number of a man; and his number is Six hundred threescore and six.

Q-6. Do these two beasts as described in Rev. 13 have relation to the subconscious and conscious minds of man?

A-6. They work in and through these influences, to be sure; the subconscious forces that become as a portion, and the consciousness that works through the elements—for self or for God. They work *through* these but not as directing, as being the beast.

Q-7. What is meant by the mark of the beast in the right hand, or forehead?

A-7. These are as signs or symbols of this or that grouping, or of the organizations that become as a part of the vows or obligations to those who have joined in with the work of the beast.

Hence the warning that if these come to mean more in the experience they stand as that which condemns, rather than that which is the helpful experience.

For having the mark of the beast and the mark of the Lamb becomes the difference between the consciousness of the indwelling presence of the Christ and the hoped for yet not seen or known.

Q-8. What is meant by the number of the beast is the number of a man, 666?

A-8. Just as has been given, that when it is taken on as being the exercise of the man without reference to or realizing the influence which has brought same—though it may be in an organization, in a group, in any influence that becomes the work of man's hands—then it is the number of a man and is numbered as may be the days of man, but lacks that consciousness of God and God alone directing.

For as in each organized work or each association, or each group—it should never be as is said as of any man, but how hath He given? God that worketh in and through Him. Thus is the mark of the beast effaced from the workings of the hand or the activities of the head, and it becomes not as the name or the number of a man but the trust alone in God.

Q-9. Explain "Here is wisdom" mentioned in this connection.

A-9. That as ye have gained by the analysis or the study of the activity and influence of the spirit of truth throughout the whole members of thy body, physical, mental and spiritual, and have come to the knowledge of that which has first been given, that there is only *one* God, *one* Christ, one faith, one baptism; or as Christ hath given—this is the whole law; to love the Lord thy God with all thy mind, thy body, thy soul; thy neighbor as thyself. This is the whole law. This is wisdom. This is knowledge. Knowing that those things which have been put on through the activities of the elements within thine own forces of thy body and mind are but as the stepping-stones to the knowledge that no man, no number, no force, is above that knowledge that God is in and through ALL—and in Him ye live and move and have thy being. When this is fully comprehended, fully understood, ye have the working knowledge of God in the earth. 281-34

Chapter 14

1. And I looked, and, lo, a Lamb stood on the Mount Sion, and with him an hundred forty and four thousand, having his Father's name written in their foreheads.

2. And I heard a voice from heaven, as the voice of many waters, and as the voice of a great thunder; and I heard the voice of harpers harping with their harps,

3. And they sung as it were a new song before the throne, and before the four beasts, and the elders: and no man could learn that song but the hundred and forty and four thousand, which were redeemed from the earth.

4. These are they which were not defiled with women; for they are virgins. These are they which follow the Lamb whithersoever he goeth. These were redeemed from among men, being the firstfruits unto God and to the Lamb.

5. And in their mouth was found no guile: for they are without fault before the throne of God.

6. And I saw another angel fly in the midst of heaven, having the everlasting gospel to preach unto them that dwell on the earth, and to every nation, and kindred, and tongue, and people,

7. Saying with a loud voice, Fear God, and give glory to him; for the hour of his judgment is come: and worship him that made heaven, and earth, and the sea, and the fountains of waters.

8. And there followed another angel, saying, Babylon is fallen, is fallen, that great city, because she made all nations drink of the wine of the wrath of her fornication.

9. And the third angel followed them, saying with a loud voice, If any man worship the beast and his image, and receive his mark in his forehead, or in his hand,

10. The same shall drink of the wine of the wrath of God, which is poured out without mixture into the cup of his indignation; and he shall be tormented with fire and brimstone in the presence of the holy angels, and in the presence of the Lamb:

11. And the smoke of their torment ascendeth up for ever and ever; and they have no rest day nor night, who worship the beast and his image, and whosoever receiveth the mark of his name.

12. Here is the patience of the saints, here are they that keep the commandments of God, and the faith of Jesus.

Q-33. Are we correct in interpreting the 144,000 who were sealed as being spiritualized cellular structure of the 12 major divisions of the body?

A-33. Correct. And this is as of a man, and the name of same.

Q-34. Are the zodiacal divisions of the body proper and do they have any relation to this?

A-34. Only relatively. For this is as we have given again and again in reference to same; for as they have been set as the zodiacal signs, correct. As they have moved in their orb or their sphere about the earth, these have just recently passed and have become—as has been indicated—a very different nature to them. 281-29

Q-1. In Rev. 14 do the harpers as mentioned symbolize the souls or spiritual beings that took part in the early attempts to stop the fall of man, but who have not entered the earth plane?

A-1. These have entered the earth plane but were those that in the beginning were as the sons of God *in* the earth plane; and hence are referred to as the first of those redeemed.

Q-2. What is the meaning of the new song of the harpers?

A-2. The new experience that comes to each soul. Let's keep it individual, see? The new experience that comes to each soul, as to the assurance of that help when necessary of the saints of the Father. 281-36

Q-7. What is meant by the four beasts?

A-7. As given, the four destructive influences that make the greater desire for the carnal forces, that rise as the beasts within self to destroy. Even as man, in his desire to make for companionship, brought those elements within self's own experience. These must be met. Even as the dragon represents the one that separated self so far as to fight with, to destroy with, those that would make of themselves a kingdom of their own. 281-16

Q-3. Please explain the symbols of the angels mentioned in Rev. 14. What is meant by the symbols of the sickles and reaping?

A-3. That those individuals who have and are a part of the active force in a material world are to work, to give forth, to give out of their strength, their selves in active service and not as those that would rest (from the material angle); but as the reapers, as the harvesters—which to the individual mind means labors for a definite purpose and service. 281-36

Q-7. What is meant by the mark of the beast in the right hand, or forehead?

A-7. These are as signs or symbols of this or that grouping, or of the organizations that become as a part of the vows or obligations to those who have joined in with the work of the beast.

Hence the warning that if these come to mean more in the experience they stand as that which condemns, rather than that which is the helpful experience.

For having the mark of the beast and the mark of the Lamb becomes the difference between the consciousness of the indwelling presence of the Christ and the hoped for yet not seen or known. 281-34

Chapter 14 continued

13. And I heard a voice from heaven saying unto me, Write, Blessed are the dead which die in the Lord from henceforth: Yea, saith the Spirit, that they may rest from their labours; and their works do follow them.

14. And I looked, and behold a white cloud, and upon the cloud one sat like unto the Son of man, having on his head a golden crown and in his hand a sharp sickle.

15. And another angel came out of the temple, crying with a loud voice to him that sat on the cloud, Thrust in thy sickle, and reap: for the time is come for thee to reap; for the harvest of the earth is ripe.

16. And he that sat on the cloud thrust in his sickle on the earth; and the earth was reaped.

17. And another angel came out of the temple which is in heaven, he also having a sharp sickle.

18. And another angel came out from the altar, which had power over fire; and cried with a loud cry to him that had the sharp sickle, saying, Thrust in thy sharp sickle, and gather the clusters of the vine of the earth: for her grapes are fully ripe.

19. And the angel thrust in his sickle into the earth, and gathered the vine of the earth, and cast it into the great winepress of the wrath of God.

20. And the winepress was trodden without the city, and blood came out of the winepress, even unto the horse bridles, by the space of a thousand and six hundred furlongs.

Q-5. Will we be punished by fire and brimstone?

A-5. That as builded by self; as those emblematical influences are shown through the experiences of the beloved in that builded, that created. For, each soul is a portion of creation—and builds that in a portion of its experience that it, through its physical-mental or spiritual-mental, has builded for itself. And each entity's heaven or hell must, through *some* experience, be that which it has builded for itself.

Is thy hell one that is filled with fire or brimstone? But know, each and every soul *is* tried so as by fire; purified, purged; for He, though He were the Son, learned obedience through the things which He suffered. Ye also are known even as ye do, and have done.

Q-3. Where are the dead until Christ comes? Do they go direct to Him when they die?

A-3. As visioned by the beloved, there are those of the saints making intercession always before the throne for those that are passing in and out of the inter-between; even as He, the Christ, is ever in the consciousness of those that are redeemed in Him.

The passing in, the passing out, is as but the summer, the fall, the spring; the birth into the interim, the birth into the material. 281-16

Q-4. What is meant by "Blessed are the dead which are in the Lord from henceforth, yea, saith the spirit, that they may rest from their labors, and their works do follow them." Rev. 14:13.

A-4. As referred to or given, the changes that have come and the assurance that has come to each individual who has recognized that the Lamb (or the Christ), or the activities of Jesus becoming the Christ are the assurance of the activity of the Christ in the passage from the material plane to the celestial. For as He preached to those bound even in the shadows of death, loosened that which made it possible for them to become again conscious of the opportunities for reconstructing of themselves in the experiences through which error had come, so blessed then are they who die in the Lord—for the body alone is bound. 281-36

Chapter 15

1. And I saw another sign in heaven, great and marvellous, seven angels having the seven last plagues; for in them is filled up the wrath of God.

2. And I saw as it were a sea of glass mingled with fire: and them that had gotten the victory over the beast, and over his image, and over his mark, and over the number of his name, stand on the sea of glass, having the harps of God.

3. And they sing the song of Moses the servant of God, and the song of the Lamb, saying, Great and marvellous are thy works, Lord God Almighty; just and true are thy ways, thou King of saints.

4. Who shall not fear thee, O Lord, and glorify thy name? for thou only art holy: for all nations shall come and worship before thee; for thy judgments are made manifest.

5. And after that I looked, and, behold, the temple of the tabernacle of the testimony in heaven was opened:

6. And the seven angels came out of the temple, having the seven plagues, clothed in pure and white linen, and having their breasts girded with golden girdles.

7. And one of the four beasts gave unto the seven angels seven golden vials full of the wrath of God, who liveth for ever and ever.

8. And the temple was filled with smoke from the glory of God, and from his power; and no man was able to enter into the temple, till the seven plagues of the seven angels were fulfilled.

Q-5. What is meant by the angels with the seven last plagues, in Rev. 15?

A-5. These are the activities that come to those who have begun and have found and have known the experiences of the activities and influences as indicated, and even have put on and become a part of—or are still in the active forces in the materiality—these see the pouring out of that which is the meeting of self in individuals yet in the earth, see? that is, the angels are the figures of that influence as of the wrath; that is, then the law, see? and this becomes necessary for the fulfilling of that "He hath not willed that any soul shall perish but hath with every ill provided a means, a way." Hence the pouring out, the meeting—and the great work or service that those may render who have named the Name, those who have known the song, those that are one with Him.

Q-6. Is the temple or tabernacle of testimony, Rev. 15:5, referring to Akashic Records?

A-6. That as you may term the Akashic Record, or the Book of Life, or the Book of Revelation; that is, of the individual, see?

Q-7. What is meant by the temple filled with smoke, Rev. 15:8? Is the temple the body and are these final steps in the process of spiritualization of the body?

A-7. These are the final steps in the abilities of the individuals for their effective service, or filled with the smoke as the glory of the Father, see? This is the temple of the body, and—as such—where the Lord hath promised to meet those that are faithful and true. 281-36

Q-7. What is meant by the four beasts?

A-7. As given, the four destructive influences that make the greater desire for the carnal forces, that rise as the beasts within self to destroy. Even as man, in his desire to make for companionship, brought those elements within self's own experience. These must be met. Even as the dragon represents the one that separated self so far as to fight with, to destroy with, those that would make of themselves a kingdom of their own. 281-16

Chapter 16

1. And I heard a great voice out of the temple saying to the seven angels, Go your ways, and pour out the vials of the wrath of God upon the earth.

2. And the first went, and poured out his vial upon the earth; and there fell a noisome and grievous sore upon the men which had the mark of the beast, and upon them which worshipped his image.

3. And the second angel poured out his vial upon the sea; and it became as the blood of a dead man: and every living soul died in the sea.

4. And the third angel poured out his vial upon the rivers and fountains of waters, and they became blood.

5. And I heard the angel of the waters say, Thou art righteous, O Lord, which art, and wast, and shalt be, because thou hast judged thus.

6. For they have shed the blood of saints and prophets, and thou hast given them blood to drink; for they are worthy.

7. And I heard another out of the altar say, Even so, Lord God Almighty, true and righteous are thy judgments.

8. And the fourth angel poured out his vial upon the sun; and power was given unto him to scorch men with fire.

9. And men were scorched with great heat, and blasphemed the name of God, which hath power over these plagues: and they repented not to give him glory.

10. And the fifth angel poured out his vial upon the seat of the beast; and his kingdom was full of darkness; and they gnawed their tongues for pain.

11. And blasphemed the God of heaven because of their pains and their sores, and repented not of their deeds.

12. And the sixth angel poured out his vial upon the great river Euphrates; and the water thereof was dried up, that the way of kings of the east might be prepared.

13. And I saw three unclean spirits like frogs come out of the mouth of the dragon, and out of the mouth of the beast, and out of the mouth of the false prophet.

14. For they are the spirits of devils, working miracles, which go forth unto the kings of the earth and of the whole world, to gather them to the battle of that great day of God Almighty.

15. Behold, I come as a thief. Blessed is he that watcheth and keepeth his garments, lest he walk naked, and they see his shame.

Q-8. What is meant by the angels with the seven vials, Rev. 16?

A-8. This again is that fulfilling of the law. This is as the carrying forth in the earth of those influences that bring the wrath in the active forces, in the experience of the individuals.

Q-9. What is the symbol of the first vial and the pouring of it?

A-9. These all are as the same, though are represented as the effective activity upon the various conditions that have become a part of the errors in those that have the mark of the beast. 281-36

Q-4. Please explain the meaning of some of the symbols in the sounding of the seven angels: (1) Hail and fire, blood and one-third of earth burned. What is the earth in this connection?

A-4. As has been intimated or given in the first interpretations of what the elements represent, that are apparent or a portion of the First Cause; as the Earth, Air, Water and the like. These are then as has just been given, ever to represent or be symbolical of the same influences or forces throughout; else we may become confused as to their place. Earth—that as we represent as being in a state of transition, or as earthy. Not necessarily lowly or unduly a condition that would belie development. But as Fire is purifying, as Hail is the crystallization of the Water, the Air and the temperaments, so all of these then represent those as figuratives of that as may be purified by the fires of Nature; as may be represented by the earth when they are met and conquered and used for the development—as in the Hail and the like becoming purifying in their natures for the crystallization and the oneness of the individual's purposes and desires.

For to go back just a bit, that we may ever keep what is the purpose of the Revelation: Was it for the purpose of confusing, of being mysterious? (This has been gone over before, to be sure.) Rather was it not to present it that each entity, each soul, might find within itself that which answers to that within, that makes the real answer to that as was before stated, "My Spirit beareth witness with thy spirit"? And until the answer is in accord, in attune, is there the consciousness of the prompting of the ability in a manifested material world to make same practical?

Then as the progress is made, as the understanding comes more and more, *never, NEVER,* does it make the manifested individual entity other than the more humble, the more meek, the more long-suffering, the more patient. Of this ye may be sure.

Then in all of the experiences of the opening of the centers as are represented, and those vibrations that find expression in the various temperaments of individual souls, these come not as justifications in *self* but justification in the Lamb of God!

Q-5. (2) Mountain of fire in sea, sea becomes blood.

A-5. Again as the body elements that become conflicting one with another, which shows the overcoming within the individual activities of the influences that are constantly warring within.

How has it been said? "O today there is life and death, good and evil—Choose thou." This may be said to be symbolical then of these conflicting forces within the influences that are ever present, or as given by another, "The Spirit is willing, the flesh is weak." These are symbolical then, one interpreting the other. 281-31

Chapter 16 continued

16. And he gathered them together into a place called in the Hebrew tongue Armageddon.

17. And the seventh angel poured out his vial into the air; and there came a great voice out of the temple of heaven, from the throne, saying, It is done.

18. And there were voices, and thunders, and lightnings; and there was a great earthquake, such as was not since men were upon the earth, so mighty an earthquake, and so great.

19. And the great city was divided into three parts, and the cities of the nations fell: and great Babylon came in remembrance before God, to give unto her the cup of the wine of the fierceness of his wrath.

20. And every island fled away, and the mountains were not found.

21. And there fell upon men a great hail out of heaven, every stone about the weight of a talent; and men blasphemed God because of the plague of the hail; for the plague thereof was exceeding great.

Q-1. Please interpret the fall of Babylon as referred to in the 14th, 17th, and 18th chapters of Revelation.

A-1. Babylon represented the individual; those periods through which every soul passes in its delving into the varied mysteries that are the experiences of the carnal-mental, the spiritual-mental forces of the body; and, as viewed from that presented, may come to the knowledge only through the *cleansing* that is shown must come to those that would be saved from the destructions that are given there. 281-16

Q-12. Does Babylon symbolize self?

A-12. Babylon symbolizes self.

Q-13. Does Rev. 18 give some idea in symbols of the effect of the fall of self—selfishness?

A-13. It does. 281-36

Q-6. (3) Great star falls from heaven. What are the one-third part of the rivers and fountains that it falls upon?

A-6. The star signifies simply the coming of the influence from without to the influences from within, as is signified by "His Star have we seen." Then this becomes that as falls upon the 3rd, or that is a 3rd portion of the bodily activities—and as interpreted in the experience of the individual, ye have made so many steps as it were along the way. 281-31

Chapter 17

1. And there came one of the seven angels which had the seven vials and talked with me, saying unto me, Come hither; I will shew unto thee the judgment of the great whore that sitteth upon many waters;

2. With whom the kings of the earth have committed fornication, and the inhabitants of the earth have been made drunk with the wine of her fornication.

3. So he carried me away in the spirit into the wilderness: and I saw a woman sit upon a scarlet colored beast, full of names of blasphemy, having seven heads and ten horns.

4. And the woman was arrayed in purple and scarlet colour, and decked with gold and precious stones and pearls, having a golden cup in her hand full of abominations and filthiness of her fornication.

5. And upon her forehead was a name written, MYSTERY, BABYLON THE GREAT, THE MOTHER OF HARLOTS AND ABOMINATIONS OF THE EARTH.

6. And I saw the woman drunken with the blood of the saints, and with the blood of the martyrs of Jesus: And when I saw her, I wondered with great admiration.

7. And the angel said unto me, Wherefore didst thou marvel? I will tell thee the mystery of the woman, and of the beast that carrieth her, which hath the seven heads and ten horns.

8. The beast that thou sawest was, and is not; and shall ascend out of the bottomless pit, and go into perdition: and they that dwell on the earth shall wonder, whose names were not written in the book of life from the foundation of the world, when they behold the beast that was, and is not, and yet is.

9. And here is the mind which hath wisdom, The seven heads are seven mountains, on which the woman sitteth.

10. And there are seven kings: five are fallen, and one is, and the other is not yet come; and when he cometh, he must continue a short space.

11. And the beast that was, and is not, even he is the eighth, and is of the seven, and goeth into perdition.

12. And the ten horns which thou sawest are ten kings, which have received no kingdom as yet; but received power as kings one hour with the beast.

13. These have one mind, and shall give their power and strength unto the beast.

Q-2. What did the angel mean when he said: "I will tell thee the mystery of the woman, and of the beast that carrieth her"?

A-2. That which is understood by those that follow in the way of the Lamb, that come to know how man separates himself through the desires to become as the procreator in the beasts; which made the necessity of the shedding of blood for redemption, for it brought sin *in* the shedding—and only through same may there be the fulfilling; and, as given, the heavens and the earth may pass, but His law, His love, His mercy, His grace, endureth for those who *will* seek to know His will. 281-16

Q-10. In Rev. 17 does the woman here symbolize the cause of the fall of spiritual man? Please explain with reference to Creation.

A-10. It represents rather that which made for the projecting of man into matter through the associations that brought carnal relationships in those very activities. Not as a spiritual but as a material giving or bringing spiritual activity in the desire of the individual or soul. 281-36

Q-1. Please interpret the fall of Babylon as referred to in the 14th, 17th, and 18th chapters of Revelation.

A-1. Babylon represented the individual; those periods through which every soul passes in its delving into the varied mysteries that are the experiences of the carnal-mental, the spiritual-mental forces of the body; and, as viewed from that presented, may come to the knowledge only through the *cleansing* that is shown must come to those that would be saved from the destructions that are given there. 281-16

Q-12. Does Babylon symbolize self?

A-12. Babylon symbolizes self.

Q-13. Does Rev. 18 give some idea in symbols of the effect of the fall of self—selfishness?

A-13. It does. 281-36

Q-8. Star from heaven, Key to bottomless pit. What are the locusts as described in this sounding? King Apollyon in this connection?

A-8. As has been given as to how each of these vibratory forces arises from the lower portion, or as has been put in another setting—that which represents in the bodily forces the most uncomely, or that from the depths of the bottomless pit, or from out the presence of God, again has the spirit of man arisen to the glory of the star as in the Son (not sun, but Son), to those glories that become as the natures of the bodily forces, and every influence as comes through the earthly natures becomes lost in that beauty in the Son. 281-31

Q-11. Do the seven heads and mountains have any reference to the spiritual centers of the body, Rev. 17:9?

A-11. These have reference to the spiritual centers, as has been indicated; and indicate and show in the latter portion of same as to how these have become purified in the redeeming forces of the Lamb. 281-36

Chapter 17 continued

14. These shall make war with the Lamb, and the Lamb shall overcome them: for he is Lord of lords, and King of kings: and they that are with him are called and chosen, and faithful.

15. And he saith unto me, The waters which thou sawest, where the whore sitteth, are peoples, and multitudes, and nations, and tongues.

16. And the ten horns which thou sawest upon the beast, these shall hate the whore, and shall make her desolate and naked, and shall eat her flesh, and burn her with fire.

17. For God hath put in their hearts to fulfil his will, and to agree, and give their kingdom unto the beast, until the words of God shall be fulfilled.

18. And the woman which thou sawest is that great city, which reigneth over the kings of the earth.

Chapter 18

1. And after these things I saw another angel come down from heaven, having great power; and the earth was lightened with his glory.

2. And he cried mightily with a strong voice, saying, Babylon the great is fallen, is fallen, and is become the habitation of devils, and the hold of every foul spirit, and a cage of every unclean and hateful bird.

3. For all nations have drunk of the wine of the wrath of her fornication, and the kings of the earth have committed fornication with her, and the merchants of the earth are waxed rich through the abundance of her delicacies.

4. And I heard another voice from heaven, saying, Come out of her, my people, that ye be not partakers of her sins, and that ye receive not of her plagues.

5. For her sins have reached unto heaven, and God hath remembered her iniquities.

6. Reward her even as she rewarded you, and double unto her double according to her works: in the cup which she hath filled, fill to her double.

7. How much she hath glorified herself, and lived deliciously, so much torment and sorrow give her: for she saith in her heart, I sit a queen, and am no widow, and shall see no sorrow.

8. Therefore shall her plagues come in one day, death, and mourning, and famine; and she shall be utterly burned with fire: for strong is the Lord God who judgeth her.

9. And the kings of the earth, who have committed fornication and lived deliciously with her, shall bewail her, and lament for her, when they shall see the smoke of her burning,

10. Standing afar off for the fear of her torment, saying, Alas, alas, that great city Babylon, that mighty city! for in one hour is thy judgment come.

11. And the merchants of the earth shall weep and mourn over her; for no man buyeth their merchandise any more:

12. The merchandise of gold, and silver, and precious stones, and of pearls, and fine linen, and purple, and silk, and scarlet, and all thyine wood, and all manner vessels of ivory, and all manner vessels of most precious wood, and of brass, and iron, and marble,

13. And cinnamon, and odours, and ointments, and frankincense, and wine, and oil, and fine flour, and wheat, and beasts, and sheep, and horses, and chariots, and slaves, and souls of men.

Q-1. Please interpret the fall of Babylon as referred to in the 14th, 17th and 18th chapters of Revelation.

A-l. Babylon represented the individual; those periods through which every soul passes in its delving into the varied mysteries that are the experiences of the carnal-mental, the spiritual-mental forces of the body; and, as viewed from that presented, may come to the knowledge only through the *cleansing* that is shown must come to those that would be saved from the destructions that are given there. 281-16

Q-12. Does Babylon symbolize self?

A-12. Babylon symbolizes self.

Q-13. Does Rev. 18 give some idea in symbols of the effect of the fall of self—selfishness?

A-13. It does. 281-36

Chapter 18 continued

14. And the fruits that thy soul lusted after are departed from thee, and all things which were dainty and goodly are departed from thee, and thou shalt find them no more at all.

15. The merchants of these things, which were made rich by her, shall stand afar off for the fear of her torment, weeping and wailing.

16. And saying, Alas, alas, that great city, that was clothed in fine linen, and purple, and scarlet, and decked with gold, and precious stones, and pearls!

17. For in one hour so great riches is come to naught. And every shipmaster, and all the company in ships, and sailors, and as many as trade by sea stood afar off,

18. And cried when they saw the smoke of her burning, saying, What city is like unto this great city!

19. And they cast dust on their heads, and cried, weeping and wailing, saying, Alas, alas, that great city, wherein were made rich all that had ships in the sea by reason of her costliness! for in one hour is she made desolate.

20. Rejoice over her, thou heaven, and ye holy apostles and prophets; for God hath avenged you on her.

21. And a mighty angel took up a stone like a great millstone, and cast it into the sea, saying, Thus with violence shall that great city Babylon be thrown down, and shall be found no more at all.

22. And the voice of harpers, and musicians, and of pipers and trumpeters, shall be heard no more at all in thee; and no craftsman, of whatsoever craft he be, shall be found any more in thee; and the sound of a millstone shall be heard no more at all in thee.

23. And the light of a candle shall shine no more at all in thee; and the voice of the bridegroom and of the bride shall be heard no more at all in thee: for thy merchants were the great men of the earth; for by thy sorceries were all nations deceived.

24. And in her was found the blood of prophets, and of saints, and of all that were slain upon the earth.

Chapter 19

1. And after these things I heard a great voice of much people in heaven, saying, Alleluia; Salvation, and glory, and honour, and power, unto the Lord our God:

2. For true and righteous are his judgments; for he hath judged the great whore, which did corrupt the earth with her fornication, and hath avenged the blood of his servants at her hand.

3. And again they said, Alleluia. And her smoke rose up for ever and ever.

4. And the four and twenty elders and the four beasts fell down and worshipped God that sat on the throne, saying, Amen; Alleluia.

5. And a voice came out of the throne, saying, Praise our God, all ye his servants, and ye that fear him, both small and great.

6. And I heard as it were the voice of a great multitude, and as the voice of many waters, and as the voice of mighty thunderings, saying, Alleluia: for the Lord God omnipotent reigneth.

7. Let us be glad and rejoice, and give honour to him: for the marriage of the Lamb is come, and his wife hath made herself ready.

8. And to her was granted that she should be arrayed in fine linen, clean and white: for the fine linen is the righteousness of saints.

9. And he saith unto me, Write, Blessed are they which are called unto the marriage supper of the Lamb. And he saith unto me, These are the true sayings of God.

10. And I fell at his feet to worship him, And he said unto me, See thou do it not: I am thy fellow servant, and of thy brethren that have the testimony of Jesus: worship God: for the testimony of Jesus is the spirit of prophecy.

11. And I saw heaven opened, and behold a white horse; and he that sat upon him was called Faithful and True, and in righteousness he doth judge and make war.

12. His eyes were as a flame of fire, and on his head were many crowns; and he had a name written, that no man knew, but he himself.

13. And he was clothed with a vesture dipped in blood: and his name is called The Word of God.

14. And the armies which were in heaven followed him upon white horses, clothed in fine linen, white and clean.

Q-14. Does the marriage of the Lamb symbolize the complete spiritualization of the body? Please explain.

A-14. As there has been given through the whole portion of Revelation; first how the symbols of the activity of the body mentally, spiritually, physically, are affected by influences in the earth—and as to how now the body has been raised to the realizations of the associations with spirit and matter through mind, the builder, and comes now to that as represented by the Lamb—or the mind, spiritual—that has now so raised the body as to become as a new being; or as was given by Him—the body is the church, the Christ Consciousness is that activity which motivates same within the individual. 281-36

Q-1. Explain Rev. 19:9-10. To whom is John talking here? Is it Peter?

A-1. That which is represented by Peter. What did Peter represent? That as had been given, "Flesh and blood hath not revealed this unto thee, but my father in heaven."

All then who have taken, who do take that which had been given as the example, as the pattern, as the manner of expression, as the acknowledgement of the activities within self, are in that position—that they have touched, do touch as it were the knowledge of God in that His ways, His laws, His love are not only a part of their individual lives but are by them manifested in their daily life, their daily conversation as one to another.

Yes, then—to the Peter in every experience of the body, the mind, the soul.

Q-2. Explain the symbols of the white horse and rider in Rev. 19. Is this the Christ?

A-2. This is the Christ in that it, as the horse, in the experiences of the awakening is the symbol of the messenger; and this is Christ, Jesus, the messenger. 281-37

Q-5. Will we be punished by fire and brimstone?

A-5. That as builded by self; as those emblematical influences are shown through the experiences of the beloved in that builded, that created. For, each soul is a portion of creation—and builds that in a portion of its experience that it, through its physical-mental or spiritual-mental, has builded for itself. And each entity's heaven or hell must, through *some* experience, be that which it has builded for itself.

Is thy hell one that is filled with fire or brimstone? But know, each and every soul *is* tried so as by fire; purified, purged; for He, though He were the Son, learned obedience through the things which He suffered. Ye also are known even as ye do, and have done. 281-16

Chapter 19 continued

15. And out of his mouth goeth a sharp sword, that with it he should smite the nations and he shall rule them with a rod of iron: and he treadeth the winepress of the fierceness and wrath of Almighty God.

16. And he hath on his vesture and on his thigh a name written, KING OF KINGS, AND LORD OF LORDS.

17. And I saw an angel standing in the sun; and he cried with a loud voice, saying to all the fowls that fly in the midst of heaven, Come and gather yourselves together unto the supper of the great God;

18. That ye may eat the flesh of kings, and the flesh of captains, and the flesh of mighty men, and the flesh of horses, and of them that sit on them, and the flesh of all men, both free and bond, both small and great.

19. And I saw the beast, and the kings of the earth, and their armies, gathered together to make war against him that sat on the horse, and against his army.

20. And the beast was taken, and with him the false prophet that wrought miracles before him with which he deceived them that had received the mark of the beast, and them that worshipped his image. These both were cast alive into a lake of fire burning with brimstone.

21. And the remnant were slain with the sword of him that sat upon the horse, which sword proceeded out of his mouth: and all the fowls were filled with their flesh.

Chapter 20

1. And I saw an angel come down from heaven, having the key of the bottomless pit and a great chain in his hand.

2. And he laid hold on the dragon, that old serpent, which is the Devil, and Satan, and bound him a thousand years,

3. And cast him into the bottomless pit, and shut him up, and set a seal upon him, that he should deceive the nations no more, till the thousand years should be fulfilled: and after that he must be loosed a little season.

4. And I saw thrones, and they sat upon them and judgment was given unto them, and I saw the souls of them that were beheaded for the witness of Jesus, and for the word of God, and which had not worshipped the beast, neither his image, neither had received his mark upon their foreheads, or in their hands; and they lived and reigned with Christ a thousand years.

5. But the rest of the dead lived not again until the thousand years were finished. This is the first resurrection.

6. Blessed and holy is he that hath part in the first resurrection: on such the second death hath no power, but they shall be priests of God and of Christ, and shall reign with him a thousand years.

7. And when the thousand years are expired, Satan shall be loosed out of his prison.

8. And shall go out to deceive the nations which are in the four quarters of the earth, Gog and Magog, to gather them together to battle: the number of whom is as the sand of the sea.

9. And they went up on the breadth of the earth, and compassed the camp of the saints about, and the beloved city: and fire came down from God out of heaven, and devoured them.

10. And the devil that deceived them was cast into the lake of fire and brimstone, where the beast and the false prophet are, and shall be tormented day and night for ever and ever.

11. And I saw a great white throne, and him that sat on it, from whose face the earth and the heaven fled away; and there was found no place for them.

12. And I saw the dead, small and great, stand before God; and the books were opened: and another book was opened, which is the book of life; and the dead were judged out of those things which were written in the books, according to their works.

Q-8. Star from heaven, Key to bottomless pit. What are the locusts as described in this sounding? King Apollyon in this connection?

A-8. As has been given as to how each of these vibratory forces arises from the lower portion, or as has been put in another setting—that which represents in the bodily forces the most uncomely, or that from the depths of the bottomless pit, or from out the presence of God, again has the spirit of man arisen to the glory of the star as in the Son (not sun, but Son), to those glories that become as the natures of the bodily forces, and every influence as comes through the earthly natures becomes lost in that beauty in the Son. 281-31

Q-3. Explain what is meant by the first and second resurrections.

A-3. The first is of those who have not tasted death in the sense of the dread of same. The second is of those who have GAINED the understanding that in Him there IS no death.

Q-4. What is the meaning of one thousand years that Satan is bound?

A-4. Is banished. That, as there are the activities of the forty and four thousand—in the same manner that the prayer of ten just should save a city, the deeds, the prayers of the faithful will allow that period when the incarnation of those only that are in the Lord shall rule the earth, and the period is as a thousand years.

Thus is Satan bound, thus is Satan banished from the earth. The desire to do evil is only of him. And when there are—as the symbols—those only whose desire and purpose of their heart is to glorify the Father, these will be those periods when this shall come to pass.

Be YE *ALL* DETERMINED within thy minds, thy hearts, thy purposes, to be of that number! 281-37

Q-4. In what form does the anti-Christ come, spoken of in Revelation?

A-4. In the spirit of that opposed to the spirit of truth. The fruits of the spirit of the Christ are love, joy, obedience, long-suffering, brotherly love, kindness. Against such there is no law. The spirit of hate, the anti-Christ, is contention, strife, fault-finding, lovers of self, lovers of praise. Those are the anti-Christ, and take possession of groups, masses, and show themselves even in the lives of men.

Q-5. Will we be punished by fire and brimstone?

A-5. That as builded by self; as those emblematical influences are shown through the experiences of the beloved in that builded, that created. For, each soul is a portion of creation—and builds that in a portion of its experience that it, through its physical-mental or spiritual-mental, has builded for itself. And each entity's heaven or hell must, through *some* experience, be that which it has builded for itself.

Is thy hell one that is filled with fire or brimstone? But know, each and every soul *is* tried so as by fire; purified, purged; for He, though He were the Son, learned obedience through the things which He suffered. Ye also are known even as ye do, and have done. 281-16

Chapter 20 continued

13. And the sea gave up the dead which were in it and death and hell delivered up the dead which were in them: and they were judged every man according to their works.
14. And death and hell were cast into the lake of fire. This is the second death.
15. And whosoever was not found written in the book of life was cast into the lake of fire.

Q-3. Where are the dead until Christ comes? Do they go direct to Him when they die?

A-3. As visioned by the beloved, there are those of the saints making intercession always before the throne for those that are passing in and out of the inter-between; even as He, the Christ, is ever in the consciousness of those that are redeemed in Him.

The passing in, the passing out, is as but the summer, the fall, the spring; the birth into the interim, the birth into the material. 281-16

Chapter 21

1. And I saw a new heaven and a new earth: for the first heaven and the first earth were passed away; and there was no more sea.

2. And I John saw the holy city, new Jerusalem, coming down from God out of heaven, prepared as a bride adorned for her husband.

3. And I heard a great voice out of heaven saying, Behold, the tabernacle of God is with men, and he will dwell with them, and they shall be his people, and God himself shall be with them, and be their God.

4. And God shall wipe away all tears from their eyes; and there shall be no more death, neither sorrow, nor crying, neither shall there be any more pain: for the former things are passed away.

5. And he that sat upon the throne said, Behold, I make all things new. And he said unto me, Write, for these words are true and faithful.

6. And he said unto me, It is done. I am Alpha and Omega, the beginning and the end. I will give unto Him that is athirst of the fountain of the water of life freely.

7. He that overcometh shall inherit all things; and I will be his God, and he shall be my son.

8. But the fearful, and unbelieving, and the abominable, and murderers, and whoremongers, and sorcerers, and idolaters, and all liars, shall have their part in the lake which burneth with fire and brimstone: which is the second death.

9. And there came unto me one of the seven angels which had the seven vials full of the seven last plagues, and talked with me saying, Come hither, I will shew thee the bride, the Lamb's wife.

10. And he carried me away in the spirit to a great and high mountain, and shewed me that great city, the holy Jerusalem, descending out of heaven from God,

11. Having the glory of God: and her light was like unto a stone most precious, even like a jasper stone, clear as crystal;

12. And had a wall great and high, and had twelve gates, and at the gates twelve angels, and names written thereon, which are the names of the twelve tribes of the children of Israel:

13. On the east three gates; on the north three gates, on the south three gates; and on the west three gates.

14. And the wall of the city had twelve foundations, and in them the names of the twelve apostles of the Lamb.

Q-8. What is meant by "a new heaven and a new earth"?

A-8. Former things have passed away, when there is beheld within self that the whole will of the Creator, the Father, the place of abode, the forces within and without, make for the *new* heaven, the *new* earth. 281-16

Q-5. In Rev. 21—What is the meaning of "a new heaven and a new earth: for the first heaven and the first earth were passed away; and there was no more sea"?

A-5. When the foundations of the earth are broken up by those very disturbances. Can the mind of man comprehend no desire to sin, no purpose but that the glory of the Son may be manifested in his life? Is this not a new heaven, a new earth? For the former things would have passed away. For as the desires, the purposes, the aims are to bring about the whole change physically, so does it create in the experience of each soul a new vision, a new comprehension.

For as has been given, it hath not entered the heart of man to know the glories that have been prepared, that are a part of the experiences of those that love ONLY the Lord and His ways.

Q-6. Please explain second through fourth verse of Chapter 21—the new Jerusalem and no more death.

A-6. Those then that are come into the new life, the new understanding, the new regeneration, there IS then the new Jerusalem. For as has been given, the place is not as a place alone but as a condition, as an experience of the soul.

Jerusalem has figuratively, symbolically, meant the holy place, the holy city—for there, the ark of the covenant, the ark of the covenant in the minds, the hearts, the understandings, the comprehensions of those who have put away the earthly desires and become as the NEW purposes in their experience, become the new Jerusalem, the new undertakings, the new desires.

Q-7. What is meant by the second death in Rev. 21:8?

A-7. Those that have passed into the understanding and then fall away, become minded of the earthly desires for self-exaltation, know the second death. 281-37

Q-5. Will we be punished by fire and brimstone?

A-5. That as builded by self; as those emblematical influences are shown through the experiences of the beloved in that builded, that created. For, each soul is a portion of creation—and builds that in a portion of its experience that it, through its physical-mental or spiritual-mental, has builded for itself. And each entity's heaven or hell must, through *some* experience, be that which it has builded for itself.

Is thy hell one that is filled with fire or brimstone? But know, each and every soul *is* tried so as by fire; purified, purged; for He, though He were the Son, learned obedience through the things which He suffered. Ye also are known even as ye do, and have done. 281-16

Q-8. What is meant by the Holy Jerusalem Rev. 21:12?

A-8. As indicated, that purpose, that estate to which there is the attaining of those who through the purifying—as has been indicated in the earlier portion—now come to the holy purpose—as the Holy Jerusalem; the Holy of Holies becomes the dwelling as it were of those.

Chapter 21 continued

15. And he that talked with me had a golden reed to measure the city, and the gates thereof, and the wall thereof.

16. And the city lieth foursquare, and the length is as large as the breadth: and he measured the city with the reed, twelve thousand furlongs. The length and the breadth and the height of it are equal.

17. And he measured the wall thereof, a hundred and forty and four cubits, according to the measure of a man, that is, of the angel.

18. And the building of the wall of it was of jasper: and the city was pure gold, like unto clear glass.

19. And the foundations of the wall of the city were garnished with all manner of precious stones. The first foundation was jasper; the second, sapphire; the third, a chalcedony; the fourth an emerald;

20. The fifth, sardonyx; the sixth, sardius; the seventh, chrysolyte; the eighth, beryl; the ninth, a topaz, the tenth, a chrysoprasus; the eleventh, a jacinth; the twelfth, an amethyst.

21. And the twelve gates were twelve pearls; every several gate was of one pearl; and the street of the city was pure gold, as it were transparent glass.

22. And I saw no temple therein: for the Lord God Almighty and the Lamb are the temple of it.

23. And the city had no need of the sun, neither of the moon, to shine in it: for the glory of God did lighten it, and the Lamb is the light thereof.

24. And the nations of them which are saved shall walk in the light of it: and the kings of the earth do bring their glory and honour into it.

25. And the gates of it shall not be shut at all by day: for there shall be no night there.

26. And they shall bring the glory and honour of the nations into it.

27. And there shall in no wise enter into it any thing that defileth, neither whatsoever worketh abomination or maketh a lie: but they which are written in the Lamb's book of life.

Q-9. What is meant by the twelve gates?

A-9. The twelve manners, the twelve ways, the twelve openings, the twelve experiences of the physical to all, and those that have all been purified in purpose for the activities with same.

Q-10. What is the significance of the twelve angels?

A-10. The twelve purposes as represented by the activities of the openings to the bodily forces for their activities in the experiences of expression in the phases of the activities of the individual.

Q-11. Please explain the twelve names which represent the twelve tribes of the children of Israel.

A-11. The same as the twelve gates, the twelve angels, the twelve ways, the twelve understandings; or the approach to ISRAEL, the seeker—all seeking not then as the expression of self but as *one* in the Holy One!

Q-12. Rev. 21:15. Please interpret—What is the golden reed to measure the city? and what is the significance of the stones of the new Jerusalem and their colors?

A-12. The new understanding, the reed to measure the city, the abilities of each. Not unto all is it given to be ministers, not unto all to be interpreters, not unto all to be this or that; but measured according to that whereunto they have purposed in their hearts. Though all are as one, remember it has been given that the purpose of the heart is to know YOURSELF to BE yourself and yet one with God even as Jesus, even as is represented in God the Father, Christ the Son, and the Holy Spirit; each knowing themselves to be themselves yet ONE!

So the measurements for those that make the vibrations within themselves that become attuned to the new purpose, the new desire, the new hopes, the new Revelation, the new understandings to do the will of the Father with the will of that made perfect in the Christ. 281-37

Chapter 22

1. And he shewed me a pure river of water of life, clear as crystal, proceeding out of the throne of God and of the Lamb.

2. In the midst of the street of it, and on either side of the river, was there the tree of life, which bare twelve manner of fruits, and yielded her fruit every month: and the leaves of the tree were for the healing of the nations.

3. And there shall be no more curse: but the throne of God and of the Lamb shall be in it; and his servants shall serve him:

4. And they shall see his face; and his name shall be in their foreheads.

5. And there shall be no night there; and they need no candle, neither light of the sun; for the Lord God giveth them light: and they shall reign for ever and ever.

6. And he said unto me, These sayings are faithful and true: and the Lord God of the Holy prophets sent his angel to shew unto his servants the things which must shortly be done.

7. Behold, I come quickly; blessed is he that keepeth the sayings of the prophecy of this book.

8. And I John saw these things, and heard them. And when I had heard and seen, I fell down to worship before the feet of the angel which shewed me these things.

9. Then saith he unto me, See thou do it not: for I am thy fellowservant, and of thy brethren the prophets, and of them which keep the sayings of this book: worship God.

10. And he saith unto me, Seal not the sayings of the prophecy of this book: for the time is at hand.

11. He that is unjust, let him be unjust still: and he which is filthy, let him be filthy still: and he that is righteous, let him be righteous still: and he that is holy, let him be holy still.

12. And, behold, I come quickly: and my reward is with me, to give every man according as his work shall be.

13. I am Alpha and Omega, the beginning and the end, the first and the last.

14. Blessed are they that do his commandments, that they may have right to the tree of life, and may enter in through the gates into the city.

15. For without are dogs, and sorcerers, and whoremongers, and murderers, and idolaters, and whosoever loveth and maketh a lie.

Q-13. Rev. 22:1. Please interpret: "And he showed me a pure river of water of life, clear as crystal proceeding out of the throne of God and of the Lamb."

A-13. As the river, the water, the life represents the active flow of the purpose of the souls of men made pure in same. Then they flow with that purpose from the throne of God itself, made pure in the blood of the Lamb—which is in Jesus, the Christ, to those who seek to know His ways.

Q-14. Rev. 22:2. What is meant by the tree of life with its twelve kinds of fruit that yielded her fruit every month and the leaves of the tree for the healing of the nations?

A-14. That as the tree planted by the water of life; that is, as the sturdiness of the purpose of the individual in its sureness in the Christ; and the leaves represent the activities that are as for the healing of all that the individual activities may contact, even in material life. And that it is CONTINUOUS, as by the month, as for the purpose, as for the activities.

Q-15. Rev. 22:10, 11. "Seal not the sayings of the prophecy," etc., and "He that is unjust, let him be unjust still; and he which is filthy be filthy still," etc.

A-15. As that period approaches when there shall be those influences of the power of those incarnated in the activities of the earth, then the purposes become set as in that indicated by the activities of each being in that to which they have then given themselves.

Q-16. Just how should this material be presented so as to be the most helpful and readable? Comment on the following:

A-16. Rather than commenting (for these touch upon the same), we would give this: First let there be not one but ALL who would purpose, who have purposed to be among that number that are called of God to give to those that seek the interpretation, compare and prepare the messages that have been given; and then choose ye they that would write, and let them—yea, by day and night—find themselves even as John, moved only by the spirit of truth. Thus preparing the message.

THEN when prepared, in one SITTING read the whole TO your source of information and receive the rejections or acceptations! 281-37

Chapter 22 continued

16. I Jesus have sent mine angel to testify unto you these things in the churches. I am the root and the offspring of David, and the bright and morning star.

17. And the Spirit and the bride say, Come. And let him that heareth say, Come. And let him that is athirst come. And whosoever will, let him take the water of life freely.

18. For I testify unto every man that heareth the words of the prophecy of this book, if any man shall add unto these things, God shall add unto him the plagues that are written in this book:

19. And if any man shall take away from the words of the book of this prophecy, God shall take away his part out of the book of life, and out of the holy city, and from the things which are written in this book.

20. He which testifieth these things saith, Surely I come quickly. Amen. Even so, come, Lord Jesus.

21. The grace of our Lord Jesus Christ be with you all. Amen.

TOWARD A BETTER UNDERSTANDING OF

The Book of
THE REVELATION

A GROUP PROJECT
Under the auspices of the
ASSOCIATION FOR RESEARCH
AND ENLIGHTENMENT, INC.
Virginia Beach, Virginia

Produced at the
NEW YORK CENTER

FOREWORD

On March 24, 1930, a physical reading was given by Edgar Cayce, the Christian mystic, for a young girl who was suffering from a severe case of nervous instability. The reading described the girl's physical condition, and at a certain point, remarked:

> For with pressure in the lumbar and sacral region . . . there is that activity to those forces as operate to and through the pineal gland to the upper portion of the body, which corresponds to those forces as are spoken of, even in that of The Revelation. BE VERY GOOD FOR THE DOCTOR HERE TO READ THE REVELATION AND UNDERSTAND IT! ESPECIALLY IN REFERENCE TO THIS BODY! (caps added)
>
> 2501-6

The Norfolk Group, three years later, took readings about the true significance of the Book of Revelation. Out of this prayerful research came a key by which the layperson might, through disciplined persistence, come to understand the message of The Revelation.

However, this took time and study. Any busy physician, psychologist, or psychotherapist would have to devote years of study to it before he or she could find out what the book was about! This before one could even begin to apply the truths contained in it even if a person wanted to with all his or her heart! This was particularly true for the layperson.

In order to make the message at least available, a group of laypeople in New York met to see if they could apply the key supplied by the Norfolk work, possibly to bring out an interpretation of The Revelation for general study. To this task these people have devoted seven years' faithful research and the following pages are the result of their labors.

THE REVELATION

Chapter 1

1. The Revelation of Jesus Christ, which God gave unto him, to shew unto his servants things which must shortly come to pass; and he sent and signified it by his angel unto his servant John:

2. Who bare record of the word of God, and of the testimony of Jesus Christ, and of all things that he saw.

3. Blessed is he that readeth, and they that hear the words of this prophecy, and keep those things which are written therein: for the time is at hand.

4. John to the seven churches which are in Asia: Grace be unto you, and peace, from him which is, and which was, and which is to come; and from the seven Spirits which are before his throne;

5. And from Jesus Christ, who is the faithful witness, and the firstbegotten of the dead, and the prince of the kings of the earth. Unto him that loved us, and washed us from our sins in his own blood,

6. And hath made us kings and priests unto God and his Father; to him be glory and dominion for ever and ever. Amen.

7. Behold, he cometh with clouds; and every eye shall see him, and they also which pierced him: and all kindreds of the earth shall wail because of him. Even so, Amen.

8. I am Alpha and Omega, the beginning and the ending, saith the Lord, which is, and which was, and which is to come, the Almighty.

9. I John, who also am your brother, and companion in tribulation, and in the kingdom and patience of Jesus Christ, was in the isle that is called Patmos, for the word of God, and for the testimony of Jesus Christ.

SYMBOLOGY

NOTE: Verses 1 to 3 form prelude to work written by someone—possibly a monk—in later centuries.

SEVEN CHURCHES —Seven spiritual centers, the endocrine system of the body, but more in a collective sense, named after the seven churches established in Asia Minor.

SEVEN SPIRITS —Seven guiding intelligences or mind cells of each "church" or center.

THRONE—Here means point of contact with the Supreme Being. (Universal).

FAITHFUL WITNESS —FIRST BEGOTTEN OF DEAD—PRINCE OF KINGS OF EARTH—The Leader Soul of mankind. First to have completed entire HUMAN EXPERIENCE.

ALPHA & OMEGA —The overself —the superconscious mind of John.

INTERPRETATION

4. John is hereby giving his REVELATION as a guide book and a testimony to the seven churches of Asia, of his own experiences while in meditation. These congregations were as despairing refugees, persecuted and some fallen away, who needed to know a way whereby they could bring into activity the forces of regeneration latent within each INDIVIDUAL body.

This was the purpose of the book, John's opening greeting serves to introduce, perhaps, the concept of the Christ Consciousness from *within* as being the true author of the book, who is now one with Jesus, the Man, who became the Christ. He it was, who first fulfilled the pattern of man's evolution and then turned to redeem and reclaim the rest of the race.

8. Alpha and Omega refers to the plan for all evolution, only partly fulfilled at present, which has within it the power to bring about a successful outcome for man in terms of experience in the world.

9. John now states his position as a fugitive also and in dire straits while living in the isle of Patmos to which he had been banished.

Chapter 1 continued

10. I was in the Spirit on the Lord's Day, and heard behind me a great voice, as of a trumpet.

11. Saying, I am Alpha and Omega, the first and the last; and, What thou seest, write in a book, and send it unto the seven churches which are in Asia, unto Ephesus, and unto Smyrna, and unto Pergamos, and unto Thyatira, and unto Sardis, and unto Philadelphia, and unto Laodicea.

12. And I turned to see the voice that spake with me. And being turned, I saw seven golden candlesticks;

13. And in the midst of the seven candlesticks one like unto the Son of man, clothed with a garment down to the foot, and girt about the paps with a golden girdle.

14. His head and his hairs were white like wool, as white as snow; and his eyes were as a flame of fire;

15. And his feet like unto fine brass, as if they burned in a furnace; and his voice as the sound of many waters.

16. And he had in his right hand seven stars; and out of his mouth went a sharp two-edged sword; and his countenance was as the sun shineth in his strength.

17. And when I saw him, I fell at his feet as dead. And he laid his right hand upon me, saying unto me, Fear not; I am the first and the last:

18. I am he that liveth, and was dead; and, behold, I am alive for evermore, Amen; and have the keys of hell and of death.

19. Write the things which thou hast seen, and the things which are, and the things which shall be hereafter;

20. The mystery of the seven stars which thou sawest in my right hand, and the seven golden candlesticks. The seven stars are the angels of the seven churches; and the seven candlesticks which thou sawest are the seven churches.

SYMBOLOGY

NOTE: John speaking.

IN THE SPIRIT—Meditation.

ALPHA & OMEGA—Overself.

CHURCHES: EPHESUS—Gonads; SMYRNA—Lyden; PERGAMOS—Adrenals; THYATIRA—Thymus; SARDIS—Thyroid; PHILADELPHIA—Pineal; LAODICEA—Pituitary.

SEVEN GOLDEN CANDLESTICKS—Same as 7 churches plus mind cells of each.

GOLDEN GIRDLE—Worth.

WHITE HAIR—Wisdom.

EYES OF FLAME—Perception.

FEET AS BRASS—Understanding.

SEVEN STARS—Control of key points of body. (These are all attributes of the Overself—Superconscious.)

TWO-EDGED SWORD—Power rising from centers applied either constructively or destructively according to the will.

N.B. DEFINITION OF THE OVERSELF: "The OVERSELF is the self-conscious, individualized portion of God, which is the unchanging core of each entity, the superconscious mind."

INTERPRETATION

10. John explains that he was in meditation on the "Lord's Day," and what follows takes place within his own body and mind. This is true of the whole book, containing all the images, symbols, and forces described here.

N.B. The instructor is to be the OVERSELF (see definition) the symbol of the higher self, the superconscious mind, which is endowed with universal consciousness and is the real entity that always survives physical death.

11. The actual physical seven churches of Asia are to be the recipients of the ensuing book, but they will also be used as symbols for the seven glandular centers in the human body, where the physical forces of the body, the mental forces and the spiritual all come together. These are the key spots throughout the body, known as the endocrine system. (A "church" is a meeting place.)

12. Through the imagery of the candlesticks, John is shown that within each center is a mind cell, the light of which would symbolize intelligence, which is in charge of the functions of each center. These in turn are in the control of the superconscious mind with supreme intelligence.

18. The OVERSELF or the superconscious mind explains that it is in perfect control of all physical and mental states and John is urged to describe his findings for the use of others, the relationships of all the parts of this own body to the whole.

CHURCH	VIRTUE	FAULTS	SEAL	VISION	SPIRITUAL CENTERS/ GLANDS	LORD'S PRAYER
EPHESUS	PATIENCE	LEFT FIRST LOVE	1	WHITE HORSE	GONADS (Desire)	BREAD

Chapter 2

1. Unto the angel of the church of Ephesus write; These things saith he that holdeth the seven stars in his right hand, who walketh in the midst of the seven golden candlesticks;

2. I know thy works, and thy labour, and thy patience, and how thou canst not bear them which are evil: and thou hast tried them which say they are apostles, and are not, and hast found them liars:

3. And hast borne, and hast patience, and for my name's sake hast laboured, and hast not fainted.

4. Nevertheless I have somewhat against thee, because thou hast left thy first love.

5. Remember therefore from whence thou art fallen, and repent, and do the first works; or else I will come unto thee quickly, and will remove thy candlestick out of his place, except thou repent.

6. But this thou hast, that thou hatest the deeds of the Nicolaitans, which I also hate.

7. He that hath an ear, let him hear what the Spirit saith unto the churches; To him that overcometh will I give to eat of the tree of life, which is in the midst of the paradise of God.

SYMBOLOGY

ANGEL OF EPHESUS—Mind cell or intelligence governing gonads.

HE WITH 7 STARS—Overself or superconscious.

FIRST LOVE—Spiritual ideal—purpose.

NICOLAITANS—Cells in this center (in this case, the gonads) that have degenerated through misuse and lascivious practices.

TREE OF LIFE—The function of supply, healing and growth, the power of regeneration as manifested through the endocrine system perfectly synchronized.

PARADISE OF GOD—The original consciousness of man, before he came into matter, and to which he will return.

INTERPRETATION

In verse 1, Chapter 2, the OVERSELF is speaking, pointing out to John the need for a cleansing and purifying of the forces of the gonads.

2. The OVERSELF is aware of the efforts of the intelligence found here to regulate and guard itself against destructive activities and pursuits, but says that the original purpose of this center has been lost. The mind cell is urged to bring about a return to the original purpose quickly, or lose its intelligence entirely. (This would mean degeneration to the point of animalistic function of this center, instinctual but without intelligence.)

7. In this verse the OVERSELF gives a clue to the great riddle of the TREE OF LIFE referred to in the Book of Genesis, a riddle of the ages in the western world.

John is told that anyone who can regain control of this center could bring about within his body and mind, as well as in his worldly circumstances, complete restoration of the law of healing and supply.

CHURCH	VIRTUE	FAULTS	SEAL	VISION	SPIRITUAL CENTERS/ GLANDS	LORD'S PRAYER
SMYRNA	SUFFERING	INSINCERITY	2	BLACK HORSE	LYDEN	TEMP-TATION

Chapter 2 continued

8. And unto the angel of the church in Smyrna write; These things saith the first and the last, which was dead, and is alive;

9. I know thy works, and tribulations, and poverty, (but thou art rich) and I know the blasphemy of them which say they are Jews, and are not, but are the synagogue of Satan.

10. Fear none of those things which thou shalt suffer: behold, the devil shall cast some of you into prison, that ye may be tried; and ye shall have tribulation ten days: be thou faithful unto death, and I will give thee a crown of life.

11. He that hath an ear, let him hear what the Spirit saith unto the churches; He that overcometh shall not be hurt of the second death.

SYMBOLOGY

ANGEL OF SMYRNA—Mind cell or intelligence governing cells of Leydig or Lyden gland.

FIRST AND LAST—Overself, or superconscious.

JEWS—Cells chosen for special development.

SYNAGOGUE OF SATAN—Unregenerate cells.

TRIBULATION 10 DAYS—Period of purification.

CROWN OF LIFE—Symbol of state of perfect control.

SECOND DEATH—Regression from partial regeneration, broadly, a relapse.

SPIRIT—Overself is speaking here.

INTERPRETATION

8. The OVERSELF instructs John to see that the "intelligence" in charge of the cells of Leydig or Lyden gland is reassured, so to speak, for the sense of inadequate creativity in their function, that their possibilities are infinite once the "unregenerate" cells which thwart and limit the activity of this center, are eliminated through a period of purification.

10. If the forces of this center will be faithful to the discipline imposed upon it, complete control will be restored to the "intelligence" in charge.

N.B. The cells of Leydig seem to be the center of what, on the mental level, is called "imagination." That is to say, the forces moving up from the gonads as pure energy take form at this point. In a mental sense again, purpose or ideals would be generated here in conjunction with the pituitary.

11. The cryptogram here seems to say that the individual who gains control of this center will not be liable to regression from partial regeneration.

CHURCH	VIRTUE	FAULTS	SEAL	VISION	SPIRITUAL CENTERS/ GLANDS	LORD'S PRAYER
PERGAMOS	FAITHFUL	STUMBLING BLOCK	3	RED HORSE	ADRENAL/ SOLAR PLEXUS	DEBTS

Chapter 2 continued

12. And to the angel of the church in Pergamos write; These things saith he which hath the sharp sword with two edges;

13. I know thy works, and where thou dwellest, even where Satan's seat is: and thou holdest fast my name, and hast not denied my faith, even in those days wherein Antipas was my faithful martyr, who was slain among you, where Satan dwelleth.

14. But I have a few things against thee, because thou hast there them that hold the doctrine of Balaam, who taught Balak to cast a stumbling block before the children of Israel, to eat things sacrificed unto idols, and to commit fornication.

15. So hast thou also them that hold the doctrine of the Nicolaitans, which things I hate.

16. Repent; or else I will come unto thee quickly, and will fight against them with the sword of my mouth.

17. He that hath an ear, let him hear what the Spirit saith unto the churches; To him that overcometh will I give to eat of the hidden manna, and will give him a white stone, and in the stone a new name written, which no man knoweth saving he that receiveth it.

SYMBOLOGY

ANGEL OF PERGAMOS—Mind cell or intelligence governing adrenals.

HE WITH SHARP SWORD—Overself, superconscious.

ANTIPAS—Martyred bishop—State of loss of control of adrenal functions.

DOCTRINE OF BALAAM—Corruption of cells, chosen for special development, through misuse and lascivious impulses.

HIDDEN MANNA—The impact of the Spirit upon the endocrine system which releases its secretions into the blood stream, creating energy.

WHITE STONE—A point of higher development, a new stage of consciousness.

A NEW NAME WRITTEN—A new sense of identification in the part for its relationship to the whole—"responsibility."

FOOTNOTE: New name is also the means by which the spiritual impact can be repeated at will.

INTERPRETATION

12. The Overself now addresses Himself to the mind cell, or "intelligence" of the adrenal center, through John. This center is commended for its adherence to its basic purposes even during periods when control of adrenal functions has sometimes been lost.

13. The adrenal intelligence is warned, however, against the misuse of its energies owing to the presence of unregenerate cells here implying the need for purification on this level also.

16. The two-edged sword symbolizes the power rising from the centers, which either blesses or curses, according to the will. Thus, the Overself promises prompt "surgery" for the cells which resist discipline on this level.

17. Now the Overself states that as a result of perfect restoration of self-control of the seven centers, the individual can renew and regenerate himself at will as the Master did, by apparently releasing hormones from the adrenal into the bloodstream directly, as a result of the impact of the Spirit upon the endocrine system. Moreover, in the resulting higher state of consciousness, the individual in knowledge of his relationship with the higher forces can effect contact with them at any time.

CHURCH	VIRTUE	FAULTS	SEAL	VISION	SPIRITUAL CENTERS/ GLANDS	LORD'S PRAYER
THYATIRA	CHARITY	FORNICATION	4	PALE HORSE	THYMUS	EVIL

Chapter 2 continued

18. And unto the angel of the church in Thyatira write; These things saith the Son of God, who hath his eyes like unto a flame of fire, and his feet are like fine brass;

19. I know thy works, and charity, and service, and faith, and thy patience, and thy works; and the last to be more than the first.

20. Notwithstanding I have a few things against thee, because thou sufferest that woman Jezebel, which calleth herself a prophetess, to teach and to seduce my servants to commit fornication and to eat things sacrificed unto idols.

21. And I gave her space to repent of her fornication; and she repented not.

22. Behold, I will cast her into a bed, and them that commit adultery with her into great tribulation, except they repent of their deeds.

23. And I will kill her children with death; and all the churches shall know that I am he which searcheth the reins and hearts: and I will give unto every one of you according to your works.

24. But unto you I say, and unto the rest in Thyatira, as many as have not this doctrine, and which have not known the depths of Satan, as they speak; I will put upon you none other burden.

25. But that which ye have already, hold fast till I come.

26. And he that overcometh, and keepeth my works unto the end, to him will I give power over the nations:

27. And he shall rule them with a rod of iron; as the vessels of a potter shall they be broken to shivers: even as I received of my Father.

28. And I will give him the morning star.

29. He that hath an ear, let him hear what the Spirit saith unto the churches.

SYMBOLOGY

ANGEL OF THYATIRA—Mind cell or intelligence governing thymus.

SON OF GOD—Overself, superconscious mind.

JEZEBEL—Symbol of misdirection of creative forces.

REINS—Controls.

HEART—Motivations.

SATAN—Unregenerate mind.

POWER OVER THE NATIONS—Control of all bodily parts and functions.

MORNING STAR—Original state of illumination or intelligence.

INTERPRETATION

The Overself is speaking to the intelligence or mind cell of the thymus center.

19. He commends its functions to date even though it is under a condition of limitation and promises that fulfillment will ultimately come about in abundance.

20, 23. Now he urges purification against the persistence of this center to misuse the divine forces for personal satisfaction. Time has been given in which to bring this about. However, if the faults are persisted in, only disintegration and decay can result. This, in turn, would automatically bring unbalance to the other centers. The Overself, being in charge, is examining constantly the controls and the motivations of each center.

24, 25. The mind cell and those cells still free from misuse, however, will not be called on for any additional duties. These are admonished to retain the ideals of their perfect pattern.

26. To the man who remains true to the perfect pattern which is within each one of us, absolute control will be given him over all parts and all functions of the body.

28. Such a man would return to his first condition in consciousness complete master of his environment.

29. "Meditate on these things."

CHURCH	VIRTUE	FAULTS	SEAL	VISION	SPIRITUAL CENTERS/ GLANDS	LORD'S PRAYER
SARDIS	FEW NOT DEFILED	IMPERFECT	5	SOULS OF PERFECT SLAIN	THYROID	WILL

Chapter 3

1. And unto the angel of the church in Sardis write; These things saith he that hath the seven Spirits of God, and the seven stars; I know thy works, that thou hast a name that thou livest, and art dead.

2. Be watchful, and strengthen the things which remain, that are ready to die: for I have not found thy works perfect before God.

3. Remember therefore how thou hast received and heard, and hold fast, and repent. If therefore thou shalt not watch, I will come on thee as a thief, and thou shalt not know what hour I will come upon thee.

4. Thou hast a few names even in Sardis which have not defiled their garments; and they shall walk with me in white: for they are worthy.

5. He that overcometh, the same shall be clothed in white raiment; and I will not blot out his name out of the book of life, but I will confess his name before my Father, and before his angels.

6. He that hath an ear, let him hear what the Spirit saith unto the churches.

SYMBOLOGY

ANGEL OF SARDIS—Mind cell or intelligence governing thyroid.

HE THAT HATH 7 SPIRITS OF GOD—7 STARS—Overself or superconscious mind.

DEAD—Unaware; Unconscious.

WHITE RAIMENT—State of purity.

BOOK OF LIFE—Collective unconscious, record of all souls.

INTERPRETATION

The OVERSELF is addressing himself to the mind cell of the thyroid center, the seat of human will.

1. The human will is an academic fact but its true function has been lost. The center is warned of its condition and is admonished not to let it go any further. Otherwise, when it is tested suddenly, it will be found imperfect.

4. The cells, however, who have adhered to their inner perfect pattern shall continue in perfection.

5. The man who OVERCOMES temptation on this level will have perpetual access to the Creative Forces.

6. "Meditate on these things!"

CHURCH	VIRTUE	FAULTS	SEAL	VISION	SPIRITUAL CENTERS/ GLANDS	LORD'S PRAYER
PHILA-DELPHIA	OPEN DOOR	NO FAULTS	6	EARTHQUAKE PERFECT	PINEAL	NAME

Chapter 3 continued

7. And to the angel of the church in Philadelphia write; These things saith he that is holy, he that is true, he that hath the key of David, he that openeth and no man shutteth; and shutteth, and no man openeth;

8. I know thy works; behold, I have set before thee an open door, and no man can shut it; for thou hast a little strength, and hast kept my word, and hast not denied my name.

9. Behold, I will make them of the synagogue of Satan which say they are Jews, and are not, but do lie; behold, I will make them to come and worship before thy feet, and to know that I have loved thee.

10. Because thou hast kept the word of my patience, I also will keep thee from the hour of temptation, which shall come upon all the world, to try them that swell upon the earth.

11. Behold, I come quickly; hold that fast which thou hast, that no man take thy crown.

12. Him that overcometh will I make a pillar in the temple of my God, and he shall go no more out: and I will write upon him the name of my God, and the name of the city of my God, which is new Jerusalem, which cometh down out of heaven from my God: and I will write upon him my new name.

13. He that hath an ear, let him hear what the Spirit saith unto the churches.

SYMBOLOGY

ANGEL OF PHILADELPHIA—Mind cell or intelligence governing pineal.

HE THAT HATH THE KEY OF DAVID—OVERSELF, superconscious mind.

OPEN DOOR—Opportunity.

NAME—Nature.

SYNAGOGUE OF SATAN—Unregenerate cells.

JEWS—Cells chosen for special development.

WORD OF MY PATIENCE—Discipline, faithful to.

EARTH—Physical body.

PILLAR IN THE TEMPLE—An evolved cell or soul in a collective sense.

NEW JERUSALEM—The new consciousness.

INTERPRETATION

7. The Overself is addressing the mind cell of the pineal center, the seat of all memory and record.

8. The pineal has apparently been true to itself and its purpose in recording all experiences of the individual and bringing them into comparison with the perfect pattern within the Soul. At this point, all imperfections and error in motivations and functions stand out in bold relief. Correction and reform must result, since the pineal is under the special custody of the Overself as it were. (The records are accurate.)

10. Because of this accuracy, this center is not subject to the instabilities of the other centers in the ways of temptations, etc., but automatically records everything good and bad. The pineal is urged to continue in its faithfulness and when it is subjected to trial it will not lose control.

11. The man who has overcome on this level the Overself says, will be in possession of his entire soul record of all his experiences in the earth and in possession of a new consciousness that will make it unnecessary for him to reincarnate any more. He will now be in complete God-consciousness.

13. "Meditate on these things!"

CHURCH	VIRTUE	FAULTS	SEAL	VISION	SPIRITUAL CENTERS/ GLANDS	LORD'S PRAYER
LAODICEA		LUKEWARM	7	SILENCE	PITUITARY	FATHER

Chapter 3 continued

14. And unto the angel of the church of the Laodiceans write; These things saith the Amen, the faithful and true witness, the beginning of the creation of God;

15. I know thy works, that thou art neither cold nor hot: I would thou wert cold or hot.

16. So then because thou art lukewarm, and neither cold not hot, I will spew thee out of my mouth.

17. Because thou sayest, I am rich, and increased with goods, and have need of nothing; and knowest not that thou art wretched, and miserable, and poor, and blind, and naked.

18. I counsel thee to buy of me gold tried in the fire, that thou mayest be rich; and white raiment, that thou mayest be clothed, and that the shame of thy nakedness do not appear; and anoint thine eyes with eyesalve, that thou mayest see.

19. As many as I love, I rebuke and chasten: be zealous therefore, and repent.

20. Behold, I stand at the door, and knock: if any man hear my voice, and open the door, I will come in to him, and will sup with him, and he with me.

21. To him that overcometh will I grant to sit with me in my throne, even as I also overcame, and am set down with my Father in his throne.

22. He that hath an ear, let him hear what the Spirit saith unto the churches.

SYMBOLOGY

ANGEL OF LAODICEA—Mind cell or intelligence governing pituitary.

THE AMEN—Overself, superconscious mind.

GOLD TRIED IN THE FIRE—Tested values.

WHITE RAIMENT—Purity.

NAKEDNESS—Faults, exposure of.

EYE SALVE—Search for truth.

INTERPRETATION

14. The Overself is addressing the mind cell of the pituitary center now. This is the MASTER gland.

15. The forces of the pituitary or MASTER gland have bogged down in materiality, so to speak, having become satisfied with limitation and circumscribed consciousness. The Overself will have no part of such a negative attitude.

18. The Overself counsels this center to enrich itself by accepting the wisdom that comes through living, vital experience—to be clothed in the purity that does not reveal any fault or inadequacy—and to gain in perception and awareness.

19. This is the advice given to all cells of all centers, that they return to their original purpose.

20. The Overself is available to any man who will accept this counsel. He says, but the individual, it is implied, must open the door. When this happens, union of the personality and the Overself is possible in the individual, just as Jesus, the universal "Christ" or Pattern was united with the Father-God.

22. "Meditate on these things!"

GLANDS	BEASTS	ELEMENTS
THYMUS	EAGLE	AIR
ADRENAL	LION	FIRE
LYDEN	MAN	WATER
GONADS	CALF	EARTH

Chapter 4

1. After this I looked, and behold, a door was opened in heaven: and the first voice which I heard was as it were of a trumpet talking with me; which said, Come up hither, and I will shew thee things which must be hereafter.

2. And immediately I was in the Spirit: and, behold, a throne was set in heaven, and one sat on the throne.

3. And he that sat was to look upon like a jasper and a sardine stone: and there was a rainbow round about the throne, in sight like unto an emerald.

4. And round about the throne were four and twenty seats: and upon the seats I saw four and twenty elders sitting, clothed in white raiment; and they had on their heads crowns of gold.

5. And out of the throne proceeded lightnings and thunderings and voices: and there were seven lamps of fire burning before the throne, which are the seven Spirits of God.

6. And before the throne there was a sea of glass like unto crystal: and in the midst of the throne, and round about the throne, were four beasts full of eyes before and behind.

7. And the first beast was like a lion, and the second beast like a calf, and the third beast had a face as a man, and the fourth beast was like a flying eagle.

8. And the four beasts had each of them six wings about him; and they were full of eyes within: and they rest not day and night, saying, Holy, holy, holy, Lord God Almighty, which was, and is, and is to come.

9. And when those beasts give glory and honour and thanks to him that sat on the throne, who liveth for ever and ever,

10. The four and twenty elders fall down before him that sat on the throne, and worship him that liveth for ever and ever, and cast their crowns before the throne, saying,

11. Thou art worthy, O Lord, to receive glory and honour and power: for thou hast created all things, and for thy pleasure they are and were created.

SYMBOLOGY

FIRST VOICE—OVERSELF—Superconscious.

OPEN DOOR IN HEAVEN—The awakening.

HE THAT SAT—Overself.

JASPER, SARDINE STONE, EMERALD—Attributes of the Overself, like healing, etc.

RAINBOW—Aura of all these things combined.

4 and 20 ELDERS—24 cranial nerves that lead to the 5 senses.

CROWNS—Positions of command, rulership.

LIGHTNINGS—THUNDERINGS—VOICES—Forces in action.

7 LAMPS—7 intelligences or mind-cells of the endocrine system.

SEA OF GLASS—Stilled emotions.

4 BEASTS—Desires of 4 lower centers: 1. Self-gratification; 2. Self-preservation; 3. Sustenance; 4. Propagation of the species.

FULL OF EYES BEFORE AND BEHIND—Aware of self.

INTERPRETATION

1. John is speaking now and he tells us that at this point, a mental awakening occurs. The OVERSELF offers himself as a guide.

2. The OVERSELF shows himself in point of control of the entire body-mind. (The stones and colors symbolize attributes—like judgment, justice, mercy, etc.) Before the control point of the superconscious mind are the lesser control points of the five senses—the 24 cranial nerves. Also the intelligences of the seven centers of the endocrine system are shown as lamps.

6. The sea of glass before the throne symbolizes the stilled emotions, the condition which will allow the OVERSELF to rule. The beasts full of eyes before and behind represent the four lower centers full of awareness of self. The attributes of these centers are: 1. Self-gratification—Thymus; 2. Self-preservation—Adrenals; 3. Sustenance—Lyden; 4. Propagation of the species—Gonads.

8. These are shown to be in a condition of complete harmony with the OVERSELF at which point the five senses relinquish their rulership over the body.

Chapter 5

1. And I saw in the right hand of him that sat on the throne a book written within and on the back side, sealed with seven seals.

2. And I saw a strong angel proclaiming with a loud voice, Who is worthy to open the book, and to loose the seals thereof?

3. And no man in heaven, nor in earth, neither under the earth, was able to open the book, neither to look thereon.

4. And I wept much, because no man was found worthy to open and to read the book, neither to look thereon.

5. And one of the elders saith unto me, Weep not: behold, the Lion of the tribe of Juda, the Root of David, hath prevailed to open the book, and to loose the seven seals thereof.

6. And I beheld, and, lo, in the midst of the throne and of the four beasts, and in the midst of the elders, stood a Lamb as it had been slain, having seven horns and seven eyes, which are the seven Spirits of God sent forth into all the earth.

7. And he came and took the book out of the right hand of him that sat upon the throne.

8. And when he had taken the book, the four beasts and four and twenty elders fell down before the Lamb, having every one of them harps, and golden vials full of odours, which are the prayers of saints.

9. And they sung a new song, saying, Thou art worthy to take the book, and to open the seals thereof: for thou wast slain, and hast redeemed us to God by thy blood out of every kindred, and tongue, and people, and nation;

10. And hast made us unto our God kings and priests: and we shall reign on the earth.

11. And I beheld, and I heard the voice of many angels round about the throne, and the beasts, and the elders: and the number of them was ten thousand times ten thousand, and thousands of thousands;

12. Saying with a loud voice, Worthy is the Lamb that was slain, to receive power, and riches, and wisdom, and strength, and honour, and glory, and blessing.

13. And every creature which is in heaven, and on the earth, and under the earth, and such as are in the sea, and all that are in them heard I saying, Blessing, and honour, and glory, and power, be unto him that sitteth upon the throne, and unto the Lamb for ever and ever.

14. And the four beasts said, Amen. And the four and twenty elders fell down and worshipped him that liveth for ever and ever.

SYMBOLOGY

HIM THAT SAT UPON THE THRONE—Overself, Superconscious Mind.

RIGHT HAND—Symbol of point of control of spiritual forces in body.

BOOK—The body.

BACKSIDE OF BOOK—Unconscious side.

SEALS—Endocrine centers in normal closed state.

LION OF TRIBE OF JUDAH—ROOT OF DAVID—CHRIST—Consciousness, perfected through experience in matter or the earth.

THE LAMB—Same.

HARPS—Alignment.

VIALS—Acknowledgement.

NEW SONG—New Understanding—a perfected relationship.

KINDRED TONGUE PEOPLE AND NATION—Ordinary cells of body, all cells.

KINGS—Ruling forces of physical cells.

PRIESTS—Control points of spiritualized cells.

10,000 times 10,000—Cells in whole physical body.

INTERPRETATION

1. John is speaking and telling of his experiences in meditation. The OVERSELF is shown at point of control of the human body—body symbolized as a book. The book is sealed, that is, the real knowledge of the body is sealed up in the control points of the endocrine system.

3. Opening these centers is beyond the ability of the average man.

5. John senses that only through the development of Christ Consciousness through *experience,* will enable him to open the centers. To the Christ-conscious man only, is the custody of the entire body entrusted.

8. Such development of an individual is attested when the lower centers and the senses acknowledge his control.

11. John is informed by the entire aggregate of bodily parts and their forces that this power over the body-mind comes only as the result of the death of the selfish-self or self-will, in the regenerating, Christ-conscious man.

N.B. The Lamb is the Symbol of the regenerating man.

SEALS	EXPERIENCES OR SOUNDS AT OPENING	GLAND	PRAYER
7	SILENCE	PITUITARY	FATHER
6	EARTHQUAKE	PINEAL	NAME
5	SOULS OF FAITHFUL SLAIN	THYROID	WILL
4	PALE HORSE	THYMUS	EVIL
3	RED HORSE	ADRENAL	DEBTS
2	BLACK HORSE	LYDEN	TEMPTATION
1	WHITE HORSE	GONADS	BREAD

Chapter 6

1. And I saw when the Lamb opened one of the seals, and I heard as it were the noise of thunder, one of the four beasts saying, Come and see.

2. And I saw, and behold a white horse: and he that sat on him had a bow; and a crown was given unto him: and he went forth conquering, and to conquer.

3. And when he had opened the second seal, I heard the second beast say, Come and see.

4. And there went out another horse that was red: and power was given to him that sat thereon to take peace from the earth, and that they should kill one another; and there was given unto him a great sword.

5. And when he had opened the third seal, I heard the third beast say, Come and see. And I beheld, and lo a black horse; and he that sat on him had a pair of balances in his hand.

6. And I heard a voice in the midst of the four beasts say, A measure of wheat for a penny, and three measures of barley for a penny; and see thou hurt not the oil and the wine.

7. And when he had opened the fourth seal, I heard the voice of the fourth beast say, Come and see.

8. And I looked, and behold a pale horse: and his name that sat on him was Death, and Hell followed with him. And power was given unto them over the fourth part of the earth, to kill with sword, and with hunger, and with death, and with the beasts of the earth.

9. And when he had opened the fifth seal, I saw under the altar the souls of them that were slain for the word of God, and for the testimony which they held:

10. And they cried with a loud voice, saying, How long, O Lord, holy and true, dost thou not judge and avenge our blood on them that dwell on the earth?

SYMBOLOGY

HORSE—Force through—White—Gonads; Red—Adrenals; Black—Lyden;
Pale—Thymus.

RIDER—Controlling intelligence.

ALTAR—Point of decision.

SOULS OF SLAIN—Latent powers.

EARTHQUAKE—Trembling of body.

STARS OF HEAVEN—Mental ideals, present concepts.

MOUNTAIN—Material attainment.

ISLAND—Limited ideas.

KINGS OF THE EARTH, etc.—Controlling intelligences of body.

INTERPRETATION

1. John perceives the energies of the gonads as this center is opened by the forces of regeneration within his own body. The intelligence of the gonads bids him "Come and see."

2. When the next center is opened, the forces of the adrenal are released. This is the main source of physical energy, which is capable of galvanizing the body into action, for constructive or destructive purposes.

5. When the regenerating will opens the Lyden center, the warning is given that for every spiritual gift there is a price and a penalty for the mis-use of each gift.

7. When the thymus is opened, the ravages of degeneration are shown through loss of consciousness and feelings of guilt as a result of self-gratification of the body.

9. The opening of the thyroid center discloses latent powers of the will, which have been immobilized through misuse, and which will have to wait for the regeneration of the other cells which are in process of being refined.

Chapter 6 continued

11. And white robes were given unto every one of them; and it was said unto them, that they should rest yet for a little season, until their fellow servants also and their brethren, that should be killed as they were, should be fulfilled.

12. And I beheld when he had opened the sixth seal, and, lo, there was a great earthquake; and the sun became black as sackcloth of hair, and the moon became as blood;

13. And the stars of heaven fell unto the earth, even as a fig tree casteth her untimely figs, when she is shaken of a mighty wind.

14. And the heaven departed as a scroll when it is rolled together; and every mountain and island were moved out of their places.

15. And the kings of the earth, and the great men, and the rich men, and the chief captains, and the mighty men, and every bondman, and every free man, hid themselves in the dens and in the rocks of the mountains;

16. And said to the mountains and rocks, Fall on us, and hide us from the face of him that sitteth on the throne, and from the wrath of the Lamb:

17. For the great day of his wrath is come; and who shall be able to stand?

12. The opening of the pineal center is accompanied by bodily trembling and loss of consciousness with the life essence centering only in the subconscious, with loss of mental impulses to the physical.

14. Old ideals are swept away together with all material attainments and limited concepts. Even the directing and controlling intelligence of the body bury themselves in matter in an attempt to avoid correction by the forces of the OVERSELF and the regenerating will.

MAJOR DIVISIONS OF THE PHYSICAL BODY				
THOSE OF CONSTRUCTION	BONES	MUSCLES	LIGAMENTS	SKIN
THOSE THAT KEEP ALIVE	LUNGS	HEART	BLOOD	LIVER
THOSE THAT INFLUENCE THAT OF THE PHYSICAL, MENTAL, AND SPIRITUAL	CENTRAL NERVOUS SYSTEM; CEREBROSPINAL; SYMPATHETIC NERVOUS SYSTEM; DUCTLESS GLANDS			

Chapter 7

1. And after these things I saw four angels standing on the four corners of the earth, holding the four winds of the earth, that the wind should not blow on the earth, nor on the sea, nor on any tree.

2. And I saw another angel ascending from the east, having the seal of the living God: and he cried with a loud voice to the four angels, to whom it was given to hurt the earth and the sea,

3. Saying, Hurt not the earth, neither the sea, nor the trees, till we have sealed the servants of our God in their foreheads.

4. And I heard the number of them which were sealed: and there were sealed a hundred and forty and four thousand of all the tribes of the children of Israel.

5. Of the tribe of Juda were sealed twelve thousand. Of the tribe of Reuben were sealed twelve thousand. Of the tribe of Gad were sealed twelve thousand.

6. Of the tribe of Aser were sealed twelve thousand. Of the tribe of Nephthalim were sealed twelve thousand. Of the tribe of Manasses were sealed twelve thousand.

7. Of the tribe of Simeon were sealed twelve thousand. Of the tribe of Levi were sealed twelve thousand. Of the tribe of Issachar were sealed twelve thousand.

8. Of the tribe of Zabulon were sealed twelve thousand. Of the tribe of Joseph were sealed twelve thousand. Of the tribe of Benjamin were sealed twelve thousand.

9. After this I beheld, and, lo, a great multitude, which no man could number, of all nations, and kindreds, and people, and tongues, stood before the throne, and before the Lamb, clothed with white robes, and palms in their hands;

10. And cried with a loud voice, saying, Salvation to our God which sitteth upon the throne, and unto the Lamb.

SYMBOLOGY

FOUR ANGELS AT FOUR CORNERS OF THE EARTH—Controlling intelligences in charge of four elements of body. 1. Physical; 2. Emotional; 3. Mental; 4. Spiritual.

ANGEL FROM EAST—Beginning of awakening of consciousness.

SEAL—As pattern, having DIVINE APPROVAL.

144,000 SEALED—Selected bodily cells bearing pattern for perfect development, evolution.

12 TRIBES—12 major portions of body.

TEMPLE—Head or the mental.

INTERPRETATION

1. John now observes the four controlling intelligences within himself. These are those which have custody of the four essences that go to make up the (a) physical body; (b) the emotional natures and all fluids; (c) the mentality; (d) the soul forces.

N.B. In the BODY, these would be bones, muscles, tendons, skin, having to do with construction. The organs of vital fluids: lungs, heart, blood, liver influences and the organs of the mental, physical, and spiritual, such as the central nervous system, brain and spinal cord. Also the cerebrospinal system including senses plus sympathetic nervous system and ductless glands.

3, 7. The four intelligences of these four general classifications are instructed to withhold action against these elements until certain principal cells throughout the body are stamped with the perfect pattern of Christ purpose. The total of these spiritualized cells throughout the body number 144,000.

9. Because of the influence of these perfect cells, the whole body, in the sum of all its cells and atoms, will be regenerated and brought into realignment with the ruling force of the developed Christ Consciousness.

Chapter 7 continued

11. And all the angels stood round about the throne, and about the elders and the four beasts, and fell before the throne on their faces, and worshipped God,

12. Saying, Amen: Blessing, and glory, and wisdom, and thanksgiving, and honour, and power, and might, be unto our God for ever and ever. Amen.

13. And one of the elders answered, saying unto me, What are these which are arrayed in white robes? and whence came they?

14. And I said unto him, Sir, thou knowest. And he said to me, These are they which came out of great tribulation, and have washed their robes, and made them white in the blood of the Lamb.

15. Therefore are they before the throne of God, and serve him day and night in his temple: and he that sitteth on the throne shall dwell among them.

16. They shall hunger no more, neither thirst any more; neither shall the sun light on them, nor any heat.

17. For the Lamb which is in the midst of the throne shall feed them, and shall lead them unto living fountains of waters: and God shall wipe away all tears from their eyes.

13. John senses that these cells have been purified and regenerated through the abrasion of their experiences in matter and can now be relied on for perfect service, without breaking down.

17. From now on, also, there will be no breakdown in their contact with the law of supply.

Chapter 8

1. And when he had opened the seventh seal, there was silence in heaven about the space of half an hour.

2. And I saw the seven angels which stood before God; and to them were given seven trumpets.

3. And another angel came and stood at the altar, having a golden censer; and there was given unto him much incense, that he should offer it with the prayers of all saints upon the golden altar which was before the throne.

4. And the smoke of the incense, which came with the prayers of the saints, ascended up before God out of the angel's hand.

5. And the angel took the censer, and filled it with fire of the altar, and cast it into the earth: and there were voices, and thunderings, and lightnings, and an earthquake.

6. And the seven angels which had the seven trumpets prepared themselves to sound.

7. The first angel sounded, and there followed hail and fire mingled with blood, and they were cast upon the earth: and the third part of trees was burnt up, and all green grass was burnt up.

8. And the second angel sounded, and as it were a great mountain burning with fire was cast into the sea: and the third part of the sea became blood;

9. And the third part of the creatures which were in the sea, and had life, died; and the third part of the ships were destroyed.

10. And the third angel sounded, and there fell a great star from heaven, burning as it were a lamp, and it fell upon the third part of the rivers, and upon the fountains of waters;

11. And the name of the star is called Wormwood: and the third part of the waters became wormwood; and many men died of the waters, because they were made bitter.

12. And the fourth angel sounded, and the third part of the sun was smitten, and the third part of the moon, and the third part of the stars; so as the third part of them was darkened, and the day shone not for a third part of it, and the night likewise.

13. And I beheld, and heard an angel flying through the midst of heaven, saying with a loud voice, Woe, woe, woe, to the inhabiters of the earth by reason of the other voices of the trumpet of the three angels, which are yet to sound.

SYMBOLOGY

SEVENTH SEAL—The pituitary.

SEVEN ANGELS—7 intelligences of endocrine system.

TRUMPETS—Impulses or vibrations which actually open centers.

GOLDEN CENSER—Pure Heart.

INCENSE—Good works. Note—These are as a result of right activity in the world.

HAIL AND FIRE MIXED WITH BLOOD—Purification through the sacrifice of ego.

SHIPS—Concepts deriving from emotional experiences.

RIVERS AND FOUNTAINS—Desires and urges from emotional level.

WORMWOOD—Disillusionment with old ideals.

SUN, MOON, AND STARS DARKENED—Loss of consciousness in all the parts.

INTERPRETATION

(Resumption after pause of opening 6 of the 7 centers.)

1. Now the OVERSELF opens the pituitary center, as a result of perfect control of the mind for half an hour. John sees the entire endocrine system being restored to the rightful position of command by the Superconscious, or OVERSELF. Next, the accumulated experience for good, won by the soul in the earth appears as a force, or intelligence itself. This mind force infuses the new material with the vitality of regeneration and injects it into the physical structure. The body reacts spasmodically.

6. As a result of the activity of pituitary, the entire endocrine system is recharged.

7. When the gonads release their hormones into the blood stream (under these conditions) purification of the organs begins, through the crystallizing of the emotions and a burning out of a portion of the growths and developments of the purely physical.

8. Next, the adrenals follow the example of the gonads in turn, removing the conflicts caused by the warring of the spiritual forces against the physical desires, and cleaning out old patterns of energy.

10. The lyden in turn, brings about correction of the ideals, which creates disillusionment with former forms and concepts.

11. The thymus activity results in partial loss of consciousness.

13. More upheavals in the body are promised as a result of the activity of the three upper centers, not yet heard from.

Chapter 9

1. And the fifth angel sounded, and I saw a star fall from heaven unto the earth: and to him was given the key of the bottomless pit.

2. And he opened the bottomless pit; and there arose a smoke out of the pit, as the smoke of a great furnace; and the sun and the air were darkened by reason of the smoke of the pit.

3. And there came out of the smoke locusts upon the earth: and unto them was given power, as the scorpions of the earth have power.

4. And it was commanded them that they should not hurt the grass of the earth, neither any green thing, neither any tree; but only those men which have not the seal of God in their foreheads.

5. And to them it was given that they should not kill them but that they should be tormented five months: and their torment was as the torment of a scorpion, when he striketh a man.

6. And in those days shall men seek death, and shall not find it; and shall desire to die, and death shall flee from them.

7. And the shapes of the locusts were like unto horses prepared unto battle; and on their heads were as it were crowns like gold, and their faces were as the faces of men.

8. And they had hair as the hair of women, and their teeth were as the teeth of lions.

9. And they had breastplates, as it were breastplates of iron; and the sound of their wings was as the sound of chariots of many horses running to battle.

10. And they had tails like unto scorpions, and there were stings in their tails: and their power was to hurt men five months.

11. And they had a king over them, which is the angel of the bottomless pit, whose name in the Hebrew tongue is Abaddon, but in the Greek tongue hath his name Apollyon.

12. One woe is past; and, behold, there come two woes more hereafter.

SYMBOLOGY

FIFTH ANGEL—Mind or intelligence of the thyroid.

BOTTOMLESS PIT—"ID," subconscious mind, area of repression.

SMOKE—Obscurity, confusion.

LOCUSTS—Repressed negative emotions.

GRASS—Growth, development.

FIVE MONTHS—Period.

KING OF BOTTOMLESS PIT—Self-will, lust.

FOUR ANGELS—Physical emotions, mental-spiritual nature.

HORSEMEN AND HORSES—Destroying forces from the "ID."

EUPHRATES—Beginning, original state.

FIRE, SMOKE, & BRIMSTONE—Process of purification through suffering.

TAILS—Regret, remorse.

DEVILS—Concepts, ideas that became Frankensteins.

IDOLS—False ideals.

MURDERS—Condemnation, slander.

SORCERIES—Manipulation for selfish gains.

FORNICATIONS—Misapplication of spiritual power.

THEFTS—Self-deception.

INTERPRETATION

1. The thyroid releases its hormone into the blood stream. Now the control of the "ID" or area of repression, is given over to the will, which deliberately releases the contents.

2. Consciousness is dimmed by the confusion brought about by the released negative repressions. Old regrets and guilt feelings are activated. Yet, these do not injure the natural growths or development, but strike at those cells which carry no pattern or program, of development in them. However "painful," this does not kill them.

7. The descriptions of the repressed thought-forms indicate malformation and a hybrid nature, *yet they carry force, in the power of their guilt feelings. These are the* creatures resulting from self will, or lusts in the body.

12. (Three mental centers are being activated here. Only the action of one has so far been given.)

Chapter 9 continued

13. And the sixth angel sounded, and I heard a voice from the four horns of the golden altar which is before God,

14. Saying to the sixth angel which had the trumpet, Loose the four angels which are bound in the great river Euphrates.

15. And the four angels were loosed, which were prepared for an hour, and a day, and a month, and a year, for to slay the third part of men.

16. And the number of the army of the horsemen were two hundred thousand thousand: and I heard the number of them.

17. And thus I saw the horses in the vision, and them that sat on them, having breastplates of fire, and of jacinth, and brimstone: and the heads of the horses were as the heads of lions; and out of their mouths issued fire and smoke and brimstone.

18. By these three was the third part of men killed, by the fire, and by the smoke, and by the brimstone, which issued out of their mouths.

19. For their power is in their mouth, and in their tails: for their tails were like unto serpents, and had heads, and with them they do hurt.

20. And the rest of the men which were not killed by these plagues yet repented not of the works of their hands, that they should not worship devils, and idols of gold, and silver, and brass, and stone, and of wood; which neither can see, nor hear, nor walk:

21. Neither repented they of their murders, nor of their sorceries, nor of their fornication, nor of their thefts.

13. The pineal now activates the latent energies retained in the 4 original elements of John's make-up, for changes in the physical, the emotional, the mental and the spiritual to be made through the practice of what he has learned.

18. A third part of the cells are purged yet those that are unaffected continue to manufacture false concepts, create Frankensteins and materiality, and go on misapplying the divine God-Force.

Chapter 10

1. And I saw another mighty angel come down from heaven, clothed with a cloud: and a rainbow was upon his head, and his face was as it were the sun, and his feet as pillars of fire:

2. And he had in his hand a little book open: and he set his right foot upon the sea, and his left foot on the earth,

3. And cried with a loud voice, as when a lion roareth: and when he had cried, seven thunders uttered their voices.

4. And when the seven thunders had uttered their voices, I was about to write: and I heard a voice from heaven saying unto me, Seal up those things which the seven thunders uttered, and write them not.

5. And the angel which I saw stand upon the sea and upon the earth lifted up his hand to heaven,

6. And sware by him that liveth for ever and ever, who created heaven, and the things that therein are, and the earth, and the things that therein are, and the sea and the things that are therein that there should be time no longer:

7. But in the days of the voice of the seventh angel, when he shall begin to sound, the mystery of God should be finished, as he hath declared to his servants the prophets.

8. And the voice which I heard from heaven spake unto me again, and said, Go and take the little book which is open in the hand of the angel which standeth upon the sea and upon the earth.

9. And I went unto the angel, and said unto him, Give me the little book. And he said unto me, Take it, and eat it up: and it shall make thy belly bitter, but it shall be in thy mouth sweet as honey.

10. And I took the little book out of the angel's hand, and ate it up; and it was in my mouth sweet as honey: and as soon as I had eaten it, my belly was bitter.

11. And he said unto me, Thou must prophesy again before many peoples, and nations, and tongues, and kings.

SYMBOLOGY

ANOTHER ANGEL—Another aspect of OVERSELF, superconscious mind.

LITTLE BOOK—The BODY.

RIGHT FOOT ON SEA—Understanding of emotional nature.

LEFT FOOT ON LAND—Understanding of physical nature.

SEVEN THUNDERS—Responses from seven centers of endocrine system.

BITTER IN THE BELLY—Difficult in experience as it is digested in application.

SWEET IN THE MOUTH—Pleasing to hear about—to contemplate.

PROPHESY—To apply.

INTERPRETATION

1. The OVERSELF is shown now in complete control of the body with all the endocrine centers open. He is shown master of the entire emotional and physical nature at this point.

3. He demonstrates his command over the seven centers.

4. John is forbidden to record the knowledge revealed in this demonstration, since he is not yet ready for a complete understanding of his divine nature.

6. Time shall be no more—4th-dimensional consciousness?

8. John is now urged to take over the body from the control and custody of the OVERSELF.

9. The OVERSELF, or Superconscious, tells him that mere knowledge of his divine-physical nature may be sweet to contemplate, but it is digested and made part of him only through the bitter experiences in the world through personal application.

10. John then found this out through his own experience.

11. He is now told that he must apply that which he has learned to all peoples, in all conditions.

Chapter 11

1. And there was given me a reed like unto a rod: and the angel stood, saying, Rise, and measure the temple of God, and the altar, and them that worship therein.

2. But the court which is without the temple leave out, and measure it not; for it is given unto the Gentiles; and the holy city shall they tread under foot forty and two months.

3. And I will give power unto my two witnesses, and they shall prophesy a thousand two hundred and three score days, clothed in sackcloth.

4. These are the two olive trees, and the two candlesticks standing before the God of the earth.

5. And if any man will hurt them, fire proceedeth out of their mouth, and devoureth their enemies; and if any man will hurt them, he must in this manner be killed.

6. These have power to shut heaven, that it rain not in the days of their prophecy; and have power over waters to turn them to blood, and to smite the earth with all plagues, as often as they will.

7. And when they shall have finished their testimony, the beast that ascendeth out of the bottomless pit shall make war against them, and shall overcome them, and kill them.

8. And their dead bodies shall lie in the street of the great city, which spiritually is called Sodom and Egypt, where also our Lord was crucified.

9. And they of the people and kindreds and tongues and nations shall see their dead bodies three days and a half, and shall not suffer their dead bodies to be put in graves.

SYMBOLOGY

ANGEL—OVERSELF, Superconscious.

REED—ROD—Conscience.

TEMPLE OF GOD—The body-mind.

ALTAR—Point of union.

COURT WITHOUT—The physical body.

GENTILE—Unspiritualized cells.

HOLY CITY—Point of overall control.

FORTY AND TWO MONTHS—1/2 period of regeneration, 3-1/2 yrs.

TWO WITNESSES—The subconscious and superconscious mind. 2 attributes of same—healing and supply.

BEAST FROM BOTTOMLESS PIT—Self-will, Lust.

SODOM AND EGYPT—Earthly experience leading to an awakening.

GRAVES—Darkness.

WOE—Trial or Test.

FOUR AND TWENTY ELDERS—The 24 cranial nerves to 5 senses.

ARK OF HIS TESTAMENT—The soul record, the akashic memory.

INTERPRETATION

NOTE: In chapter 11, the OVERSELF is showing John his relationship to *all Mankind,* in a collective sense; that the pattern of the Collective Soul follows the structure of the individual.

1. The OVERSELF instructs John to evaluate man's mind at the point of union between the human and the Divine. The physical intellect, however, is given over to conditions of limitation, which for a time will crush to earth the innate ideals. During this period, all results of these conditions are recorded and judged by the function of the subconscious and superconscious minds, bringing about cycles of natural retribution.

6. The subconscious and superconscious are the vehicles of the law of healing and supply and when their forces are wasted by the activities of lust and self will, their original function is lost for a time.

8. However, they are latent, not completely lost.

Chapter 11 continued

10. And they that dwell upon the earth shall rejoice over them, and make merry, and shall send gifts one to another; because these two prophets tormented them that dwelt on the earth.

11. And after three days and a half the Spirit of life from God entered into them, and they stood upon their feet; and great fear fell upon them which saw them.

12. And they heard a great voice from heaven saying unto them, Come up hither. And they ascended up to heaven in a cloud; and their enemies beheld them.

13. And the same hour was there a great earthquake, and the tenth part of the city fell, and in the earthquake were slain of men seven thousand: and the remnant were affrighted, and gave glory to the God of heaven.

14. The second woe is past; and, behold, the third woe cometh quickly.

15. And the seventh angel sounded; and there were great voices in heaven, saying, The kingdoms of this world are become the kingdoms of our Lord, and of his Christ; and he shall reign for ever and ever.

16. And the four and twenty elders, which sat before God on their seats, fell upon their faces, and worshipped God.

17. Saying, We give thee thanks, O Lord God Almighty, which art, and wast, and art to come; because thou has taken to thee thy great power, and hast reigned.

18. And the nations were angry, and thy wrath is come, and the time of the dead, that they should be judged, and that thou shouldest give reward unto thy servants the prophets, and to the saints, and them that fear thy name, small and great; and shouldest destroy them which destroy the earth.

19. And the temple of God was opened in heaven, and there was seen in his temple the ark of his testament; and there were lightnings, and voices, and thunderings, and an earthquake, and great hail.

10. The body now freed from these restricting factors now gives itself over to complete indulgence.

11. When these latent functions are reawakened, however, great changes in the body follow.

14. John's experience in regeneration has been completed, the pattern of Collective man's experience with the law of healing and supply has been laid out and now comes the redemption of the whole race as it acknowledges God as the source of all supply and healing, through a purging of the senses and universal enlightenment.

Chapter 12

1. And there appeared a great wonder in heaven; a woman clothed with the sun, and the moon under her feet, and upon her head a crown of twelve stars.

2. And she being with child cried, travailing in birth, and pained to be delivered.

3. And there appeared another wonder in heaven; and behold a great red dragon, having seven heads and ten horns, and seven crowns upon his heads.

4. And his tail drew the third part of the stars of heaven, and did cast them to the earth; and the dragon stood before the woman which was ready to be delivered, for to devour her child as soon as it was born.

5. And she brought forth a man child, who was to rule all nations with a rod of iron; and her child was caught up unto God, and to his throne.

6. And the woman fled into the wilderness, where she hath a place prepared of God, that they should feed her there a thousand two hundred and threescore days.

7. And there was war in heaven: Michael and his angels fought against the dragon; and the dragon fought and his angels.

8. And prevailed not; neither was their place found any more in heaven.

SYMBOLOGY

WOMAN—The soul, the record in a collective sense as the soul of Mankind, collective unconscious.

SUN, MOON, UNDER HER FEET—In control of vital forces, instincts.

CROWNED WITH 12 STARS—Perfect state.

CHILD—Active mental principle, the conscious mind.

RED DRAGON—Urges for rebellion on spiritual level.

SEVEN HEADS AND SEVEN CROWNS—Rebellious urges in control of endocrine centers.

TEN HORNS—Aggressive urges for self-gratification through senses.

ROD OF IRON—Symbol of control.

WILDERNESS—Below level of consciousness.

1260 DAYS—Period of passive state.

MICHAEL AND ANGELS—Protective forces.

WINGS OF EAGLE—Mental ability to rise above physical conditions.

WATER AS A FLOOD—Destructive emotions.

REMNANT OF HER SEED—Established ideals.

INTERPRETATION

N.B. John is now given a picture of the soul of Man in its development since the beginning in a historical sense—showing the relationship of the conscious mind to the subconscious, and which came first.

1. "The great wonder" is symbolic of the human soul, fully illumined and in control of consciousness, crowned with the twelve basic patterns of Man. Her child is the active principle of mind, the "conscious mind," as we call it. None of this is as yet come into materiality.

3. Simultaneously, a parallel activity takes place. With the coming of the conscious mind, the rival force of Self Will occurs, which brings about recurring periods of rebellion in Man.

5. However, through Divine intervention, the conscious mind is taken into "protective custody" while the unconscious mind from which it has sprung, is withdrawn below the conscious level, where it continues to be supplied for a period. (See Genesis 1, 2, 3—"Fall of Man.")

Chapter 12 continued

9. And the great dragon was cast out, that old serpent, called the Devil, and Satan, which deceiveth the whole world; he was cast out into the earth, and his angels were cast out with him.

10. And I heard a loud voice saying in heaven, Now is come salvation, and strength, and the kingdom of our God, and the power of his Christ; for the accuser of our brethren is cast down, which accused them before our God day and night.

11. And they overcame him by the blood of the Lamb, and by the word of their testimony; and they loved not their lives unto the death.

12. Therefore rejoice, ye heavens, and ye that dwell in them. Woe to the inhabiters of the earth and of the sea for the devil is come down unto you, having great wrath, because he knoweth that he hath but a short time.

13. And when the dragon saw that he was cast unto the earth, he persecuted the woman which brought forth the man child.

14. And to the woman were given two wings of a great eagle, that she might fly into the wilderness, into her place, where she is nourished for a time, and times, and half a time, from the face of the serpent.

15. And the serpent cast out of his mouth water as a flood after the woman, that he might cause her to be carried away of the flood.

16. And the earth helped the woman, and the earth opened her mouth, and swallowed up the flood which the dragon cast out of his mouth.

17. And the dragon was wroth with the woman, and went to make war with the remnant of her seed, which keep the commandments of God, and have the testimony of Jesus Christ.

9. The forces of rebellion are removed from the levels of mentality and now have their place in the body.

10, 11. It is now the duty of the human mind to control the rebellious urges coming from the physical as a result of experience in the world.

13. Rebellion from the physical next brings conflict into the soul (persecution) but the soul can remain above it by remaining concealed from the forces of Self-Will.

15. The emotions coming as a result of the struggles between the soul and Self-Will are absorbed by the body, but there remains ever the danger of continued attacks upon all established ideals.

Chapter 13

1. And I stood upon the sand of the sea, and saw a beast rise up out of the sea, having seven heads and ten horns, and upon his horns ten crowns, and upon his heads the name of blasphemy.

2. And the beast which I saw was like unto a leopard, and his feet were as the feet of a bear, and his mouth as the mouth of a lion; and the dragon gave him his power, and his seat, and great authority.

3. And I saw one of his heads as it were wounded to death; and his deadly wound was healed; and all the world wondered after the beast.

4. And they worshipped the dragon which gave power unto the beast: and they worshipped the beast, saying, Who is like unto the beast? Who is able to make war with him?

5. And there was given unto him a mouth speaking great things and blasphemies; and power was given unto him to continue forty and two months.

6. And he opened his mouth in blasphemy against God, to blaspheme his name, and his tabernacle and them that dwell in heaven.

7. And it was given unto him to make war with the saints, and to overcome them: and power was given him over all kindreds, and tongues, and nations.

8. And all that dwell upon the earth shall worship him, whose names are not written in the book of life of the Lamb slain from the foundation of the world.

9. If any man have an ear, let him hear.

10. He that leadeth into captivity shall go into captivity; he that killeth with the sword must be killed with the sword. Here is the patience and the faith of the saints.

SYMBOLOGY

SANDS OF SEAS—Detached state of observation.

BEAST—Emotional urges for expression of SELFISH desires.

ATTRIBUTES: LEOPARD—Treacherous. FEET OF BEAR—Blundering. MOUTH OF LION—Boastful. WOUND HEALED—Able to perform miracles.

WORLD—Mankind.

PATIENCE AND FAITH OF SAINTS—Experience in world.

ANOTHER BEAST—Mind on conscious level with power of choice between good and evil.

MARK OF BEAST—Pattern of animalistic behavior shown.

FOREHEAD—In mental, and HANDS—Creative activities.

NUMBER OF BEAST—666.

NUMBER OF MAN—666—The natural man as opposed to the evolved man.

INTERPRETATION

1. From a point of detached observation, John now perceives how forces for the expression of selfish desires arise through the emotions which are capable of ruling man. Attributes of these forces are treachery, error, and boastfulness. The power springs from the Self Will of the unspiritualized intellect of Man.

3. Because of ability of this force to bring about certain miraculous transformation, the world worships the intellect as a "symbol of success."

5. During the period of its apparent unobstructed license to indulge itself, the human intellect, lacking spiritual orientation, cuts itself off from all that is Divine.

7. Yet, so great is its influence that it begins to take control of all those in the world who have no particular belief in a higher power, who don't actually know in what they truly believe.

10. However, those who have overcome through experience in the world know that whatever appears to be happening, the law of Cause and Effect goes on perpetually and inexorably.

Chapter 13 continued

11. And I beheld another beast coming up out of the earth; and he had two horns like a lamb, and he spake as a dragon.

12. And he exerciseth all the power of the first beast before him, and causeth the earth and them which dwell therein to worship the first beast, whose deadly wound was healed.

13. And he doeth great wonders, so that he maketh fire come down from heaven on the earth in the sight of men,

14. And deceiveth them that dwell on the earth by the means of those miracles which he had power to do in the sight of the beast; saying to them that dwell on the earth, that they should make an image to the beast, which had the wound by a sword, and did live.

15. And he had power to give life unto the image of the beast, that the image of the beast should both speak, and cause that as many as would not worship the image of the beast should be killed.

16. And he causeth all, both small and great, rich and poor, free and bond, to receive a mark in their right hand, or in their foreheads:

17. And that no man might buy or sell, save he that had the mark, or the name of the beast, or the number of his name.

18. Here is wisdom. Let him that hath understanding count the number of the beast: for it is the number of a man; and his number is Six hundred threescore and six.

11. The unspiritualized mentality is shown as a deceiving intelligence which persuades mankind to embrace false values of what is wonderful and miraculous in the world, to set up discriminations against those who retain their spiritual values.

16. Thus all are forced to bind themselves to the institutions of the world and its systems.

18. The intellect can be either the instrument of man's salvation or his degeneration.

Chapter 14

1. And I looked, and, lo, a Lamb stood on the mount Sion, and with him an hundred forty and four thousand, having his Father's name written in their foreheads.

2. And I heard a voice from heaven, as the voice of many waters, and as the voice of a great thunder; and I heard the voice of harpers harping with their harps,

3. And they sung as it were a new song before the throne, and before the four beasts, and the elders: and no man could learn that song but the hundred and forty and four thousand, which were redeemed from the earth.

4. These are they which were not defiled with women; for they are virgins. These are they which follow the Lamb whithersoever he goeth. These were redeemed from among men, being the firstfruits unto God and to the Lamb.

5. And in their mouth was found no guile: for they are without fault before the throne of God.

6. And I saw another angel fly in the midst of heaven, having the everlasting gospel to preach unto them that dwell on the earth, and to every nation, and kindred, and tongue, and people,

7. Saying with a loud voice, Fear God, and give glory to him; for the hour of his judgment is come: and worship him that made heaven, and earth, and the sea, and the fountains of waters.

8. And there followed another angel, saying, Babylon is fallen, is fallen, that great city, because she made all nations drink of the wine of the wrath of her fornication.

9. And the third angel followed them, saying with a loud voice, If any man worship the beast and his image, and receive his mark in his forehead, or in his hand,

10. The same shall drink of the wine of the wrath of God, which is poured out without mixture into the cup of his indignation; and he shall be tormented with fire and brimstone in the presence of the holy angels, and in the presence of the Lamb:

11. And the smoke of their torment ascendeth up for ever and ever; and they have no rest day nor night, who worship the beast and his image, and whosoever receiveth the mark of his name.

SYMBOLOGY

LAMB—Christ Consciousness as developed through experience in the earth.

SION—Pituitary, point of contact with the superconscious.

144,000—Perfected souls of Mankind.

NEW SONG—Results of new experiences.

FIRST FRUITS—First manifestation of regeneration.

BABYLON—Ideals for earthly pleasures, self-gratification.

WINE OF THE WRATH OF HER FORNICATION—Consequences of prostitution of higher faculties.

WINE OF THE WRATH OF GOD—Workings of conscience.

FIRE AND BRIMSTONE—Remorse.

WHITE CLOUD—Collective unconscious.

SICKLE—Termination, cutting off.

VINE OF THE EARTH—Mankind.

GRAPES—Fruits, rewards.

WINEPRESS—Process for refining.

HORSEBRIDLES—Point of control.

1600 FURLONGS—Period of trial.

INTERPRETATION

1. John now observes, within the collective mind of man, the higher forces going into action. As the forces of Christ Consciousness in the world are maintained through the 144,000 perfect souls in the world, new experiences come about, not only in the presence of the Universal Forces, but also in that of the lower natures and the senses. However, the new experience that comes to each soul of the immanence of God as the source of all supply is limited to those who have exercised self-control throughout.

6. Worship of God is urged and recommended.

8. As the teachers in the world seek to have mankind glorify God, it is shown at a point that the pattern for earthly riches and success in the gratification of the senses is breaking up as the forces for balance in the world bring men into contact with the consequences of their prostitution of their higher faculties and talents.

Chapter 14 continued

12. Here is the patience of the saints, here are they that keep the commandments of God, and the faith of Jesus.

13. And I heard a voice from heaven saying unto me, Write, Blessed are the dead which die in the Lord from henceforth: Yea, saith the Spirit, that they may rest from their labours; and their works do follow them.

14. And I looked, and behold a white cloud, and upon the cloud one sat like unto the Son of man, having on his head a golden crown and in his hand a sharp sickle.

15. And another angel came out of the temple, crying with a loud voice to him that sat on the cloud, Thrust in thy sickle, and reap: for the time is come for thee to reap; for the harvest of the earth is ripe.

16. And he that sat on the cloud thrust in his sickle on the earth; and the earth was reaped.

17. And another angel came out of the temple which is in heaven, he also having a sharp sickle.

18. And another angel came out from the altar, which had power over fire; and cried with a loud cry to him that had the sharp sickle, saying, Thrust in thy sharp sickle, and gather the clusters of the vine of the earth: for her grapes are fully ripe.

19. And the angel thrust in his sickle into the earth, and gathered the vine of the earth, and cast it into the great winepress of the wrath of God.

20. And the winepress was trodden without the city, and blood came out of the winepress, even unto the horse bridles, by the space of a thousand and six hundred furlongs.

12. Yet, as even these realized their mistakes and seek to change, realizing that only the body is bound, these find redemption, too.

14. As the OVERSELF of the collective unconscious judges the world, each soul reaps according to what he has sown, and the experience each has had in the world is now refined and ennobled to be made acceptable in the light of the Christ Pattern, by bringing these under control also during the period of trial.

Chapter 15

1. And I saw another sign in heaven, great and marvellous, seven angels having the seven last plagues; for in them is filled up the wrath of God.

2. And I saw as it were a sea of glass mingled with fire: and them that had gotten the victory over the beast, and over his image, and over his mark, and over the number of his name, stand on the sea of glass, having the harps of God.

3. And they sing the song of Moses the servant of God, and the song of the Lamb, saying, Great and marvellous are thy works, Lord God Almighty; just and true are thy ways, thou King of saints.

4. Who shall not fear thee, O Lord, and glorify thy name? for thou only art holy: for all nations shall come and worship before thee; for thy judgments are made manifest.

5. And after that I looked, and, behold, the temple of the tabernacle of the testimony in heaven was opened:

6. And the seven angels came out of the temple, having the seven plagues, clothed in pure and white linen, and having their breasts girded with golden girdles.

7. And one of the four beasts gave unto the seven angels seven golden vials full of the wrath of God, who liveth for ever and ever.

8. And the temple was filled with smoke from the glory of God, and from his power; and no man was able to enter into the temple, till the seven plagues of the seven angels were fulfilled.

SYMBOLOGY

SEVEN LAST PLAGUES—Trials in which the soul may overcome its Karma.

SEA OF GLASS MINGLED WITH FIRE—Emotions stilled through purification.

THE SONG OF MOSES—The Law.

THE SONG OF THE LAMB—Regeneration.

TEMPLE of the TABERNACLE of the TESTIMONY—Individual akashic record—Soul memory.

SEVEN ANGELS—Intelligence of the seven centers of the endocrine system of Man.

FOUR BEASTS—4 lower centers of the endocrine system.

SMOKE—from the GLORY OF GOD—Ability to forget.

INTERPRETATION

1. John perceives now within the soul of Man, or that known as the collective unconscious, the souls of individual men are purified and tested on seven levels of consciousness (as he has already found in his own experience).

2. The 144,000 perfect souls by reason of their own integrated state of emotional and spiritual natures, remain stable in the face of any eventuality because they bear within themselves the stamp of Law—that is to say, Divine Law, or purpose.

5. John perceives that all men encounter the condition sooner or later, where the experience of the four lower centers, the mentality of same that is, come against the perfect patterns for those centers.

N.B. This might be described as the activation of conscience—since the discrepancies between the perfect pattern and the actual experiences are now shown up in bold relief.

8. The final steps of the individual for perfect service take place within the mind as all guilt feelings, which result from these sevenfold tests, arise to cloud the mind for this period. When all seven levels have been purified, then and only then can a man achieve mastery of himself.

Chapter 16

1. And I heard a great voice out of the temple saying to the seven angels, Go your ways, and pour out the vials of the wrath of God upon the earth.

2. And the first went, and poured out his vial upon the earth; and there fell a noisome and grievous sore upon the men which had the mark of the beast, and upon them which worshipped his image.

3. And the second angel poured out his vial upon the sea; and it became as the blood of a dead man: and every living soul died in the sea.

4. And the third angel poured out his vial upon the rivers and fountains of waters, and they became blood.

5. And I heard the angel of the waters say, Thou art righteous, O Lord, which art, and wast, and shalt be, because thou hast judged thus.

6. For they have shed the blood of saints and prophets, and thou hast given them blood to drink; for they are worthy.

7. And I heard another out of the altar say, Even so, Lord God Almighty, true and righteous are thy judgments.

8. And the fourth angel poured out his vial upon the sun; and power was given unto him to scorch men with fire.

9. And men were scorched with great heat, and blasphemed the name of God, which hath power over these plagues: and they repented not to give him glory.

SYMBOLOGY

GREAT VOICE—Overself, superconscious mind.

VIALS of the WRATH of GOD—Karma—Consequences.

NOISOME and GRIEVOUS SORE—Results of misuse of creative forces.

BLOOD of a DEAD MAN—Loss of sensitivity—Deadened emotions.

RIVERS and FOUNTAINS—Sources of life and energy.

SAINTS and PROPHETS—Spiritualized cells devitalized.

SUN—Consciousness.

FIRE—Remorse.

SEAT of the BEAST—Animal instincts.

HIS KINGDOM (Beasts)—Thyroid area—Will.

DARKNESS—Unconsciousness.

EUPHRATES—Boundary.

KINGS OF THE EAST—New beginnings.

UNCLEAN SPIRITS LIKE FROGS—Distortions of intellect.

ARMAGEDDON—Conflict.

AIR—Mental level.

GREAT CITY BABYLON—Man's established systems.

ISLAND—State of limitation.

MOUNTAIN—Conferred, but unearned authority.

FALSE PROPHET—Self-delusion.

INTERPRETATION

1. Instructions are now issued for the purification of the gonads, which John witnesses. Physical diseases follow as a result of the misuse of the sex forces, in opposition to the pattern of perfection carried with them.

3. The misuse of the forces of the adrenals result in sapped energies and the misuse of the forces of leydig bring about a shutting off of the powers of natural healing and supply.

5. This has always been sensed by man through his emotional and mental-spiritual nature as the law governing each. (In other words, "this has always been generally known.")

8. Misapplied love, as on the thymus level, reacts as a consuming force upon the individual. (Love must go out, not in.)

Chapter 16 continued

10. And the fifth angel poured out his vial upon the seat of the beast; and his kingdom was full of darkness; and they gnawed their tongues for pain.

11. And blasphemed the God of heaven because of their pains and their sores, and repented not of their deeds.

12. And the sixth angel poured out his vial upon the great river Euphrates; and the water thereof was dried up, that the way of kings of the east might be prepared.

13. And I saw three unclean spirits like frogs come out of the mouth of the dragon, and out of the mouth of the beast, and out of the mouth of the false prophet.

14. For they are the spirits of devils, working miracles, which go forth unto the kings of the earth and of the whole world, to gather them to the battle of that great day of God Almighty.

15. Behold, I come as a thief. Blessed is he that watcheth and keepeth his garments, lest he walk naked, and they see his shame.

16. And he gathered them together into a place called in the Hebrew tongue Armageddon.

17. And the seventh angel poured out his vial into the air; and there came a great voice out of the temple of heaven, from the throne, saying, It is done.

18. And there were voices, and thunders, and lightnings; and there was a great earthquake, such as was not since men were upon the earth, so mighty an earthquake, and so great.

19. And the great city was divided into three parts, and the cities of the nations fell: and great Babylon came in remembrance before God, to give unto her the cup of the wine of the fierceness of his wrath.

20. And every island fled away, and the mountains were not found.

21. And there fell upon men a great hail out of heaven, every stone about the weight of a talent; and men blasphemed God because of the plague of the hail; for the plague thereof was exceeding great.

10. Also, misuse of the thyroid forces bring about the penalties of self-will. (Stubbornness, bull-headedness, etc.)

12. When the Stream of Memory is dried up, on the pineal level in its turn (cosmic memory on conscious level) new beginnings are possible for the physical, the emotions, and the mental.

13. Propaganda (distortions) stemming from wrong emotional, mental and physical action, become ranged in time against universal truth. This brings about conflict in the world between groups and government.

17. Completion of the seven ordeals comes when man's institutions and structures (financial, educational, etc.) collapse, concepts and achievements are swept away, because universal truth is fixed, or crystallized.

Chapter 17

1. And there came one of the seven angels which had the seven vials and talked with me, saying unto me, Come hither; I will shew unto thee the judgment of the great whore that sitteth upon many waters;

2. With whom the kings of the earth have committed fornication, and the inhabitants of the earth have been made drunk with the wine of her fornication.

3. So he carried me away in the spirit into the wilderness: and I saw a woman sit upon a scarlet colored beast, full of names of blasphemy, having seven heads and ten horns.

4. And the woman was arrayed in purple and scarlet colour, and decked with gold and precious stones and pearls, having a golden cup in her hand full of abominations and filthiness of her fornication.

5. And upon her forehead was a name written, MYSTERY, BABYLON THE GREAT, THE MOTHER OF HARLOTS AND ABOMINATIONS OF THE EARTH.

6. And I saw the woman drunken with the blood of the saints, and with the blood of the martyrs of Jesus: And when I saw her, I wondered with great admiration.

7. And the angel said unto me, Wherefore didst thou marvel? I will tell thee the mystery of the woman, and of the beast that carrieth her, which hath the seven heads and ten horns.

8. The beast that thou sawest was, and is not; and shall ascend out of the bottomless pit, and go into perdition: and they that dwell on the earth shall wonder, whose names were not written in the book of life from the foundation of the world, when they behold the beast that was, and is not, and yet is.

9. And here is the mind which hath wisdom, The seven heads are seven mountains, on which the woman sitteth.

SYMBOLOGY

ONE OF SEVEN ANGELS—Intelligence on level of Pituitary.

JUDGMENT—The fate of the GREAT WHORE—Lust, desire.

WILDERNESS—Collective unconscious.

WOMAN—WHORE OF BABYLON—Lust.

SCARLET-COLORED BEAST—the Dragon—Urges for rebellion on spiritual level.

GOLDEN CUP of ABOMINATIONS—Fruits of lust.

BABYLON the GREAT—Manmade patterns of self-gratification.

DRUNKEN WITH THE BLOOD of SAINTS—Has drained energy from mind cells or intelligences.

SEVEN MOUNTAINS—Seven levels of endocrine activity dominated by self-gratification.

SEVEN KINGS—Seven periods of rulership—Phases.

THE BEAST—Manmade ideals.

TEN HORNS—Urges.

INTERPRETATION

1. John is to be shown the fate of Man's own lusts, his concepts of what would be pleasurable and satisfying in the world, as experienced through the emotions in all peoples.

2. The controlling intelligences of the body as well as the senses have been brought low by misapplication of the spiritual forces through lust.

3. In the depths of the collective "ID" so to speak, John is shown the archetype of lust and the emotional forces of rebellion that feed it and keep it alive.

6. These emotional forces are drawn from the energies of the mind centers within all parts of Man's body, thus depriving or limiting the normal supply for bodily parts.

7. It is explained to John that the influences from the "ID" as shown in the beast, have taken control of the seven centers of Man's endocrine system and through this, man is possessed and ruled.

Chapter 17 continued

10. And there are seven kings: five are fallen, and one is, and the other is not yet come; and when he cometh, he must continue a short space.

11. And the beast that was, and is not, even he is the eighth, and is of the seven, and goeth into perdition.

12. And the ten horns which thou sawest are ten kings, which have received no kingdom as yet; but received power as kings one hour with the beast.

13. These have one mind, and shall give their power and strength unto the beast.

14. These shall make war with the Lamb, and the Lamb shall overcome them: for he is Lord of lords, and King of kings: and they that are with him are called and chosen, and faithful.

15. And he saith unto me, The waters which thou sawest, where the whore sitteth, are peoples, and multitudes, and nations, and tongues.

16. And the ten horns which thou sawest upon the beast, these shall hate the whore, and shall make her desolate and naked, and shall eat her flesh, and burn her with fire.

17. For God hath put in their hearts to fulfil his will, and to agree, and give their kingdom unto the beast, until the words of God shall be fulfilled.

18. And the woman which thou sawest is that great city, which reigneth over the kings of the earth.

10. As a result, seven successive cultural cycles are rotated throughout history through the actions of collective man, each one embodying the strengths and weakness contained in the pattern of each center. (As within, so without.) These are the urges that keep peace from the earth—basic urges of man—which result.

14. However, as the highest forces of evolving man overcome the forces of self, even the ten basic urges will, in time, fulfill the Divine pattern.

18. The archetype of destructive intelligence which rules man through the senses, is manmade.

Chapter 18

1. And after these things I saw another angel come down from heaven, having great power; and the earth was lightened with his glory.

2. And he cried mightily with a strong voice, saying, Babylon the great is fallen, is fallen, and is become the habitation of devils, and the hold of every foul spirit, and a cage of every unclean and hateful bird.

3. For all nations have drunk of the wine of the wrath of her fornication, and the kings of the earth have committed fornication with her, and the merchants of the earth are waxed rich through the abundance of her delicacies.

4. And I heard another voice from heaven, saying, Come out of her, my people, that ye be not partakers of her sins, and that ye receive not of her plagues.

5. For her sins have reached unto heaven, and God hath remembered her iniquities.

6. Reward her even as she rewarded you, and double unto her double according to her works: in the cup which she hath filled, fill to her double.

7. How much she hath glorified herself, and lived deliciously, so much torment and sorrow give her: for she saith in her heart, I sit a queen, and am no widow, and shall see no sorrow.

8. Therefore shall her plagues come in one day, death, and mourning, and famine; and she shall be utterly burned with fire: for strong is the Lord God who judgeth her.

9. And the kings of the earth, who have committed fornication and lived deliciously with her, shall bewail her, and lament for her, when they shall see the smoke of her burning,

10. Standing afar off for the fear of her torment, saying, Alas, alas, that great city Babylon, that mighty city! for in one hour is thy judgment come.

11. And the merchants of the earth shall weep and mourn over her; for no man buyeth their merchandise any more:

12. The merchandise of gold, and silver, and precious stones, and of pearls, and fine linen, and purple, and silk, and scarlet, and all thyine wood, and all manner vessels of ivory, and all manner vessels of most precious wood, and of brass, and iron, and marble,

SYMBOLOGY

ANGEL—Intelligence.

BABYLON—Manmade ideals of patterns for self-gratification.

BLOOD of the PROPHETS and of SAINTS—Divine energies that were taken over and used for selfish purposes.

INTERPRETATION

1. The Instructor enlightens John that, at a point, the archetype for self-gratification which man has created for himself, bogs down through the very complicity and intricacies of its own creations.

3. All people and all human institutions have been deluded and weakened through following a course of self-gratification.

4. The divine nature in Man is withdrawn from the archetype which is abandoned to its own destruction.

9. The senses will record a sense of loss of the stimulations and excitements of the archetype for selfish expression, but by implication, adjustment to the new conditions is called for.

Chapter 18 continued

13. And cinnamon, and odours, and ointments, and frankincense, and wine, and oil, and fine flour, and wheat, and beasts, and sheep, and horses, and chariots, and slaves, and souls of men.

14. And the fruits that thy soul lusted after are departed from thee, and all things which were dainty and goodly are departed from thee, and thou shalt find them no more at all.

15. The merchants of these things, which were made rich by her, shall stand afar off for the fear of her torment, weeping and wailing.

16. And saying, Alas, alas, that great city, that was clothed in fine linen, and purple, and scarlet, and decked with gold, and precious stones, and pearls!

17. For in one hour so great riches is come to naught. And every shipmaster, and all the company in ships, and sailors, and as many as trade by sea stood afar off,

18. And cried when they saw the smoke of her burning, saying, What city is like unto this great city!

19. And they cast dust on their heads, and cried, weeping and wailing, saying, Alas, alas, that great city, wherein were made rich all that had ships in the sea by reason of her costliness! for in one hour is she made desolate.

20. Rejoice over her, thou heaven, and ye holy apostles and prophets; for God hath avenged you on her.

21. And a mighty angel took up a stone like a great millstone, and cast it into the sea, saying, Thus with violence shall that great city Babylon be thrown down, and shall be found no more at all.

22. And the voice of harpers, and musicians, and of pipers, and trumpeters, shall be heard no more at all in thee; and no craftsman, of whatsoever craft he be, shall be found any more in thee; and the sound of a millstone shall be heard no more at all in thee.

23. And the light of a candle shall shine no more at all In thee; and the voice of the bridegroom and of the bride shall be heard no more at all in thee: for thy merchants were the great men of the earth; for by thy sorceries were all nations deceived.

24. And in her was found the blood of prophets, and of saints, and of all that were slain upon the earth.

24. The energies drawn from useful bodily, mental and spiritual functions in man are shown to have been the nourishment upon which this pattern of Man's collective selfishness has fed.

Chapter 19

1. And after these things I heard a great voice of much people in heaven, saying, Alleluia; Salvation, and glory, and honour, and power, unto the Lord our God:

2. For true and righteous are his judgments; for he hath judged the great whore, which did corrupt the earth with her fornication, and hath avenged the blood of his servants at her hand.

3. And again they said, Alleluia. And her smoke rose up for ever and ever.

4. And the four and twenty elders and the four beasts fell down and worshipped God that sat on the throne, saying, Amen; Alleluia.

5. And a voice came out of the throne, saying, Praise our God, all ye his servants, and ye that fear him, both small and great.

6. And I heard as it were the voice of a great multitude, and as the voice of many waters, and as the voice of mighty thunderings, saying, Alleluia: for the Lord God omnipotent reigneth.

7. Let us be glad and rejoice, and give honour to him: for the marriage of the Lamb is come, and his wife hath made herself ready.

8. And to her was granted that she should be arrayed in fine linen, clean and white: for the fine linen is the righteousness of saints.

9. And he saith unto me, Write, Blessed are they which are called unto the marriage supper of the Lamb. And he saith unto me, These are the true sayings of God.

SYMBOLOGY

FOUR and TWENTY ELDERS—The senses.

FOUR BEASTS—4 lower centers.

MARRIAGE of the LAMB—Union of the evolved self with the OVERSELF, on superconscious level.

WIFE—Overself —so described because of its passive role.

MARRIAGE SUPPER of the LAMB—Mastery of the Law.

VOICE out of THRONE—Overself, superconscious Mind.

FAITHFUL and TRUE on WHITE HORSE—OVERSELF, united with evolved self, now able to *act* as one.

WORD of GOD—CHRIST the LOGOS—Fulfilled pattern.

KING of KINGS and LORD of LORDS—Same.

FOWLS—Thoughts.

FLESH—Earthly experiences.

LAKE OF FIRE BURNING WITH BRIMSTONE—"ID" subconscious area of repression.

INTERPRETATION

N.B. In chapter 11, what was the final salvation of the bodily, mental, spiritual forces in John as an individual, now are shown to take place in collective man.

1. When Man instinctively recognizes the Divinity within him *as* the controlling force in the world, and turns away from his own selfish pattern of living for self alone, the pattern disappears and the senses together with the four lower centers are realigned with the Creative Forces.

N.B. The Intelligence who takes over John's instruction now is the OVERSELF of collective Man, the Pattern for Mankind.

7. This instructor points out that the merging of the evolved self with the Overself which has taken place with him (John) must also take place in all men.

Chapter 19 continued

10. And I fell at his feet to worship him, And he said unto me, See thou do it not: I am thy fellow servant, and of thy brethren that have the testimony of Jesus: worship God: for the testimony of Jesus is the spirit of prophecy.

11. And I saw heaven opened, and behold a white horse; and he that sat upon him was called Faithful and True, and in righteousness he doth judge and make war.

12. His eyes were as a flame of fire, and on his head were many crowns; and he had a name written, that no man knew, but he himself.

13. And he was clothed with a vesture dipped in blood: and his name is called The Word of God.

14. And the armies which were in heaven followed him upon white horses, clothed in fine linen, white and clean.

15. And out of hls mouth goeth a sharp sword, that with it he should smite the nations and he shall rule them with a rod of iron: and he treadeth the winepress of the fierceness and wrath of Almighty God.

16. And he hath on his vesture and on his thigh a name written, KING OF KINGS, AND LORD OF LORDS.

17. And I saw an angel standing in the sun; and he cried with a loud voice, saying to all the fowls that fly in the midst of heaven, Come and gather yourselves together unto the supper of the great God;

18. That ye may eat the flesh of kings, and the flesh of captains, and the flesh of mighty men, and the flesh of horses, and of them that sit on them, and the flesh of all men, both free and bond, both small and great.

19. And I saw the beast, and the kings of the earth, and their armies, gathered together to make war against him that sat on the horse, and against his army.

20. And the beast was taken, and with him the false prophet that wrought miracles before him with which he deceived them that had received the mark of the beast, and them that worshipped his image. These both were cast alive into a lake of fire burning with brimstone.

21. And the remnant were slain with the sword of him that sat upon the horse, which sword proceeded out of his mouth: and all the fowls were filled with their flesh.

10. John seeks to worship his instructor, but is warned against it, having a mission to perform as John has. He is told to worship God (the unformed) for the stamp of the Christ pattern is in the constant application of Divine truth.

11. The fulfilled pattern of evolved Man, the Christ, is shown now in a position of stability, power and judgment. All rulership of divine and worldly forces are turned over to Him. He is in control of the law of cause and effect—karma. He is able to feed his mind on all that is best in earth experience and draw sustenance from it, but to reject the former lusts and errors. (Individualized Man has merged with collective self.)

Chapter 20

1. And I saw an angel come down from heaven, having the key of the bottomless pit and a great chain in his hand.

2. And he laid hold on the dragon, that old serpent, which is the Devil, and Satan, and bound him a thousand years,

3. And cast him into the bottomless pit, and shut him up, and set a seal upon him, that he should deceive the nations no more, till the thousand years should be fulfilled: and after that he must be loosed a little season.

4. And I saw thrones, and they sat upon them and judgment was given unto them, and I saw the souls of them that were beheaded for the witness of Jesus, and for the word of God, and which had not worshipped the beast, neither his image, neither had received his mark upon their foreheads, or in their hands; and they lived and reigned with Christ a thousand years.

5. But the rest of the dead lived not again until the thousand years were finished. This is the first resurrection.

6. Blessed and holy is he that hath part in the first resurrection: on such the second death hath no power, but they shall be priests of God and of Christ, and shall reign with him a thousand years.

7. And when the thousand years are expired, Satan shall be loosed out of his prison.

8. And shall go out to deceive the nations which are in the four quarters of the earth, Gog and Magog, to gather them together to battle: the number of whom is as the sand of the sea.

9. And they went up on the breadth of the earth, and compassed the camp of the saints about, and the beloved city: and fire came down from God out of heaven, and devoured them.

10. And the devil that deceived them was cast into the lake of fire and brimstone, where the beast and the false prophet are, and shall be tormented day and night for ever and ever.

11. And I saw a great white throne, and him that sat on it, from whose face the earth and the heaven fled away; and there was found no place for them.

SYMBOLOGY

A GREAT CHAIN—Restraint.

FIRST RESURRECTION—Rebirth of advanced souls.

GOG and MAGOG—Worldly influences.

GREAT WHITE THRONE—Universal point of emanation and return of souls.

THE DEAD IN JUDGMENT—Returning souls.

BOOK of LIFE—Akashic record.

SEA—Emotions.

DEATH—Unconscious state.

HELL—Remorse and frustration.

SECOND DEATH—Destruction of all manmade Frankenstein conditions.

INTERPRETATION

1. Now the archetype of Man's continual rebellions, the self-willed intellect, itself is confined for a time in the collective ID.

4. During this thousand year period only the evolved souls incarnate in the earth. (With these souls all in perfect balance they would bring balance into the very forces of earth itself, perfect peace and harmony to Nature itself.)

5. At the close of the thousand year period, the remaining souls begin to incarnate, bringing with them their unsatisfied ambitions and desires. This, of course, brings about the former conditions of imbalance. (Wars—plagues.)

9, 10. Now the evolved souls are surrounded and their activities curtailed by the unregenerate souls, who only succeed in destroying their physical selves through tampering with natural forces. Once again they must await reincarnation.

11. Here John beholds the universal point of Divine emanation as the point of Judgment which is unbiased by material ideals or considerations.

Chapter 20 continued

12. And I saw the dead, small and great, stand before God; and the books were opened: and another book was opened, which is the book of life; and the dead were judged out of those things which were written in the books, according to their works.

13. And the sea gave up the dead which were in it and death and hell delivered up the dead which were in them: and they were judged every man according to their works.

14. And death and hell were cast into the lake of fire. This is the second death.

15. And whosoever was not found written in the book of life was cast into the lake of fire.

12. Before this judgment, not only are the individual soul records scanned but also the record for Collective Man, Akasha.

13. Those souls entrapped by uncontrolled emotions, as well as those trapped by their own frustrations and remorse are now freed.

14. These conditions, all manmade, are now themselves eliminated and all creatures, mental forms and patterns, not formed by Divine Will are purged.

Chapter 21

1. And I saw a new heaven and a new earth: for the first heaven and the first earth were passed away; and there was no more sea.

2. And I John saw the holy city, new Jerusalem, coming down from God out of heaven, prepared as a bride adorned for her husband.

3. And I heard a great voice out of heaven saying, Behold, the tabernacle of God is with men, and he will dwell with them, and they shall be his people, and God himself shall be with them, and be their God.

4. And God shall wipe away all tears from their eyes; and there shall be no more death, neither sorrow, nor crying, neither shall there be any more pain: for the former things are passed away.

5. And he that sat upon the throne said, Behold, I make all things new. And he said unto me, Write, for these words are true and faithful.

6. And he said unto me, It is done. I am Alpha and Omega, the beginning and the end. I will give unto Him that is athirst of the fountain of the water of life freely.

7. He that overcometh shall inherit all things; and I will be his God, and he shall be my son.

8. But the fearful, and unbelieving, and the abominable, and murderers, and whoremongers, and sorcerers, and idolaters, and all liars, shall have their part in the lake which burneth with fire and brimstone: which is the second death.

9. And there came unto me one of the seven angels which had the seven vials full of the seven last plagues, and talked with me saying, Come hither, I will shew thee the bride, the Lamb's wife.

10. And he carried me away in the spirit to a great and high mountain, and shewed me that great city, the holy Jerusalem, descending out of heaven from God,

11. Having the glory of God: and her light was like unto a stone most precious, even like a jasper stone, clear as crystal;

SYMBOLOGY

A NEW HEAVEN—A perfected state of consciousness.

A NEW EARTH—A perfected integrated body.

NEW JERUSALEM—State of the evolved soul.

TABERNACLE of GOD—Superconscious.

12 GATES; 12 ANGELS; 12 TRIBES; 12 FOUNDATIONS—12 basic patterns of action.

3 GATES to a SIDE—3 dimensional; time, space, motion.

FOURSQUARE—Perfection in 3 dimensions.

MEASURE of a MAN; MEASURE of the ANGEL—144 perfect units (Man now in a state of complete superconsciousness).

12 APOSTLES—12 active principles of same.

12,000 FURLONGS - Measurement of perfection.

144 CUBITS—Perfected man angel-spiritual pattern.

12 PRECIOUS STONES—12 fruits of active principles of 12 basic patterns.

INTERPRETATION

1. John envisions a perfected state of consciousness and a regenerated body, with the elimination of all unstable emotional behavior.

2. As a result of these conditions, the completed fulfilled soul record of Man moves into place containing all the riches of earthly experience in presentable order.

3. It is explained that the Divine touches Man at the level of the superconscious in indissoluble union with man. (In a collective sense, as well as individual.)

4. In the new state, an end is brought to the "abrasion" of natural experience in the world. The formed conditions have passed.

5. The Collective Superconscious calls attention to his powers for regeneration and bids John record the fact. The Superconscious is custodian of all Supply, and when an individual establishes self control, supply control will be restored to him.

8. The fearful, the unbelieving, the impostors, etc., do not experience this since they have cut themselves off.

9. The OVERSELF, speaking on the level of the pituitary offers to explain John's relationship to himself.

10. The soul record of Man is reviewed which contains twelve basic human patterns in terms of recorded time, space and motion.

Chapter 21 continued

12. And had a wall great and high, and had twelve gates, and at the gates twelve angels, and names written thereon, which are the names of the twelve tribes of the children of Israel:

13. On the east three gates; on the north three gates, on the south three gates; and on the west three gates.

14. And the wall of the city had twelve foundations, and in them the names of the twelve apostles of the Lamb.

15. And he that talked with me had a golden reed to measure the city, and the gates thereof, and the wall thereof.

16. And the city lieth foursquare, and the length is as large as the breadth: and he measured the city with the reed, twelve thousand furlongs. The length and the breadth and the height of it are equal.

17. And he measured the wall thereof, a hundred and forty and four cubits, according to the measure of a man, that is, of the angel.

18. And the building of the wall of it was of jasper: and the city was pure gold, like unto clear glass.

19. And the foundations of the wall of the city were garnished with all manner of precious stones. The first foundation was jasper; the second, sapphire; the third, a chalcedony; the fourth an emerald;

20. The fifth, sardonyx; the sixth, sardius; the seventh, chrysolyte; the eighth, beryl; the ninth, a topaz, the tenth, a chrysoprasus; the eleventh, a jacinth; the twelfth, an amethyst.

21. And the twelve gates were twelve pearls; every several gate was of one pearl; and the street of the city was pure gold, as it were transparent glass.

22. And I saw no temple therein: for the Lord God Almighty and the Lamb are the temple of it.

23. And the city had no need of the sun, neither of the moon, to shine in it: for the glory of God did lighten it, and the Lamb is the light thereof.

24. And the nations of them which are saved shall walk in the light of it: and the kings of the earth do bring their glory and honour into it.

25. And the gates of it shall not be shut at all by day: for there shall be no night there.

26. And they shall bring the glory and honour of the nations into it.

27. And there shall in no wise enter into it any thing that defileth, neither whatsoever worketh abomination or maketh a lie: but they which are written in the Lamb's book of life.

15, 17. Its perfection is gauged according to the standard always carried within the Superconscious—OVERSELF, and the attributes listed which symbolize man's perfected experiences in the world.

22, 27. Man's mind at this point is now divine in the perfection of control and is free of outside limitation.

Chapter 22

1. And he shewed me a pure river of water of life, clear as crystal, proceeding out of the throne of God and of the Lamb.

2. In the midst of the street of it, and on either side of the river, was there the tree of life, which bare twelve manner of fruits, and yielded her fruit every month: and the leaves of the tree were for the healing of the nations.

3. And there shall be no more curse: but the throne of God and of the Lamb shall be in it; and his servants shall serve him:

4. And they shall see his face; and his name shall be in their foreheads.

5. And there shall be no night there; and they need no candle, neither light of the sun; for the Lord God giveth them light: and they shall reign for ever and ever.

6. And he said unto me, These sayings are faithful and true: and the Lord God of the Holy prophets sent his angel to shew unto his servants the things which must shortly be done.

7. Behold, I come quickly; blessed is he that keepeth the sayings of the prophecy of this book.

8. And I John saw these things, and heard them. And when I had heard and seen, I fell down to worship before the feet of the angel which shewed me these things.

9. Then saith he unto me, See thou do it not: for I am thy fellowservant, and of thy brethren the prophets, and of them which keep the sayings of this book: worship God.

10. And he saith unto me, Seal not the sayings of the prophecy of this book: for the time is at hand.

11. He that is unjust, let him be unjust still: and he which is filthy, let him be filthy still: and he that is righteous, let him be righteous still: and he that is holy, let him be holy still.

12. And, behold, I come quickly: and my reward is with me, to give every man according as his work shall be.

13. I am Alpha and Omega, the beginning and the end, the first and the last.

SYMBOLOGY

PURE RIVER, etc.—Combined will of God and Man.

STREET of it—Channel.

TREE OF LIFE—Function of supply, healing and generation within the soul.

12 MANNER OF FRUITS—Supply for 12 major portions of body mind and soul.

EVERY MONTH—Regularly.

CURSE—(Adamic)—Limitation of Man.

THRONE of GOD and the LAMB—Man in complete superconsciousness as his normal state.

SERVANTS—Those forces under an individual's control—abilities.

ANGEL of the Lord—Highest self of the individual.

ANGEL of JESUS—Highest self of collective man.

SPIRIT and the BRIDE—Union of OVERSELF with personality.

INTERPRETATION

1. John is shown the flowing forces which come from the combined will of God and the will of man flowing from a point at which man merges with the Divine.

2. This energy nourishes the system for healing and supply in the physical, regularly, and the age old limitations of man are to be removed as a result, as all things are brought into perfect order.

5. The merging of Man's conscious mind with the Christ mind will bring about sufficient illumination for perfect service.

6. This knowledge needs to be passed on to those who will make use of it.

7. To those who apply themselves to the study of this knowledge, the instructor-Superconsciousness comes quietly.

8, 9, 10. John, again, seeks to worship the figure emblematically shown and is told to worship God only.

11, 12. Judgment on the world will come quickly as each individual is found deep in his own earthly activity for good or evil, wherever he may be.

Chapter 22 continued

14. Blessed are they that do his commandments, that they may have right to the tree of life, and may enter in through the gates into the city.

15. For without are dogs, and sorcerers, and whoremongers, and murderers, and idolaters, and whosoever loveth and maketh a lie.

16. I Jesus have sent mine angel to testify unto you these things in the churches. I am the root and the offspring of David, and the bright and morning star.

17. And the Spirit and the bride say, Come. And let him that heareth say, Come. And let him that is athirst come. And whosoever will, let him take the water of life freely.

18. For I testify unto every man that heareth the words of the prophecy of this book, if any man shall add unto these things, God shall add unto him the plagues that are written in this book:

19. And if any man shall take away from the words of the book of this prophecy, God shall take away his part out of the book of life, and out of the holy city, and from the things which are written in this book.

20. He which testifieth these things saith, Surely I come quickly. Amen. Even so, come, Lord Jesus.

21. The grace of our Lord Jesus Christ be with you all. Amen.

14. Those operating within the DIVINE law will be found in control of all healing and supply from within and/or in possession of their souls or God-conscious.

16. The OVERSELF reveals the source of his knowledge.

18, 19. The "Book" is the body, which is the vehicle for human experience in the world. Through it the lessons of the soul are learned. There can be no shortcuts or meanderings without dire consequences to it.

THE END

COMMENTARY

The mental-physical anatomy of Man as outlined here by John seems to show much the same understanding of the functions of the body-mind relationships as modern science has found. However, where modern science has only begun to develop an understanding of the effects of mental attitudes upon the body through the study of psychosomatics and its therapy, John's record declares that the state of the mind, its thoughts, its desires and its conflicts, etc. are reflected at all times in the state of the body. And, of course, the state of the body has its effect on the mental outlook. The way, then, to change and heal the body is to change the mind and its attitudes. The first bodily organs to feel and respond to this, John says, will be the endocrine system, keys to all bodily changes.

If we can accept this, then Man is responsible not only for how he thinks and feels on the conscious level but also what happens to him as a result of what his unconscious attitudes attract. However, the greater part of his mind lies beyond his reach, so to speak. This would seem a complete and final obstacle to any aspirations he might have towards establishing total self control. Or so it seems.

John suggests that the key to this dilemma lies in the superconscious mind. By putting the forces of the body-mind back in order, this level of consciousness is released into action, first as a guide and instructor during the processes of cleansing and purification and finally merging with the personality and operating on the conscious level. Any man acting in complete superconsciousness, the implication is, would be as a god. This has been the goal of all mystics through the ages and the story of their seeking. This is the explanation of the state of Christhood, the archetype of the evolved man.

To the psychologist who has spent long years in the study of the human mind in action, it becomes increasingly clear that present-day knowledge is inadequate for dealing with the problems of people who have become victims of their own tensions and conflicts. Most exploration, so far, seems to have been in the area of the subconscious, the repository of all patterns of repeat actions, of a mechanistic nature. By bringing to the surface something of the residue of this area, it is hoped that the individual will recognize the cause of his problems and be automatically released from his tensions.

In many cases this appears to work very well indeed. In an equal number of cases, however, the results are completely unpredictable.

If John's information is worth study by the scientific men, as the readings suggest, it may be found that the present assumption that an individual's mentality on the conscious level as the only yardstick to be considered in treatment may have to be abandoned. This may prove not to be in accord with the true situation at all! What if, over the conscious thinking mind of the individual sits a greater mind in judgment, a mind possessing universal scope, which is observing all that is happening and perhaps bringing about its own conflicts as its own yardstick for the well-being of the individual is violated?

The Book of the Revelation implies a course of action. To read it, if only in its interpretation as given here, means nothing. The real "Book" of the Revelation is the body-mind of Man and his true nature is studied and absorbed only by putting the suggested course of action into practice—in everyday living. In the ensuing experience alone, in the overcoming of everyday problems in self can Man be freed to know himself and in knowing himself to become what he truly is and to fulfill his vast breathtaking destiny as outlined by John.

BOOK OF REVELATION—GLOSSARY

by Esther Wynne—used at 8/58 A.R.E. Summer School

Chapter 1

SEVEN CHURCHES—Seven spiritual centers; the endocrine glands
- EPHESUS—Gonads
- SMYRNA—Lyden (cells of Leydig)
- PERGAMOS—Adrenal or Solar Plexus
- THYATIRA—Thymus
- SARDIS—Thyroid
- PHILADELPHIA—Pineal
- LAODICEA—Pituitary

SEVEN SPIRITS BEFORE THE THRONE—Helpful influences without.
IN SPIRIT ON THE LORD'S DAY—In meditation.
SEVEN GOLDEN CANDLESTICKS—Seven churches, the seven spiritual centers.
SEVEN STARS—The seven angels of the seven churches, the messengers of the seven spiritual centers. "Listen to what the Spirit says to the Churches."
ONE LIKE UNTO THE SON OF MAN—The Christ.
SHARP TWO-EDGED SWORD—Power rising through the centers, either blesses or curses, according to the use or misuse of it.
THE REVELATION OF JOHN—John's revelation of his experience and interpreted by others through application in the mental, physical, and spiritual.

Chapter 2

THOSE WHO CALL THEMSELVES APOSTLES AND ARE NOT—Self-righteousness.
LEFT FIRST LOVE—The fall from the spiritual Ideal.
NICOLAITANS—Those who practised and defended immorality and lasciviousness. (*Webster*)
DO THE FIRST WORKS—(That purpose which directs—the Ideal.) Those which manifest the Ideal.
TREE OF LIFE—Endocrine system—the seven spiritual centers of the body.
PARADISE OF GOD—Where peace may be found.
THOSE WHO SAY THEY ARE JEWS AND ARE NOT—Make false claims.
SYNAGOGUE OF SATAN—Falseness in self.
SECOND DEATH—Falling away, after having passed into the understanding.
ANTIPAS—(Std. Ref. Bible) Martyr at Pergamos, and by tradition, bishop of that place. (Flavius Josephus: Book IV, Chap. 3:4, Martyr at Jerusalem, A.D. 66-70.)
WHERE SATAN DWELLETH—Where there is jealousy, greed, hate, etc.
DOCTRINE OF BALAAM—Blind to higher morality; the reward sought through popularity; applause; worldliness.
HIDDEN MANNA—Spiritual food: "Ye shall not live by bread alone, but by every word that proceedeth from the mouth of the Father."

NAME—Shows a definite period in the evolution of the entity in the material plane unless named for selfish motives.

* JEZEBEL (unwed)—Those who are false to the cause they espouse, and those who would lead others astray.

THE MORNING STAR—An awakening, Light, spiritual awareness.

POWER OVER THE NATIONS—Power over the whole of the physical body, the unspiritualized cells of the physical body.

Chapter 3

OPEN DOOR—The awakening (Lyden—Pineal centers).

THRONE—Within the head of the physical body. Where we meet the Father.

FOUR AND TWENTY ELDERS—The twenty-four cranial nerves that control the five senses of the body.

BOOK OF LIFE—The Christ's Record. Those written in are those who have not climbed up some other way.

BEGINNING OF THE CREATION OF GOD—The First Son.

WHAT THE SPIRIT SAITH UNTO THE CHURCHES—Listen in meditation, in prayer, always to the Voice of God.

Chapter 4

SEVEN LAMPS—7 spirits of God; helpful influences without.

FOUR BEASTS—Physical desires of the 4 lower centers.

1. Self-preservation
2. Sustenance
3. Propagation of species
4. Self-gratification

Chapter 5

BOOK OF SEVEN SEALS—The physical body with the seven spiritual centers.

SEVEN SEALS—Seals of the seven centers. (They may be closed or opened.)

LAMB—The Christ, or the activities of Jesus becoming the Christ.

A NEW SONG—A new understanding.

Chapter 6

FOUR HORSES—Emotions.

WHEAT AND BARLEY—Physical.

OIL AND WINE—Spiritual.

SOULS OF THE FAITHFUL SLAIN—That which the soul has experienced in the earth.

EARTHQUAKE; SUN BLACK; MOON AS BLOOD; STARS OF HEAVEN DEPART; FIG TREE CASTETH FIGS; MOUNTAIN MOVES; etc.—Experiences that affect the physical, mental and spiritual man.

Chapter 7

FOUR ANGELS AT FOUR CORNERS OF EARTH—Four influences in the nature of man from his source, as environment, heredity, as of the earth, mental and spiritual.
144,000 SEALED—Spiritualized cellular structure of the twelve major divisions of the body.
GREAT MULTITUDE—Cells within yet to be spiritualized.

Chapter 8

SOUNDING OF SEVEN ANGELS—Experiences during physical purification.
ANGEL WITH GOLDEN CENSER—Influence of good that goes out from each soul.
INCENSE—Activities from individuals who seek.
EARTH—That in state of transition.
HAIL—Crystallization of the water. Purification of the individuals.
FIRE—Purifying, burning up dross.
MOUNTAIN OF FIRE IN SEA, SEA BECOMES BLOOD—Body elements conflicting one another.
GREAT STAR FROM HEAVEN—Influences from without, as "His Star have we seen."
1/3 PART OF THE RIVERS AND FOUNTAINS—A third part of bodily activities. (Getting a little better.) (Less of Self.)
1/3 PART OF SUN AND STARS SMITTEN—Vibrations and emotions being aroused. (Getting a little better, less and less of self.)

Chapter 9

BOTTOMLESS PIT—Roots of the tree of life: the gonads.
SMOKE ARISING—Vibratory forces.
LOCUSTS—Spirit of man arising to the glory of the son.
MEN—Influence; that which comes through the physical forces.
KING APOLLYON—(Std. Ref. Bible. Gr.) "a destroyer" rendering of Hebrew Abaddon, the angel of the bottomless pit.
VOICE FROM THE FOUR HORNS OF THE ALTAR—From four influences in the experiences of the individual soul.

4 ANGELS BOUND IN EUPHRATES—4 influences that are as Air, Earth, Fire, Water.

EUPHRATES—Boundary of a beginning, or an end, from material standpoint.

HORSES AND HORSEMEN WHICH WERE TO KILL 1/3 PART OF MEN—Emotions in which changes are wrought by the application of those forces in the experience.

7 ANGELS—Spiritual forces governing the various dimensional planes through which souls pass between incarnations on earth.

Chapter 10

ANGEL WITH THE LITTLE BOOK—Guardian force, or ability to use or abuse that which has been combined in the book (Chapter 1).

BOOK—Body; or the understanding of the emotions and the needs of the body.

PROPHECY—Apply (What will ye do with it?)

TIME—The inclination of the individual mind in materiality to set metes and bounds.

Chapter 11

REED LIKE A ROD—Power given each to set metes and bounds as to what his heaven shall be (limitations).

TEMPLE—Mental body, in which is the pattern as of the tabernacle.

COURT WITHOUT THE TEMPLE—Environ without the body.

GENTILES—Those who, being very devout without, have grown smaller within.

2 WITNESSES—The subconscious and the superconscious.

EGYPT—Release from bondage.

SODOM; GOMORRAH—A reckoning with sin.

REVIVING OF WITNESSES—Renewing, by the abilities of the soul to take hold upon the witnesses of life itself.

Chapter 12

CHILD—Outgrowth of the application of the Word or the Book upon self, born of application of the elements in the body of the individual.

WOMAN—The mother, earth; the source from which all materiality is to become a conscious thing.

DRAGON—That through which man's rebellious forces rise. Lord of Darkness.

MICHAEL—Lord of the Way.

WINGS OF AN EAGLE (given the woman)—Flight from materiality, for rest. Transitions from various spheres of mental experience.

BOOK OF LIFE—The record of God, of the soul within and the knowledge of same. That which we have recorded on the skeins of time.

Chapter 13

FLOOD CAUSED BY THE SERPENT—Emotions upon the influences of the body.

BEAST LIKE A LEOPARD, WITH 7 HEADS AND 10 HORNS—Self's own interest.

7 HEADS and 10 HORNS—Influence of the knowledge gained through the various forces and centers of the body.

2ND BEAST WITH 2 HORNS—Power as attained by the study that has been shown in the first portion. May be applied unworthily.

2 HORNS—2 WAYS—Doublemindedness, as showing wonders in the earth for self-aggrandizement, self-indulgence, self-glorification.

MARK OF THE BEAST—Symbol of this or that grouping, that become as a part of the obligations to those who have joined with the work of the beast.

MARK OF THE LAMB—Consciousness of the indwelling presence of the Christ.

NUMBER OF THE BEAST, NUMBER OF THE MAN (9)—The exercise of the man without realizing that influence which has brought same, lacking consciousness of God directing.

Chapter 14

HARPERS—Those souls that in the beginning were as the sons of God in the earth plane.

THE NEW SONG—New experience that comes to each soul, as to the assurance of that help when necessary of the saints of the Father.

ANGELS (in Rev. 14)—Those influences making aware of the necessity for work or active service.

Chapter 15

ANGELS WITH 7 LAST PLAGUES—Influences of the law, pouring out that which is the meeting of self in individuals yet in the earth.

TEMPLE OF THE TABERNACLE OF THE TESTIMONY—Akashic record, or Book of Life of the individual.

VIALS OF WRATH—Effective activity upon the various conditions that have become a part of the errors in those that have the mark of the beast.

TEMPLE FILLED WITH SMOKE—Final steps in the spiritualization of the body.

ANTI-CHRIST—Spirit of that opposed to the spirit of truth. Spirit of hate, contention, strife, faultfinding, lovers of self, lovers of praise.

Chapter 17

BABYLON—Self.

SCARLET-COLOURED BEAST—That which made for the projecting of man into matter, through the associations that brought carnal relationships.

7 HEADS AND MOUNTAINS—7 spiritual centers.

THE GREAT TRIBULATION—Experiences of every soul, arising from influences created by man.

Chapter 19

WHITE HORSE—Symbol of the messenger in the awakening.

RIDER—Jesus Christ, the messenger.

BRIDE—The body, so raised as to become a new being, one with the Christ.

MARRIAGE OF THE LAMB—Attainment through the Christ Consciousness, Holy Spirit.

Chapter 21

FIRST RESURRECTION—Of those who have not tasted death, in the sense of the dread of same.

SECOND RESURRECTION—Of those who have GAINED the understanding, that in HIM there is no death.

NEW JERUSALEM—New life, understanding, regeneration, desires, purpose.

12 GATES, ANGELS, TRIBES—12 ways, experiences of the physical, activities of the openings to the bodily forces.

GOLDEN REED TO MEASURE THE CITY—Abilities of each.

A NEW HEAVEN AND A NEW EARTH—No desire to sin, no purpose but that glory of the Son to be manifested.

FIRE AND BRIMSTONE—That as builded by self. Purification, purging.

Chapter 22

RIVER OF WATER OF LIFE—The active flow of the purpose of the souls of men made pure in the blood of the Lamb.

TREE OF LIFE—Tree planted by the water of life, the sturdiness of the purpose of the individual in its sureness in the Christ. (The 7 spiritual centers of Man.)

LEAVES OF THE TREE—Continuous activities for the healing of all contacted in material life.

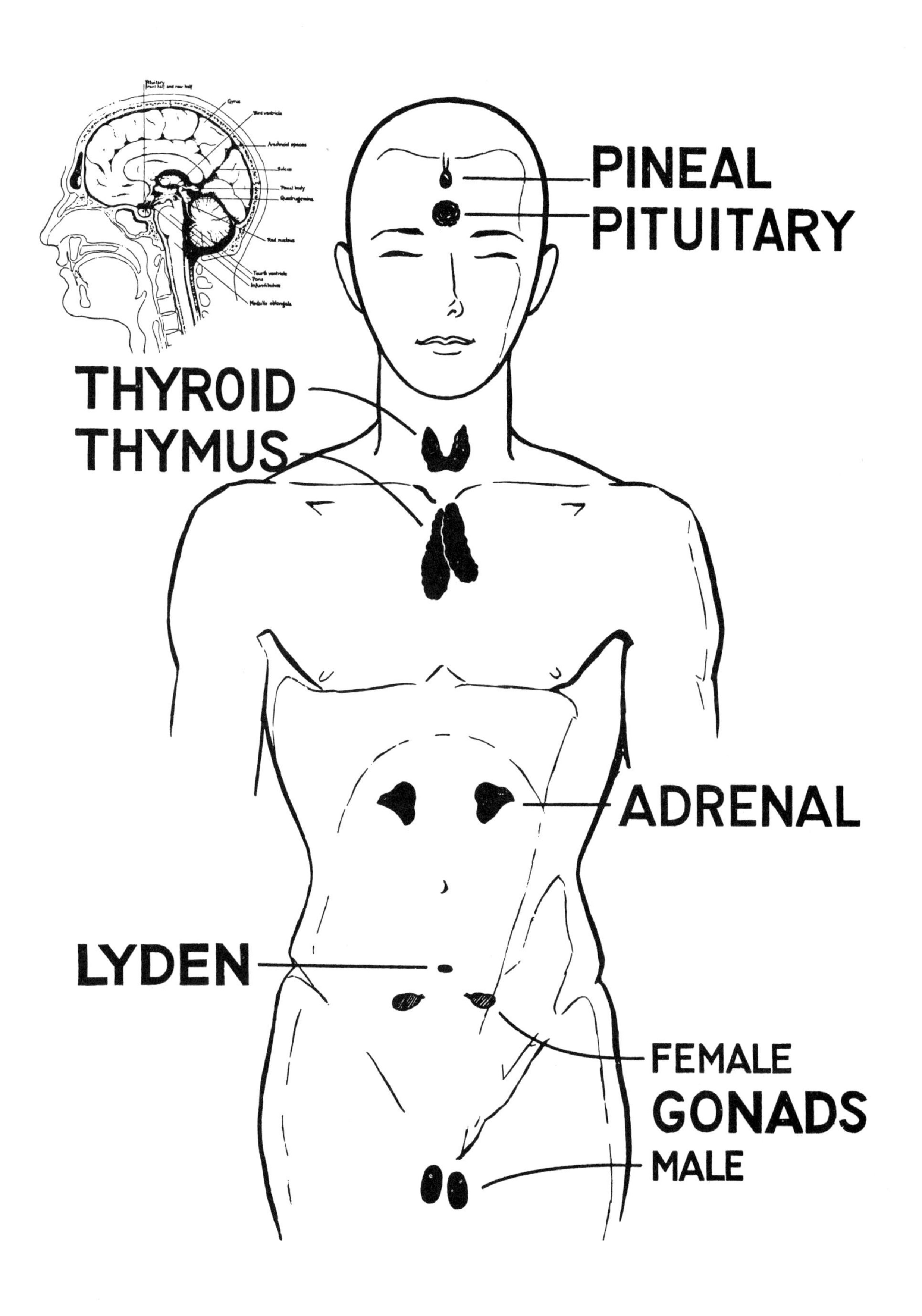
Pituitary
front half and rear half
Gyrus
Third ventricle
Arachnoid spaces
Sulcus
Pineal body
Quadrugemina
Red nucleus
Fourth ventricle
Pons
Infundibulum
Medulla oblongata
PINEAL
PITUITARY
THYROID
THYMUS
ADRENAL
LYDEN
FEMALE
GONADS
MALE

REVELATION READINGS #281 MASTER INDEX

(The numbers for each index entry refer to the second set of numbers in the 281 readings series. For example, in the Bible, "Acts 2:17 58," the number "58" refers to reading 281-58.)

What Is A.R.E.?

The Association for Research and Enlightenment, Inc. (A.R.E.®), is the international headquarters for the work of Edgar Cayce (1877-1945), who is considered the best-documented psychic of the twentieth century. Founded in 1931, the A.R.E. consists of a community of people from all walks of life and spiritual traditions, who have found meaningful and life-transformative insights from the readings of Edgar Cayce.

Although A.R.E. headquarters is located in Virginia Beach, Virginia—where visitors are always welcome—the A.R.E. community is a global network of individuals who offer conferences, educational activities, and fellowship around the world. People of every age are invited to participate in programs that focus on such topics as holistic health, dreams, reincarnation, ESP, the power of the mind, meditation, and personal spirituality.

In addition to study groups and various activities, the A.R.E. offers membership benefits and services, a bimonthly magazine, a newsletter, extracts from the Cayce readings, conferences, international tours, a massage school curriculum, an impressive volunteer network, a retreat-type camp for children and adults, and A.R.E. contacts around the world. A.R.E. also maintains an affiliation with Atlantic University, which offers a master's degree program in Transpersonal Studies.

For additional information about A.R.E. activities hosted near you, please contact:

A.R.E.
67th St. and Atlantic Ave.
P.O. Box 595
Virginia Beach, VA 23451-0595
(804) 428-3588

A.R.E. Press

A.R.E. Press is a publisher and distributor of books, audiotapes, and videos that offer guidance for a more fulfilling life. Our products are based on, or are compatible with, the concepts in the psychic readings of Edgar Cayce.

We especially seek to create products which carry forward the inspirational story of individuals who have made practical application of the Cayce legacy.

For a free catalog, please write to A.R.E. Press at the address below or call toll free 1-800-723-1112. For any other information, please call 804-428-3588.

A.R.E. Press
Sixty-Eighth & Atlantic Avenue
P.O. Box 656
Virginia Beach, VA 23451-0656